LIMA 3

LIMA 3

HARRY FERGUSON

BLOOMSBURY

First published in Great Britain 2005

This paperback edition published 2006

Bloomsbury Publishing Plc, 36 Soho Square, London W1D 3QY

A CIP catalogue record for this book is available from the British Library

ISBN 0 7475 7970 9
ISBN-13 9780747579700

10 9 8 7 6 5 4 3 2 1

All papers used by Bloomsbury Publishing are natural, recyclable products made from
wood grown in well-managed forests. The manufacturing processes conform to the
environmental regulations of the country of origin.

Typeset by Palimpsest Book Production Ltd,
Polmont, Stirlingshire

Printed in Great Britain by
Clays Ltd, St Ives plc

www.bloomsbury.com/harryferguson

For Mum and Dad

AUTHOR'S NOTE

Although this is a true story, some names and other details
have been changed in order to protect the operational
security of HM Customs and Excise.

The Investigation Division (ID) became the National
Investigation Service (NIS) in 1996.

ACKNOWLEDGEMENTS

I would like to thank three groups of people who have helped me to write this book. First, the staff at Bloomsbury. Two years ago they were just strangers working in a crowded London HQ crammed behind countless boxes stuffed with books. Today, the offices are still crowded and the boxes are still there, but far fewer of the staff are strangers. I would like to thank them all for their friendship, for their support and for their hard work.

Then there are the men and women of the National Investigation Service. Although my career with them is over, they are still out there at all hours and in all weathers fighting an increasingly sophisticated and well-armed enemy. The government now has plans for them to be absorbed into the new Serious Organised Crime Agency (SOCA) and the ID/ NIS as I knew it will cease to exist. But the name of the organisation doesn't really matter: the people will remain the same and they are the organisation's most valuable asset. My hope is that more members of the public will become aware of the difficult work they do; work which has gone unrecognised for too long. I cannot fully pay tribute to their dedication and sacrifice. I would especially like to thank the six officers who took time to read and vet the text before publication (although I must emphasise that this in no way means that HM Customs and Excise have endorsed the book or its contents).

Last (and definitely not least), I would once again like to thank my family for their love, for their support and for ignoring the sounds of cursing coming from the study late at night. I couldn't have written this book without them.

But their coffee isn't any better . . .

H.F.
February 2005

CONTENTS

1

Declaration of War

It was raining on the night they came to deal with Danny Mulligan.

Danny had no idea they were after him and no way to protect himself when they did. According to all the rules of the game he shouldn't even have been considered as a target. But in Liverpool in the early 1990s, after two decades' worth of drugs money had fuelled increasingly vicious and powerful smuggling organisations, the rules had changed. The old school villains, who had seen drugs as a soft touch compared with armed robbery and other areas of crime, had gradually been replaced by heavily armed gangs with international connections. These gangs had learned to use ruthlessness and extreme violence to defend their turf from other criminals and it had been on the cards for a long time that they would use the same tactics to hit back at either the police or Customs. Danny was destined to be the first target in this new approach to the drugs war.

Even other criminals agreed that the incident should never have happened; above all it was stupid. Up until that night everyone knew how the game was supposed to be played. There were so many gangs bringing illegal drugs into the country that your chances of getting away with it were pretty good to start with. Even if Customs or the police finally caught you,

you were at least safer than if one of your gangland rivals turned on you. Unlike the police, Customs were never armed so there was no risk of getting shot and if you didn't put up a fight you wouldn't even get hurt. You went away, did some easy time on remand and then you had your say in court. At the end of the trial you still had a better-than-evens chance of getting away with it: your lawyer would get as much of the evidence excluded as possible and there was always the possibility of bribing or intimidating a member of the jury. Even if you were convicted, you simply did your time and then, after doing about half the sentence, you went straight back to work. In fact many criminals were able to continue running their smuggling activities from inside prison. That was the nature of the game and that was also the smart way to do things because if you hit back, if you made it personal, then you could guarantee that either Customs or the police would mark you as a grade A target and would move heaven and earth to bring you down.

But in 1992 one gang in Liverpool stopped thinking this way. They learned that they were under investigation by a Customs and Excise investigation team and rather than just wait for the hand on the shoulder they decided that they would do something to hit back. It may seem strange to say but they didn't see the attack as anything personal. The gang leader who had ordered the attack had no idea who the target was; Danny was only a low-level officer on a Customs and Excise investigation unit. But when they put out the word to local informers for names and addresses of any Customs officers who were working in the area, it was Danny's details that got passed. And that was why the gang had hired some men to break into his house that night.

The four thugs who had been paid to do the job were from out of town. They were typical of the sort of gangland muscles who get taken on as door security in clubs or as enforcers in business deals wherever they could get the work. But it was precisely their need for money and a willingness to take on any job which made them unpredictable and dangerous. They had been hired out of Manchester in the hope that it would make them harder to trace and to an extent it had worked. It was some months before an informant told us exactly who they were and what had happened that night. And violence comes cheap these days: the four of them were paid just a few hundred pounds upfront, with the rest to follow when the job was done. They spent most of the evening watching a football match at a quiet pub in the south of the city before setting out. The landlord was in the pay of the local syndicate and they had been told that it was a safe place for them to hang around until they thought the time was right. Even after last orders were called and the pub was supposedly closed, they stayed for the 'lock in' with the locals, knocking back whisky and playing pool.

If they had been more professional they would have kept watch on Danny's house to make sure that he was at home. But none of the gang fancied sitting in a car on a dank November night, getting cold and bored and worrying that at any moment they might be spotted by a suspicious neighbour. They figured that as long as they got the job done no one would be worried whether or not they had sat around outside for a few hours. Get in, get out, get it done, that was their philosophy.

Finally, at about two in the morning, they drove to Danny's house in an old B-reg Mercedes. They had bought the car for cash so that it could be dumped and burned after they had done the job. A little hatchback might have been handier for nipping away through the back streets afterwards, but they chose the Merc because in a big car with four doors they could be in and out with no messing.

When they arrived, the house was in darkness just as they had expected. There were one or two lights on in the upstairs windows of neighbouring houses, but that didn't bother them. At this late hour on a Sunday night everyone would be in bed. For normal people tomorrow was a working day. For this mob, tomorrow would mean their usual long lie-in before gathering at the local pub for the first drinks of the day.

They had done a recce of the area the week before. Danny lived in a quiet cul-de-sac of semi-detached houses. There would be almost no chance of late-night traffic or pedestrians to disturb them. They had made a note of the colour and make of Danny's car, but there was no sign of it outside on the drive as they pulled up. For a moment they glanced at their boss wondering if he had made a mistake. He was the one who was going to do the job. They knew he had an old Tokarev automatic pistol, wrapped in a tea towel and tucked under his belt at the back of his jacket, which he intended to use to kneecap Danny, putting a round through the back of both of his legs once he had been given a severe beating. It was up to him to call it off if there was anything that he didn't like. They sat there for a few moments in the dark, watching the house as the rain drummed on the roof of the car. But then the boss climbed out of the car and two of the others quickly followed. The three of them crept up the drive, keeping to the grass verge to muffle their footsteps. They waited for a moment in the driveway, but there was no sound other than the steady patter of the drizzle and the engine of the Mercedes rumbling quietly in the road behind them.

There was a small garage standing to one side of the house. The wooden doors were old; they were rotting in places and there was a row of grimy glass panels along the tops of both doors. One of these panels had been broken many years before. Shining his torch through the hole where the glass had once been, the leader could see Danny's car parked inside. He turned and nodded to the two men behind him. They opened the small wooden side gate and made their way silently around the back of the darkened house. They knew from their previous visit that Danny didn't have a dog.

The leader nodded to one of the others who pulled a crowbar from under his jacket and used it to force open the back door. There was only a single lock and it popped open easily. The wood around the lock split slightly, but not enough to cause a significant amount of noise. They waited for a moment, but there was no sign of lights going on upstairs. Even if somebody was now lying awake in the dark, wondering what the noise was, the gang knew they would be up the stairs before anyone had a chance to react. Together they dashed through the kitchen and sprinted up the stairs, making as much noise as possible. They each had a knife or a club at the ready and the leader burst in through the first door he came to. But he'd chosen the wrong one – it was the kids' room. The others quickly kicked open the next two doors, still making as much noise as possible to scare the wits out of anyone who might think of putting up a fight, but they found themselves staring into the empty rooms. And it was then that the truth suddenly dawned on them.

There was no one in the house.

By sheer chance, on the one night they'd decided to carry out the attack, Danny Mulligan wasn't home. In fact he was about a hundred miles away, spending the weekend in a hotel with his family following a wedding. They stood in the darkness of the hallway wondering what to do. Finally the leader made a decision. They had been paid to deliver a warning and they had better do something.

'Trash the place.'

The gang went through a well-practised routine, rooting clothes out of drawers, emptying cupboards, overturning furniture and grabbing anything that was easily carried and looked like it was worth something. One of them even took a mini hi-fi system from one of the bedrooms as they made their way back downstairs.

As they were leaving through the kitchen, the leader of the gang saw empty milk bottles lined up on the window ledge and suddenly had an idea.

'Grab those,' he said to the youngest one.

The youth picked up two bottles and the three of them left the house quickly through the front door. They crossed the front lawn back to the car. The gang was getting nervous now. Nothing had gone to plan so far and they hadn't counted on this sort of delay. Although the road was still quiet, there was always the chance that someone had heard something and had already made a call to the police. Most nervous of all was the driver, who was actually out on bail for another offence. He had been parked at the end of the road watching the other houses and waiting for the sound of a shot or a scream, but he had heard nothing. When he saw the others come running out of the house he thought the job was done. He revved the engine hard, accelerated forwards and screeched to a halt at the end of the drive.

But instead of climbing into the car, the leader of the gang wrenched open one of the rear doors and grabbed a container of petrol from the seat, which they had brought for torching the car after they dumped it. He stood on the pavement and quickly filled the two bottles half-full as the younger lad held them and the driver shouted at him, demanding to know what was going on. Curtains around the close began to twitch as neighbours woke up and wondered what all the noise was. The leader grabbed some rags from the floor of the car and stuffed them into the tops of the bottles. Then he pulled a lighter out of his pocket and set light to both rags.

As he moved to the front of the car and climbed in next to the driver, he said to the youngest one:

'Do it!'

The youth ran back towards the garage, terrified that the Molotov cocktails might suddenly go off in his hands. He slipped over on the rain-soaked grass but somehow managed to land on one knee, keeping both the bottles upright. He carefully got back to his feet and hurled the first bottle. It hit the garage door near the bottom and sent up a sheet of flame. He was surprised by the force of the explosion and for a moment thought the entire car had gone up. The sheet of bright orange light blinded him. He quickly turned and threw the other bottle at the doorway of the house. But this time his aim was even worse, and the seemingly indestructible milk bottle bounced off the brickwork at the side of the porch and came back towards him. Leaping backwards, he only just avoided the bottle as it smashed on the drive and scattered flaming liquid across the lawn. He sprinted back towards the car. The engine of the Merc roared loudly for one last time and the gang sped off into the night with tyres squealing. Fortunately, neighbours called the fire brigade quickly and the house was saved before the fire seriously took hold. But the car and the garage were burned to the ground.

In the darkness no one had seen the registration number of the car. The gang were able to get to some waste ground and dump it before switching to another one and disappearing into the night. The police found the torched Mercedes just a few hours later. The blackened and melted remains of Danny's hi-fi were still on the back seat.

News of the attack appeared to spark an abrupt change in the Liverpool drugs world. Some of the more high-profile criminals seemed to think that they no longer had to simply sit and wait for the hand upon their shoulder. Suddenly it seemed possible to go on the offensive against the authorities, just as gangsters had done during Prohibition in 1920s America. Once some of them began to think seriously about what they might be able to get away with it wasn't long before another attack was being planned: this time against a different target, but by a far more serious outfit than the men who had gone after Danny Mulligan.

There is a hierarchy in the Liverpool drugs world: above the street dealers and the chancers there are the professional smugglers and distribution gangs, many of whom control their own 'patch' within the city. But above even these career criminals there are a handful of notorious characters who consider themselves the godfathers of the Liverpool drugs trade. Many of them are known to local people, though none dare name them and even the police and Customs tread warily around them. They are numbered amongst the two hundred plus 'untouchable' major criminals which the National Crime Squad estimates are at large in the UK.

One of these, known to those who dealt with him as simply 'the Fixer', provided money-laundering facilities to many of the criminal gangs in the city. But in the past year his organisation had suffered a number of setbacks as a result of investigations by Customs and Excise against gangs working for him. The Fixer needed to stop this haemorrhage and at the same time demonstrate to his rivals that he was still a force to be reckoned with. Using his own network of informants, he was soon able to pinpoint the officer responsible for many of the operations which had been mounted in the city: a senior Customs investigator called Eddy Knowles. Whereas most of the personnel on the investigation teams came from London, Eddy was based near Bradford, easily within reach – and this made him a very tempting target. It wasn't long before the Fixer had a considerable dossier of intelligence on Knowles's movements including his home address. As soon as he was sure that the information was good and that the risk to himself would be minimal, the Fixer gave the word for an attack.

Unlike the amateurs from Manchester who had attacked Danny's house, the man he selected to do the job was a seasoned criminal, recently released from a long stretch in prison for attempted murder. The reward for a successful attack was said to be in five figures. This time the job was going to be done right.

So it was that, three weeks later, the scene which had occurred outside Danny Mulligan's house happened again. This time there were four men in two cars which pulled up outside the house in the early hours of the morning. They all got out and quickly crossed the silent street. Once more they made their way around to the back of the house. By chance, the door had been left unlocked and they were able to walk straight inside. Two of the men were armed with Heckler & Koch MP5 machine guns. Swiftly and silently they made their way up to the main bedroom.

But this time no one was going to get hurt. One of the men was Eddy Knowles, the senior Customs officer who had been targeted by the Liverpool gangster. The others were armed police who had been detailed to go with him and help him get his family to safety. Knowles quickly woke his wife and children, helped his wife to pack a few belongings and then led them downstairs. He put his family into one of the cars; the children still wrapped in blankets. Then, with the armed police shadowing them in the other vehicle, they set off into the night. They were heading for the dubious safety of the police witness protection programme. Until the man who had been sent after them was stopped, they wouldn't be going home again.

HM Customs and Excise Investigation Division, known within the law enforcement world simply as 'the ID', had moved fast that night. Only a few hours earlier they had received a tip-off from one of their intelligence sources that there was a plan to hit Knowles and his family. All ID units have an intelligence team attached to them and these teams have access to a wide range of resources ranging from informants to telephone taps on leading targets. There are also excellent liaisons with British and foreign police forces as well as NCIS, the National Criminal Intelligence Service which is staffed by both police and Customs officers. Somewhere on this vast intelligence net, news of the planned attack had been picked up and was quickly relayed to the ID's senior operational management team.

The report which arrived at their late night meeting made it clear that a contract had been put out on the life of Knowles. According to the report, which had a grade 'A' reliability rating, the attack was believed to be imminent. The information was so specific that there was no chance of it being a hoax. Clearly something had to be done immediately to protect Knowles and his family.

The next thing Knowles knew was that two Divisional officers were dispatched to pull him off the late night stakeout he was working on. As he was whisked away, he was told by the senior officer what had happened and that his family was being moved to a safe house as a security measure.

ID intelligence teams worked hard for the rest of the night to confirm their information and by the next day the picture had become worse rather than better. The threat was in deadly earnest and, according to one unconfirmed report, the hit man had already visited Knowles's home and found it empty.

The very next day, the senior management of the Investigation Division held a council of war. It was clear to them that events were spinning out of control in Liverpool. Although officers had been killed or injured on operations before, this was the first time that the life of a case officer had been deliberately targeted. Clearly the hit man had to be found and stopped, but this was more than just a matter of protecting the life of one officer. At the same time as protecting Knowles, something needed to be done to break the power of the drugs barons in Liverpool.

The Fixer was a careful strategist and had survived in the city for years by staying well away from direct involvement in crime. But the ID intelligence teams had another target that might offer a way into his network. This was a major heroin importation and distribution gang run by a criminal called John Haase. Haase's gang was the biggest source of heroin in Liverpool and taking it out would be a major victory for Customs and Excise and, at the same time, the intelligence teams believed that targeting his gang might yield clues that would bring them closer to nailing the Fixer. The management team considered the file on Haase that was before them.

John Haase was born in 1948, had achieved a long criminal career even as a teenager, and in his twenties had graduated to a series of armed robberies of Post Offices. When he was caught in 1973 he was sent to prison for seven years. It was a hard blow but, with the contacts he made whilst he was inside, Haase confirmed himself as a rising star amongst major criminals. When he got out he moved straight into armoured-car robberies. The gang he joined was known as 'The Transit Mob'. They were notorious for their organisation, their ruthlessness and their readiness to use terrifying levels of violence. But eventually this stage of his career also came to an end. The gang was betrayed by an informer and caught. In 1982 Haase was sent down again, this time for fourteen years. Even with time off for remand and good behaviour it was a yet another serious dose of prison time.

If the experience changed him, it seemed to be in one respect only: when he came out Haase was determined never to go back inside again. He formed a new gang and this time he moved into the lucrative area of drugs trafficking, using a new set of contacts he had formed whilst in prison. These contacts, coupled with his reputation for brutality, quickly took him to the top. He had access to firearms stashed around the city and soon earned a reputation as a man who would use them without a second thought if he was crossed. To make sure that there were no leaks in his new organisation he trusted only one other man, his nephew Paul Bennett. Soon Haase and Bennett were controlling the major supply route for heroin into Liverpool and making a fortune.

One of the puzzles about the Haase/Bennett gang was where they managed to get their supply of high-grade heroin and how they managed to get so much of it safely into the country time after time. It was suspected that there must be a powerful international organisation working with them, but so far there were no leads. One of the benefits of a successful operation against the Haase/Bennett gang might be that this other organisation would be exposed and possibly even damaged. The management team had to consider that the gang would be very tough opposition – they were experienced, ruthless and cautious. But the possible rewards for law enforcement in Liverpool, and indeed in the UK, were high.

The Chief Investigation Officer and his advisers decided that an ID team should be assigned to end the reign of the Haase/Bennett gang. The question was, of the sixty or so fifteen-man investigation teams which made up the Division, which was the right one? Amongst the five administrative groups which make up the Investigation Division, Group 'A', the operational drugs group, is divided into referred teams and target teams. Referred teams are immediate-response units. They get called in whenever drugs are found at a port or airport, or whenever last minute intelligence reports that a drugs run is imminent. The other type of ID team are the target teams. Each of these is assigned to watch a known major smuggler and keep him under almost constant surveillance, building up a detailed picture of his entire organisation. When they think they have enough evidence, they move in. Officers on these teams have usually served a long apprenticeship on a referred team before being selected for this work. They are specialists in long-term surveillance, their skills honed by being out on the streets doing close surveillance almost every day. The problem is that there are always far more targets than there are target teams to work on them.

A lot of work had already been done on the Haase/Bennett gang by local Customs teams, but there was no telling how much more would need to be done before they could be arrested, so it was decided to appoint a target team to the job even though this might mean abandoning other work. There was only one natural choice: a team known by the designation 'Drugs F/L'. This was the Division's frontline heroin target team. Because it only took on the hardest jobs, the team was composed of two normal ID units, the 'Foxtrots' and the 'Limas', giving it over thirty officers to call on.

The next issue was the choice of case officer to lead the team. After a short discussion an ID officer called Patrick 'Paddy' Clark was chosen. He had extensive experience of working against drug gangs and excellent knowledge of the underworld in Liverpool. There was a slight risk in that it was believed he was known to some members of the gang, but that was offset by his skills as case officer. His deputy would be Terry Banks, a former SAS soldier and urban surveillance specialist already serving with Drugs F/L.

The second problem was that the F/Ls were severely under strength. Several experienced officers were due to leave for other posts and there was a shortage of volunteers because of the arduous work and long hours the team was expected to put in. Senior officers were told to nominate any suitable candidates who might be available for an immediate transfer. There was no sudden rush of people offering to make the move; the work on Drugs F/L was as tough as it gets on the Division and the team had a reputation for not suffering anyone who didn't meet their high standards.

At the time the call went out I was a surveillance officer on the 'Kilos', one of the referred drugs teams. I had transferred to the Division from MI6 just two years earlier. Technically I was a senior officer, an HEO (Higher Executive Officer), one of the half-dozen or so officers who help the SIO (Senior Investigation Officer) run the team and organise the EOs (Executive Officers), who make up the bulk of the team. Despite my seniority I had been doing little more than learning the ropes on my current team, but I now felt that the apprentice-ship was over and I was ready to move on. I had asked my SIO for a chance to be posted to another team just a few days before. I remember that I had requested somewhere 'nice and quiet' because my wife was still unhappy with the irregular hours which drugs work demanded. He always did have a strange sense of humour.

Within a few days of my request the papers arrived on my desk saying that I was to be transferred to the F/Ls, where I would be posted as officer 'Lima 3'. That's how I became part of the operation against the Haase/Bennett gang, a case which has since become the most notorious investigation in the history of the Division.

My wife, Nicky, worked for a big financial institution in the City. We had married straight out of university and she had been convinced that she wanted to stay at home, be a wife and mother and have a large family. But a few years later it became clear that she was desperately unhappy as a housewife. At the time I was working for MI6 and was due to be posted abroad. There was no way Nicky could have a career if she was following me around the world. Eventually we came up with a compromise which we thought might make everyone happy: I took a two-year sabbatical to look after the children and give her time to get some qualifications; that way she would be able to work during our postings abroad. We thought we had solved the problem. Everything worked according to plan until I re-applied to join MI6 at the end of the sabbatical. During my two years away the Berlin Wall had come down and the Cold War had all but ended. Staff numbers were being cut. They turned me down.

After two years of looking after our (otherwise wonderful) children I knew that I could never become a permanent 'house-husband'. I desperately looked around for something else and that was when I was lucky enough to join the ID, doing work which had a lot in common with espionage but was in many ways even better. In the meantime Nicky had become an inter-national businesswoman, frequently flying out to America or the Far East to set up high-powered deals or other projects. Now, after my first two years at the ID, it was becoming clear that the conflict I had always feared was going to happen anyway. The long hours we both worked meant that we hardly saw each other, and the fact that I was never sure of where I would be working from one day to the next meant that she found it hard to plan for the demands of her highly competitive career. We were slowly being pulled apart.

With hindsight it is easy to see the mess we were in, but at the time we were both so frantically busy that there only seemed to be time to keep pushing forward and hope that everything would turn out right in the end. Nicky knew that I was due to change job soon and she hoped that, after two years chasing round southern England with the Kilos, I was going some-where quiet. But then the F/L job came up and, although I didn't know anything about Haase or Bennett, I knew that I would be working on something special. It seemed like too good a chance to ignore. I took the job and kept my fingers crossed that we would sort something out – after all, we always had before.

Nicky had been an ID wife long enough to know that being the new officer on an operational team would mean working long hours and taking any spare work on offer. Although she wasn't sure what a 'target team' was, she knew that this was going to be worse than the Kilos. To make matters even more difficult, this was all happening at a time when she was hoping for a promotion which would mean a new job in another part of the country. When I told her about the job I had been offered we talked about it long into the night, trying to balance the future of our two careers and the needs of the children, but there just wasn't any way round the problem. It seemed as if the only thing to do was to keep going and hope that somehow it would all sort itself out. We didn't realise just how bad things were going to become.

2

The All-Stars

I arrived in the office bright and early on that first Monday morning, determined to make a good impression. Like all ID teams, Drugs F/L was based in Custom House on Lower Thames Street. The building is right on the north bank of the Thames and just a short walk upriver from the Tower of London. The F/L's office was at the eastern end of Custom House. Although most of the building dates from the reign of Queen Anne, this part of the building had been demolished by a bomb during World War II and rebuilt with a far more modern interior, unlike the antique rooms which the Kilos occupied. There were no ornate plaster mouldings or panelled doors here. Instead there were grey walls, suspended ceilings and integrated strip lighting – it had about as much character as a hospital ward.

I knew that the F/Ls worked long hours even by the standards of the Investigation Division, so I arrived at half past seven. If it was like most teams on the Division, there were bound to be one or two people in, even at that hour. But when I got there the room was empty and dark. I flicked a switch by the door and, row by row, the strip lights flickered into life away down the length of the room.

The fifteen men and women on the Kilos had been squeezed into two tiny rooms which were an untidy maze of equipment, desks and papers. This single room was home to twice that number, but was enormous and completely free from clutter. Desks were clear and equipment was neatly stowed away. At the time I was impressed, thinking that this team must be much more disciplined than we had been. It was only later that I discovered that the tidiness was because they were hardly ever in the office.

I threw my kitbag on to an empty desk and wandered around, reading the papers pinned to the walls, glancing at photographs from previous Christmas parties, trying to form a picture of what they were all like. I knew the team by reputation. Everybody on the Division did. They were the nearest we had to a team of 'All-Stars' and even when I was a fairly new officer on the Division I could have named five or six of the more notorious characters, officers who were so good you heard about them long before you met them.

Unlike other teams, Drugs F/L had two SIOs because it was a double team, although the one who had served on the joint team the longest was usually considered the senior and made most of the command decisions. Here that was John Bradley, a no-nonsense, old-school investigator, more like a police officer than the usual ID middle manager. Theoretically, he was in charge of ten HEOs and eighteen EOs, plus a couple of administration officers. However, although this was the strength of the team on paper, it was rarely up to that number because of the high demands of target work and the lack of volunteers.

The senior HEO (and therefore also the senior operational officer, since SIOs almost never went out on the ground), was Gareth MacKay. He was thought by many to be one of the outstanding officers in the Division – renowned for never taking leave and almost living in the office. The gossip was that he would often work a full day and then take a car out to a target address and wait, hoping to spot an unscheduled meeting or some other clue which would otherwise have been missed. According to the stories, he would just stay in the car, sleeping, watching and monitoring the radio to see what other teams were doing. Apparently he had managed to crack several cases this way, and he had certainly turned up to help on one of the Kilos' knocks because he 'happened to be in the area'.

He was once famously charged with the assault of three Turkish men who were completing the sale of a suitcase full of heroin in a London hotel room. The Limas had been monitoring the room with concealed microphones and Gareth had called the knock just as the exchange was about to take place. The trouble was that the rest of the team were too far away, so when Gareth burst into the room and told them that they were 'nicked', the Turks quickly realised that he was alone. They tried to rush him and he knocked all three of them out cold in the ensuing fight. At their pre-trial hearing the Turks' defence lawyers tried to allege that Gareth's simply saying 'you're nicked' was not sufficient to place their clients in a state of arrest because they hadn't been properly cautioned, that they had therefore been unlawfully assaulted, that all subsequent evidence seized was inadmissible and that they should be released. They even used the tapes from the hidden microphones to back up their case. Having listened carefully to what had happened in the hotel room the judge famously ruled:

'In the circumstances, I think that the phrase "you're nicked" followed by a solid right hook to the jaw is sufficient to notify any suspect that he is under arrest'.

I had met Gareth once or twice when I was on the Kilos and he was an intimidating man. He was only about 5'9" tall, but he seemed to wear a permanent frown, his language was foul and there was always a tension around him as if he were on the point of thumping someone. I've often thought that if someone were to play him in a film of his life it would have to be the actor Sean Bean. Gareth was like Carl, an officer on the Kilos – he was a man for whom the drugs war was a personal crusade and he had little time for people who didn't exhibit the same level of commitment and determination.

Another notorious figure on the team was Derek, one of the few openly homosexual men on the ID. Derek was so open about his homosexuality and so good at his job that any normally homophobic members of the Division just seemed to accept him. In fact, I always found that the ID was fairly tolerant of sexual differences, which was surprising considering it was staffed by some pretty macho types. It seemed that the unwritten rule that you always defended other members of your team gave officers from gay backgrounds or ethnic minorities a level of protection they might not have had in other jobs. Even so, I was puzzled by how Derek had managed to get on to such a high profile team as Drugs F/L. The story was that he had been a senior officer on another team which had been sent to arrest a well-known East End hood following his implication in a smuggling run. Two carloads of officers turned up at this hood's local boozer, only to find that he was in there with members of his gang and his family, celebrating his birthday. In gangland a local pub is like a fortress, where plenty of the locals can be counted on to wade in on the side of their 'boys' if there is any trouble. Seeing as it was his birthday as well, an attempt to arrest him was likely to turn into a full-scale ruck.

Apparently Derek arrived and found the cars parked a little way up the road from the pub. He got out, walked over to them and asked:

'Why are we all mooching around out here like a bunch of wet fairies?'

One of the other officers explained the situation and the imminent prospect of World War III if they went into the pub. They wondered if they should call for armed back-up.

'Oh for God's sake!' muttered Derek in disgust. 'You get a car to the door. I'll go and fetch him out'.

The other officers watched Derek cross the road and disappear into the pub. Then they waited for him to come back out through the window.

But after a few minutes nothing had happened.

Now they faced a crisis of conscience – should they go in and back him up, or just wait and fill in an accident report later? Unsure of what to do, they did at least park a car just outside the pub, with its rear doors open. A moment later Derek dived through the doors of the pub with the suspect in handcuffs and a baying mob just behind him. He quickly bundled his man into the back of the vehicle and they accelerated away down the street, followed by a shower of bottles and beer glasses.

When they had got the target safely locked away in a nearby police station, Derek explained what had happened. Apparently he had gone into the pub and had seen his target standing at the bar with his cronies. He had walked straight up to him and tapped him on the shoulder. The goon had swung round, looked Derek up and down, and snarled:

'What the fuck do you want?'

'Is your name Terry Wilkins, ducky?' asked Derek, with one hand on his hip and a limp wrist waving in the air.

'Well, what of it?'

Derek pulled out his ID badge.

'Well my name's Derek Wilson, I'm a Customs officer and you are under arrest.'

Then Derek proceeded to caution him.

For a moment there was shocked silence. Then laughter broke out because it was so obvious that this limp-wristed 'faggot' could not be a real Customs officer. One of his mates was setting him up as a birthday prank. The cronies all joined in the laughter, looking around and wondering which of them had arranged all this.

'Now turn round, handsome, and put your hands behind

your back,' said Derek, 'because I am going to handcuff you and we're going to have a little fun'.

Still laughing, Wilkins put down his cigar and did as he was asked. Derek cuffed him, took him by the arm and led him towards the door.

But by now the laughter had started to die down as his mates looked around at each other, beginning to realise that none of them had anything to do with this. They started to dash after the rapidly disappearing pair. But it was too late. Derek and his prisoner were at the door and within moments were roaring away into the night.

It was one of the bravest things I ever heard of while I was on the Division, and a man who had the courage to do that would have earned his place on any team, even if he had been a raving queen with bright red lipstick and six-inch stiletto heels. Mind you, he would have stood out on surveillance.

Every team has to have an 'enforcer', someone big and intimidating who can handle himself in a fight. Their job is to step in when an arrest gets rough. Drugs F/L had three such men. The first two were 'Mac' and 'Slapper', sometimes known on the team as the 'gruesome twosome'. Slapper was from Yorkshire, where he had been a doorman before joining the Division. He was tall, wide and bald-headed, hence his nickname. Like many big men he was quietly spoken and actually kind and good-natured once you got to know him. Mac was quite the opposite: he was just a headcase. He wasn't physically as big as Slapper, but he made up for his size with sheer aggression. He was always waiting for it to 'kick off' and if there was trouble at a knock you could always count on him to back you up. He wore heavy-rimmed glasses and in a bad light looked like Michael Caine. Mac and Slapper constantly took the mickey out of each other; they didn't always much like each other, but at a dangerous knock they worked together as if they'd rehearsed. In addition they both played in the second row of the scrum for the Divisional rugby team. At an arrest, their job was to tidy up, to make sure that anyone expected to be violent was kept under control.

To complete the trio we had Ripper, who played full back for the same rugby team. He was fairly short, about 5'7", but seriously into weight-training and karate. At first glance he didn't have the size or presence of the other two but, my God, he could have a ruck. His nickname came from a knock where he'd been attacked by a dealer carrying a machete. They'd ended up wrestling on the floor of the lock-up and the only way Ripper could get the guy to drop the weapon was to bite his arm. The dealer later tried to sue the Division for personal injury. He lost.

Then there were drivers. In the Division high-speed surveillance driving is the most important part of the job, and almost every officer likes to consider himself better than anyone else. But it was generally acknowledged that the frontline heroin team needed the best and there were at least two who fitted the bill: the first was Billy Wright, a 5'6" streak of nothing. He was stick-thin and looked as if he might blow away in a strong wind, but he was also reputedly the best driver on the Division. Before joining he had been a motorcycle paramedic in London, and this is where he had learned his skills. He seemed to have the ability to swerve at high speeds through the middle of packed city traffic, without even touching the brakes. Riding with Billy was like being on a rollercoaster: it was as scary as hell as you were thrown from side to side, but you never felt you were in any danger.

If Billy was arguably the best driver on the Division, then there was another officer on the team who came a close second. Jess had a head start over most of us because his hobby was amateur rally driving. He had been appointed to the Division after an arrest at Heathrow airport: an Australian student had been detained at inward controls in one of the terminals after they found several kilos of cocaine strapped to his body. The student was actually an Australian Rules football player and, knowing that he was facing a long term of imprisonment, he suddenly barged his escorts out of the way and made a run for it as he was being led out from the terminal to a car. He hadn't been cuffed because up to that point he had seemed so docile, and now he put that advantage to good use.

He sprinted away, dodging through the heavy airport traffic which squealed to a stop to avoid running him down. He was chased by half a dozen uniformed Customs officers. The Australian knew he was fast and, after several hundred yards, glanced back and saw that he was outpacing all of the officers except one. He didn't know the layout of the airport and ran all over the place trying to lose his pursuers, vaulting over security barriers and desperately searching for an unlocked door. A few moments later he glanced back and saw that only one officer was left in the chase, but that officer was Jess, who had been on his lunch break when he saw the chase start. Not only was Jess still with the Australian, he was gaining on him. Jess was extremely fit and, after leaving school, had tried out for a professional football team before joining Customs. Finally, in desperation, the Australian ran into the road tunnel which leads from the M4 into the airport, against the flow of traffic. He reasoned it was so dangerous that no one would dare follow him.

A hundred metres into the tunnel, with traffic roaring past only inches away on either side, Jess caught him, knocked him to the ground with a flying tackle and cuffed him before the other officers managed to stop the traffic so that he could be led out safely. ID officers who worked at the airport regularly soon heard about the incident and decided that an officer who showed that kind of determination deserved more than a career on the baggage benches.

The team had its share of good female officers as well. Any

woman who worked on the male-dominated Division had to be tough, but the women who worked on the F/Ls had to be special. Donna, Sarah and Natty were three of the women who had worked there the longest and they all had the same 'Essex girl' sense of humour. They were affectionately known to the rest of the team as 'the coven' because they occupied three desks at one end of the room and always looked out for each other on the predominantly male team. Two of them were married to guys on other teams and they were always the first to hear any gossip which was going around. Amongst the banter of a full-time surveillance team they could give as good as they got, and their biting comments made many a male officer wish he'd kept his mouth shut.

Although technically the junior rank on any team, the Administration Officer (AO) is actually one of its most important members. It is the AO's job to find kit and liaise with other teams and agencies, as well as carrying out routine background checks on any suspicious individuals spotted during surveillance operations. On some occasions the AO even has to act as an extra surveillance officer on the team, although strictly speaking this is against the rules as they aren't trained. They might have to go out on the ground to man an OP or sit in a car logging observations made by the rest of the team. They are also the unofficial grapevine of the Division: because of their contacts with other AOs in the personnel and administration departments, they always seem to know what is going before it is officially announced.

As with any large organisation, none of the systems ran smoothly. There were always long queues for checks on systems like the Police National Computer or for kit such as bugging devices or spare parts for radios. If your cars were getting a bit 'toasty' on an operation and you needed to swap yours for some fresh ones from another team it was easy enough to do a swap. However, if you didn't want to end up with some old car which was a pile of junk, you needed your AO to do a deal with the AO of the other team. So these officers also had to be good scroungers and the F/Ls had two of the best. They were both called Dave, both were ardent West Ham supporters and, like a couple of dodgy East End market traders, the 'two Daves' could always get you whatever you wanted, whether it was a covert transmitter for a suspect's car or a check done on the computer records, without going through the official channels.

Knowing that there were characters like this on the team, it wasn't surprising that I was feeling apprehensive. But I had been trained by the Widow, who was one of the best HEOs on the Division, and I had two years under my belt, including some pretty tricky cases, so I thought that I was ready. In fact I was even looking forward to it. I felt that I had completed my apprenticeship; now I was impatient to see what the next level was like.

But eight o'clock came and went and there was still no sign of anyone. I knew that this team were usually early starters, but the room remained empty. It didn't make sense. I wandered around the room again, looking at posters on the wall. There was a photograph of a crashed car atop a six-foot-high brick wall, with the uninjured driver giving a thumbs up out of the driver's side window. The caption below the photograph read: 'Mac tries not to show out'. On the wall next to Gareth's desk was pinned a thick sheaf of unpaid parking tickets, below which sat a plastic cup with a notice that read 'Please give generously'. It had a wad of worthless Turkish notes and a prostitute's advertising card stuffed into it. I found the corner of the room which I decided must belong to the coven. Someone had photocopied 'The Fat Slags' from Viz and altered the speech balloons to read as though it was about them, and there was a calendar of some half-naked beefcake US firemen hanging on the wall beside it.

At the far end of the room there were three rows of battered and dented lockers, the only old or tatty furniture in the room. I found the one marked 'Lima 3' and noticed that the lock was broken. I briefly wondered who the previous Lima 3 had been and what had happened to him or her. I dumped my kitbag in it, made myself a cup of coffee and then sat and waited. At one stage I thought that perhaps there had been a shout and they had been called out on the ground without anyone telling me. I rang Control, the central operations room which monitors all team activities out on the ground, but they assured me that F/L weren't out anywhere. So I sipped my coffee and sat and waited.

At about ten past nine the first officer finally wandered in. He was a short, pudgy-faced guy with wire-framed glasses, who looked like Harry Potter would if he reached forty and let himself go a bit. He was carrying a holdall which he dumped on a desk. After glancing at some papers that were on it he looked up and caught sight of me sitting at the far end of the room. He ambled over and shook my hand.

'Morning,' he yawned. 'I'm Phil. HEO. Lima 5. You must be the new sacrificial victim.' He smiled as he slumped into a nearby seat and scratched at several days' worth of stubble on his chin.

'Sorry about the lack of welcome, but we were out on the ground until half-four this morning. Technically speaking you were on the strength of the team from midnight and we could have called you out, but Gareth said not to. He said he'd let you get one last night of beauty sleep.' He leaned forwards and looked at me closely. 'Doesn't look as if it worked though,' he grinned.

'Look,' he continued, 'give me a few minutes. I've got some calls to make so just kick around for a bit. The SIOs are up at the Home Office sorting out some warrants. Once the others are in, I'll find someone to give you the rundown.'

Over the next hour or so a line of zombie-like individuals drifted in. They didn't look like the crack surveillance unit I'd been led to expect. They looked hollow-eyed and tired, most of them clutching steaming mugs of coffee like talismans. I recognised some of the better known ones who had been pointed out to me by the Kilos. Some of them came over and said hello; some didn't seem to be fully awake yet. Soon there were about twenty officers milling around, phoning, laughing, chatting, fiddling with cameras or radio equipment, or dozing with their heads on the desk, grabbing the last few possible minutes of kip.

It was like the first morning at a new school, not knowing anyone, not fitting in, not knowing the jokes or the gossip. I wandered round saying hello, trying to join in the conversations. I could see one or two of them eyeing me up occasionally, trying to work out which of the new guys I was. As soon as I mentioned the call-sign Kilo 17 they knew I was 'the ex-spy'. At one stage I got drawn in towards the coven. They were as ferocious as their reputation. They knew who I was and they had already heard my old team nickname, given to me because I had worn a suit on my first day working in the office, rather than the usual ID uniform of jeans and bomber jacket.

'Morning, Mr Chumley Warner,' chuckled one, nudging her friend.

An older one, with shoulder-length curly hair, looked me up and down pointedly.

'Is that how you normally dress? You'll need to get a better surveillance kit than that.'

Before I could answer, the third one said, 'So where have you sprung from, then?'

'Kilos, working cannabis down in Dover.' I hoped that she would be impressed, but she shook her head as if she'd never heard of them. Noticing my disappointment, one of the others said:

'Ah well, never mind love. We'll make a man out of you here.'

A male voice added: 'And if they don't, I will sweetie!'

That had to be Derek. He had just entered the room and swept past. He dumped his kitbag on a desk and then returned to shake my hand. As he did so he said quietly: 'Don't worry about them, love, they're like that with everyone.'

Behind us the three of them cackled together. I smiled politely and decided to move on. A hulking officer I recognised as Slapper, one of the enforcers, came over.

'All right Harry? Fancy coming to the garage to carry out the weekly checks? I'll let you see what we've got in the line-up.' He was heavily freckled and had a Yorkshire accent that was so strong it was almost comical. But he didn't look like someone who would appreciate it if you took the mickey.

I was glad of the chance to escape the awkwardness of all the first-time introductions. I followed Slapper out of the office and down the stairs to the underground garage beneath Custom House, which is where all the sensitive surveillance vehicles are kept. I was impressed by the range of vehicles available. The team was twice the size of a standard ID team so it had twice the number of cars, but the quality and range was far better, including a couple of very nice BMWs and a Mercedes. There were also plenty of little hatchbacks for nipping through the backstreets. As for the rest, they were usual, nondescript family saloons, but whereas the Kilos would have had fairly standard, middle of the range cars so as not to arouse attention, these were Gti versions, definitely built for speed. There was also a battered old estate car, although I was to learn that beneath the dented and rusted bodywork the engine was in top condition and it could really shift. It was known as the 'war wagon' because it carried all the necessary bulky equipment like cameras and observation post equipment which we couldn't fit into other cars. It could also operate as a radio base station if our vehicles were really spread out, such as when covering a target in a rural area.

We checked the oil levels and tyre pressures of each of the cars, running through a set checklist which Slapper had on a clipboard. Although the cars had only been used the night before it was important to check that none of them had picked up a slow puncture or was showing signs of a fluid leak – you never knew whether that day would see you racing around on a motorway surveillance at more than a hundred miles an hour and, with cars that got driven as hard as ID vehicles did, daily vehicle checks were an important part of the job.

Not only were the cars more powerful than those I was used to, but their level of disguise was higher as well. There were several sets of false licence plates in the boot of every car, known in the trade as 'ghost plates'. The Kilos had rarely been in the same place long enough to need this sort of thing, but on intensive target surveillance where the same criminals are followed day after day and often note down the registrations of anything suspicious, ghost plates are an important part of the arsenal for whenever a particular vehicle gets too 'toasty'. I had heard that they weren't officially authorised and that officers on the team had paid for the plates to be made up themselves. But whatever the truth of the story, the management trusted that the teams knew what was needed out on the streets and turned a blind eye to the practice. There were also other little tricks designed to throw suspicious viewers off the scent, from nodding dogs right down to child seats and a carry cot containing an enormous doll which could go on a back seat and pass for a sleeping child.

By the time we had finished doing the weekly checks John, the SIO, had returned to his office. He soon stuck his head round the door of the office and said: 'My room, Harry, in five minutes.'

He was slim, of average height, and in his late forties, with dark but receding hair. Whenever I had seen him around the building he was always smartly dressed and today he was wearing a sharply pressed, grey chalkstripe suit with a blue silk lining. For a moment I wondered (I later realised unfairly) if he might be more concerned with his appearance than with the job, but officers I respected said that during his career he had shown he could work the tough shifts with the best of them. He had quite a temper if you got on the wrong side of him: he wouldn't suffer fools on the team at all and thought little of dismissing anyone he considered wasn't up to the mark. One of the reasons that the team was short-handed was because he would only accept officers who could reach the standards he expected, regardless of what they might have achieved elsewhere on the Division.

He was watering a pot plant on the top of a filing cabinet when I tapped on the open door, exactly five minutes later. He didn't seem too menacing, standing there with his little watering can. Having waved me towards a seat in front of his desk, he sat down and opened what appeared to be a summary of my personnel file.

'The first thing you will make sure you remember is that we're not like any other team on the Division. On your old team you might have talked about whatever case you were on with your old mates. We've all done it. It doesn't do any harm and sometimes you learn something useful, but you don't do it here, all right? Nothing, and I mean *nothing*, goes off the team. These are top-level heroin targets and the maximum sentence for heroin importation is prison for life, same as murder. The bastards we play against will think nothing of putting a bullet in one of us if they figure they can get away with it. We can't risk even one tiny bit of information getting out. If I find out you've broken that rule, there will be no excuses, no second chances, you will be out. Simple as that.'

He gave me a hard stare. When we had met before to discuss

me moving to the team it had just been a pleasant chat, but now he was my boss. I nodded to show that I'd got the message.

'I'm told you're the case officer who brought down Frank Davies,' he said.

The statement sounded harmless enough, but I knew it was a challenge. He wanted to see if I was going to boast about any success I might have had so that he could take me down a peg or two. It was the sort of trick the Widow would have used. But she had also taught me that when you started on a new team, the cases you had worked on before counted for nothing. You had to prove yourself all over again.

'I just did the paperwork,' I replied. 'We had a few bits of luck and my name was on the case file when he got killed.'

He considered this for a short while and then nodded.

'Let's hope you get as lucky while you're here then. OK. Now for the job.'

He opened a different file and passed two photographs across the desk.

'The one on the right is John Haase; on the left is Paul Bennett. Zulus 1 and 2 on this operation, code-name Florr.'

Haase had a heavy-set face, clean-shaven with a close-cropped head of tightly curled hair. His eyes stared blankly at the camera and his mouth was unsmiling. Although it was only an upper-body shot, he looked tanned and muscular and certainly not like a man in his mid-forties, as the date of birth on the photograph made him out to be. Bennett, on the other hand, looked overweight, with a bloated face and a thin growth of beard. It was hard to believe the two of them were related. John briefly outlined Haase's criminal record then continued:

'Haase is your typical, old-style Scouse hard man. He always carries a knife and he'll reach for a gun like it's second nature. He's not sophisticated but he's as tough as they come, and cunning. Bennett is his nephew and from the same mould. They're both highly cautious and surveillance aware.'

He explained about the contract that was out on Knowles. Intelligence sources thought they had traced the leaking of Knowles's home address to a junior clerk in a Customs office in Leeds. John stressed how sensitive that little piece of information was and that it was strictly for team members only.

'We are only in the very early stages of the investigation, but Haase's associates are a close-knit crew. It means a lot of work in Liverpool and that has its own problems: officers from the south of England stand out as soon as they open their mouths up there. At the moment we are rotating half the team at a time for duty in the city, but wherever possible we are borrowing Liverpool officers. On some of the estates up there even the local kids are paid cash if they spot a surveillance officer. So far we know that Haase and Bennett are being supplied by a powerful Turkish syndicate. That syndicate has a contact working somewhere out of London, but we don't know where yet.

'For this job to be a success we've got to do more than just wrap up Haase and Bennett. It would be a big feather in our caps, but they will just be replaced by some other gang of dealers. What we really want is to trace the Turks as well, round them up and cut off the supply of heroin. That means working against them in London at the same time as we are working against Haase in Liverpool. Most important of all is keeping Knowles and his family alive. We know that someone is still out there waiting for the vital piece of information that will track Knowles down. Our biggest problem is that we don't know who the assassin is. If you're the senior officer out on the ground and you get any sort of lead on him, that takes priority over everything else, even the drugs. Understood?'

I nodded.

'As you can see, we've got our work cut out. I hope you're prepared for some hard work. Paddy Clark, the HEO acting as case officer, is in Liverpool at the moment, but hopefully you'll meet him soon.'

He sat back from the folder and gave me a moment to take all this in.

'You came here straight from MI6?' he asked.

I nodded. I had hoped to gloss over this bit of my past without too many questions being asked.

'I spent a couple of years looking after the kids,' I volunteered.

I knew that he would already have found all this out, but he still frowned and asked: 'What? Cooking and stuff?'

I nodded again.

He burst into a short, harsh laugh.

'Jesus! Well don't let the coven find out about it or they'll have you for breakfast.'

His face softened and with a trace of a smile he said, 'I understand that on the Kilos you didn't have any management responsibility?'

'That's right.'

'Well around here, my old son, you pull your weight,' he said, but the look on his face showed that he meant it kindly. Giving me an EO to be responsible for was a sign of his confidence.

'I'm giving you two experienced officers to manage. One is Jackie Dunmall, Lima 10. She came to us from one of the airport teams. She may not look like anything special, but don't let that fool you. She is particularly good at close surveillance. Her big problem is that she hasn't settled in too well. She likes to act the loner and I suspect the team makes her suffer for it. I know she's been thinking about going to an EO post on another team where life would be easier, but I want to see her stay here and move up to be an HEO. That's what I want you to do. Get her to become more of a team player and try and teach her some of those analysis skills you're supposed to have.'

'OK.'

'The other officer is our motorcyclist. He's . . .' John tried to put his thoughts into words and gave up. 'He's Ralph. You'll soon find out. He thinks he's a live wire; sometimes he's charming, but a lot of the time he's just bloody irritating. Oh, and he doesn't take orders. If you tell him to go somewhere on a plot, don't expect him to turn up there. He likes to do things his own way. Calm him down a bit. He's a bloody good biker, he could make a good senior officer and we can't afford to let him go. The trouble is that he knows that.'

I wasn't surprised to hear that he was a bit of a maverick – all of the bikers on the ID were. They were an élite cadre of officers within the organisation. No one could cut through really heavy traffic as fast as they could, so they spent a lot of time out of radio communication with the rest of the team, often conducting surveillance single-handed. As for going where they were told, none of the bikers thought that someone sitting in a nice warm car knew better than them where they should go – and they were usually right.

John passed over the slim personnel files for my new charges. 'What's your driving like?'

'Pretty poor,' I said, with a grin.

'Well you'll get plenty of chance to practise round here, starting today in all probability. As I said, Paddy is away at the moment hoping to get some new intelligence. Something's brewing and the intelligence teams keep promising that one of their sources will have something for us any day now. Come on. I'll introduce you formally to the rest of the team.'

Phil was waiting outside John's office. I don't know if he had been listening at the door but, as we passed by, he grinned at me and, in a passable imitation of Sean Connery, said 'Do you know what a blood oath is Mr Ness? 'Cos you just took one.' I knew that this was a line from the film, *The Untouchables*, when Eliot Ness, a mild-mannered Treasury investigator, has just agreed to take on Al Capone's gang in 1930s Chicago. Phil was forever quoting lines out of movies. I grinned back at him and gave him a single finger salute.

The highlight of my morning was having my name put up on the team board. Now I was officially Lima 3. The Kilo 17 call-sign which, because all the teams comprised fifteen officers, had always marked me down as an outsider was gone for ever. I noticed that Paddy Clark was Lima 2. He would be away in Liverpool most of the time and one of the other HEO slots was vacant. That just left me and Phil, who was Lima 5, as the Lima HEOs in London.

It was shortly after lunch, as I was reading through the case files on Haase and his organisation, when Phil slumped on the edge of my desk and said:

'Better call your wife and tell her you're going away for a few days.'

'Sure. What's going on?'

'Oh, we're just going down to the coast for a few days,' he grinned. 'A little holiday to make sure that you and some of the new guys are nicely rested before we let you hit the streets.'

With a team like the F/Ls you couldn't just turn up and join in a live surveillance. They worked to a system and to a standard. Although all Customs surveillance teams use the same basic system there are always small differences, little things which the team expects and you have to get used to that before you can be let out on the streets for real. These differences can be important. I knew an experienced officer who was loaned to another team for a day. As he and a driver with whom he had never worked before approached a junction, he saw a sports car racing up from the left-hand side. He called out 'No!', which meant 'Stop!' on his team, but in that team the navigator was supposed to call out 'Go!' if the way was clear. The driver misheard him, pulled out and they were hit broadside at fifty miles an hour by the sports car. It was a miracle that no one was killed, but both of them spent several months in hospital. On high-speed surveillance even the slightest mistake can prove fatal.

As well as providing training in their procedures, the team needs to know that they can trust new recruits. With a drugs surveillance you only get one chance – as soon as the opposition spot you and suspect that they are under surveillance they will simply close down. All that effort has been wasted. So Phil and a couple of the more-experienced surveillance officers were taking us down to Bournemouth for three days to make sure that we were up to standard. To make up the numbers we were also taking a couple of officers from the Yankee and November teams. Those teams handled referred heroin cases rather than the target work which we did. But as sister teams to F/L they always got called on first if we needed extra manpower, so it was important that their personnel know our routines and were capable of operations up to our standards. Then came the bad news: Gareth was going to be in charge of the training. We would have to be on our toes and if Gareth thought anyone wasn't up to standard, they would be off the team.

I called Nicky, knowing that she wouldn't be happy about the lack of notice. As soon as she found out I was going to be away for a while she sighed heavily but said that she would do her best. I apologised as much as I could and said that I would make it up to her, but I had enough to worry about just then. Within twenty minutes of making the call we were on our way.

Right from the word go Gareth put the pressure on. I figured something was up when he insisted that all the new officers get behind the wheel and appointed regular team members to be our navigators. My co-driver was called Tony; he'd been out on the ground that morning so we hadn't even had the

37

chance to say hello. We were barely clear of Central London when I noticed the pace of the target car increasing, then Gareth started calling us through to different positions, or sending us off on alternate routes. Soon we were on the motorway heading south. If you were called through to the eyeball position (the car closest to the target, responsible for commentating on all of the target vehicle's movements) you would have to accelerate past all the other vehicles who were already travelling at 90–100 mph. We all knew what he was doing; he was testing our nerve, making sure that we were comfortable under pressure. You can't have people who dither at these kinds of speeds; it would mean danger for the public as well as ourselves.

But it's no good getting the vehicles to where the target is if the footmen are no good. At the motorway services, Gareth suddenly pulled in. The rest of us had to cover the car park and deploy as footmen in order to follow Gareth around the buildings. As we roared away again ten minutes later, Gareth was already growling over the radio:

'Too fucking slow! I want a footman out within fifteen seconds of the target leaving his vehicle. I want someone checking the registration numbers of all suspect vehicles in the car park. I want someone covering possible routes to the other side of the drag.' ('Drag' was one of the Division's terms for a motorway.)

It was always a nightmare if the target was trying to throw surveillance and used one of the service stations with a foot-bridge across to the other side. They would then jump into a waiting vehicle and roar off in the other direction. It was possible to cover that kind of trick, but you had to work like hell.

'I don't expect to have to tell you what to do, this is not fucking primary school and I'm not your fucking mother. Call it out so the rest of the team knows what you're doing. If someone beats you to it, tough. Take the next job and call it out. At the next services we're going to do it all again. Lima 12 you're eyeball. Move up.'

This continued for the rest of the day until we arrived in Bournemouth. By taking us all over southern England, Gareth managed to make a two-hour car journey last almost three times as long. We were all exhausted from the constant concentration demanded by high-speed driving. We hoped that we would have the evening off to recover, after all it was the first day, but after a short break we went out again, this time to practise night driving. Afterwards there was just time for a pint in the hotel bar before collapsing into bed. Gareth didn't join us at the bar. He was on the phone, checking on the progress of the rest of the team in Liverpool and London. I thought about ringing Nicky to see how she was, but I knew she would already be in bed and, besides, I was too tired for an argument.

The next day we started late, to let the early morning rush-hour traffic clear and to give us a break after the night before. Gareth was out early, planning a training route for the day. He had detailed Phil to give us a quick briefing on the team's drills to cover target stops at road junctions, car parks and so on. It was like being back in basic training all over again, but this time the emphasis was on speed, discipline and taking responsibility. On most normal teams there would be a plot commander who would tell the rest of the team where to plot up and take overall control. Now you were expected to make that decision for yourself and be aware of where everyone else was. No one could afford to relax.

Soon we were off again. Right from the start Gareth was on our backs. This time one of the experienced officers would ride in each vehicle with three of us 'new boys', each of us taking turns as driver and navigator. Our car got Marcus, a giant of man with a mane of dark, shaggy hair who looked more like a Hell's Angel than a Customs officer. He was often away working undercover but when he was on the team he always acted as Gareth's deputy, and the two of them had been posted to several teams together during their careers. He was actually a genial, easygoing sort of person compared with the driven personality of his partner. Although he worked us just as hard as Gareth, we had a lot more fun as he wasn't afraid to crack a joke or two as we hurtled around the countryside.

Gareth was in the target vehicle once again. In our vehicle I was first up as driver. I wasn't worried; this was tiring, but the Widow's teaching had been every bit as tough and I thought I could cope with it. However, I soon got a wake-up call when it came to the first junction. I was responsible for 'clipping' Gareth's car, that is, timing my approach so that I just caught sight of him and confirmed that he was across it. But he must have accelerated and I just missed him. When I raced ahead to pick him up further down the road he was nowhere to be seen. The bastard had done a sudden turn down an alleyway just after the junction and lost me.

'Too slow, Lima 3!' bellowed Gareth's voice over the radio. 'Use that fucking accelerator, it's not a fucking milk float!'

As the only new HEO on the training course I felt that he was deliberately trying to show me up, so I hit the next junction spot on and passed control of the target to the next vehicle. I thanked the Widow for all those times she'd taken me out of the office to work on my driving skills. After about an hour at the wheel, I handed over the driver's position to one of the others. It wasn't a particularly warm day, but as I climbed in the back of the car I realised that sweat was dripping off me from the exertion of the driving. The back of my shirt was soaked through and I hadn't even noticed.

Steve, the new driver, had just come out of the army. He was good and for the first half-hour hit every mark spot on. But nobody's perfect. We had just plotted up to cover yet another stop by Gareth. Marcus looked around from the front passenger seat to see how visible we were to other vehicles and was nodding approvingly.

'Yeah, good position Steve.'

The call came over the radio that Gareth was on the move again. It had been a 'ghost stop', a move by criminals designed to catch the surveillance team out by moving off suddenly just after footmen would have been deployed.

'OK, take us away then,' said Marcus.

Steve put the car into gear and hit the accelerator. There was a squeal of tyres and a sickening crunch as we disappeared backwards into a ditch. We were left with the car sticking up into the air at an angle of about forty-five degrees. Although this was Steve's error, we all braced ourselves for the tirade of foul-mouthed abuse which would surely follow. But instead, in a voice filled with mock child-like wonder, Marcus pointed up at the broad expanse of sky which now filled the windscreen and said, 'Cor, look at those fascinating cloud formations.'

We all collapsed into hysterics in sheer relief.

A tow-rope and the brute strength of fourteen other officers got us out of the ditch. Of course it was something that Steve would never be allowed to forget, but I noticed that Gareth didn't look too displeased. At the frantic pace of modern surveillance this sort of thing was bound to happen and everyone had the occasional accident. As long as no one was hurt it was all part of a day's work. Even so, like the rest of us, he'd be as well not to do it twice.

We all had our mishaps but one recruit was twice as bad as anybody else. An academic type who had been transferred from a VAT investigation team. In any batch of transfers you're bound to get one who just isn't up to the mark. He just didn't seem to have any aptitude for the job at all. You might have thought that Gareth would simply chuck him off the team and call for a replacement – he had the power to do it and that was what everyone expected – but rather than scream and rage at the recruit for his stupid mistakes, Gareth took more time with him than the rest of us and actually appeared to be sympathetic and understanding about his floundering efforts. It was as though he really wanted everyone on the course to pass. I began to realise why Gareth had such a good reputation. He tried really hard to help the unfortunate recruit, even taking him out the following evening and doing extra driving practice with him. But in the end Gareth had to send him on his way, telling him that he needed another couple of years on a referred team before he applied to join F/L again.

All in all, Gareth squeezed about a week's worth of training into three days and it seemed only a matter of hours before we were roaring back up the motorway towards London again. The team was so stretched with all the targets we needed to cover that we just couldn't afford time away for further training. Any remaining problems would have to be sorted out on the team. It was gone midnight when I got back home. I was so tired that I simply climbed straight onto bed and fell asleep fully clothed. I had only meant to lie down for a moment. When I woke in the morning, Nicky was leaving the house. We had hardly had time to say two words to each other before it was time for work again.

Back in the office the morning was used for a refresher course in 'arrest and restraint training'. This had been something which was never taken very seriously on the Kilos. We had tended to rely on sheer weight of numbers against anyone who resisted arrest and the expectation was that they wouldn't be armed when the consignment was cannabis. But on the F/Ls it was different. Suspects were usually armed and, seeing as they were facing a life sentence anyway, there was no reason for them not to have a go with either a gun or a knife. We were supposed to call for armed police backup if we thought weapons might be present at a knock, but all the old hands told us that there either wouldn't be time or the armed police would be committed to a job elsewhere so, just as with surveillance, our training was stepped up. We worked in pairs to ensure that all targets were covered at an arrest site. We would hit the target high and low, usually from a sprint, bring them to the ground and cuff them. We never carried guns on the Division and our only hope was that the speed of attack would get us through before anyone recovered from the shock long enough to pull a weapon. Frankly, it didn't sound like much of a defence to me and I hoped we'd never have to put it to the test.

After lunch we sat around the office. The word was that some important information was expected from Paddy and that all routine surveillance by the team had been cancelled. So there was nothing to do but wait. Those who had been training were tired and those who had been out working the night before were even more tired. There wasn't a lot of talking. Most people just dozed or read the newspaper. There was no telling how long we would be out on the ground once it kicked off. Occasionally one of us would glance at the phone, wondering why Paddy hadn't called yet. Looking around the office made me think of a Battle of Britain airfield, the pilots dog-tired and bored but waiting for a call which could mean that they would be suddenly scrambling into action again.

Phil and I were playing chess on a pocket set from my kitbag when Paddy's phone finally rang at about two in the afternoon. Everyone in the room looked up as Terry Banks, Paddy Clark's deputy, crossed the room and picked up the receiver. After a few moments and some mumbled comments, whilst he made some notes in his notebook, Terry put the receiver down and turned round. We were all waiting. John had obviously heard the phone ring from his office and came through the doorway.

'That was Paddy on the phone,' said Terry. 'Haase is sending Zulu 3 and a minder towards London. According to Paddy, they've just set off and are heading for a meet with their Turkish connection.' He looked over at John, who was leaning against a pillar in the centre of the room with his hands in his pockets. 'Paddy says this is the one we've been waiting for.' John nodded and stepped forward.

'All right, boys and girls, we need to cover this meeting. Zulu 3 is Haase's bag man. He sets up the deals so that Haase won't be personally involved. These Turks will be bringing the gear in and we know that, whoever they are, they are a big enough crew to supply more than just Haase, so this job and probably several others hang on identifying these contacts today. I want three things. One, get out fast and plot up as far north as you can. The minder will be looking out for surveillance all the way down and Haase might have sent other vehicles with them. The last thing we want to do is burn any of the Liverpool vehicles.

'Two, take the bag man to the meet and identify the Turkish contacts. This is the most important thing today – if we identify them then we can work on them. Miss this and we might not get another face to face meeting for months. Three, take the Turkish contacts to an address. But don't risk everything by going too close. OK? Gareth, take them out.'

I hadn't even realised Gareth had arrived. He did a quick count of the available officers.

'Right, Slapper, Trev, Derek. You'll all drive one up and I'll be calling on you three first if I want someone close on the target vehicles. Mac, you and Steve take the war wagon and try and keep up. The rest of you pair up and get going. Speed counts.'

Ralph was up in Liverpool, but Jackie, my other EO, was on the far side of the room. She was about 5'2" with straight, blonde, shoulder-length hair, dressed smartly in grey slacks and a dark blue jacket. Her face was plain and she wore no make-up. I had seen her around the office during the morning and the one thing I had noticed was that she hadn't smiled once.

I signalled to her and she nodded. She grabbed the keys to one of the better cars, just before Ripper made a dive for them. We met up on the stairs down to the garage.

'Mind if I drive?' I asked. I hoped she couldn't hear the tremor in my voice.

'Sure.' She threw the keys across the roof of the BMW she had selected as I climbed into the driver's side.

This was it: the first time out on the ground with a target team. Now I'd know if the Widow's training over the last two years had been any good.

Jackie powered up the radio sets and grabbed the map books from the back seat as I reversed the car out of its parking space. In a moment we were roaring up the ramp out of the underground car park and into dazzling sunshine. It was a fairly typical February day, clear and bright but freezing cold. Gareth was just ahead of us, driving 'one-up' in a flash Mercedes. As we followed him up the ramp, the afternoon sun blinded me for a moment and I almost ran into the back of his car as it stopped ahead of me. We jolted to a halt as I jumped on the brakes.

'Easy, tiger,' murmured Jackie, without looking up from her map book.

I breathed a sigh of relief as Gareth moved on again and thought for a moment what a great start it would have been to have smashed two team cars in my first minute out on the ground. But there was no time to worry. Soon we were out on to the quay at the back of Custom House and accelerating towards the gates.

It was time to go to work.

3

The Invisible Girl

Jackie and I sat in our car on a motorway bridge above the M1 and waited. There was only static on the radio because all other mobiles were out of range, but we knew they were out there somewhere, just like us, sitting, watching, waiting.

During our frantic drive out of London and then north on the motorway Gareth had been on the mobile phone, constantly monitoring the progress of the other surveillance team heading towards us from Liverpool. This was another piece of technology which had revolutionised the job in my first two years. When I started almost no one had a mobile phone, now three or four were issued to every team. In this current age of tiny flip-top models which can access the internet and display movies, it's hard to remember how big and cumbersome the early models were, with their batteries the size and weight of house bricks. The Division's technical experts were aware of how easy they were to intercept, so if there was sensitive information – such as asking Control (the central operations control room in London) to run some urgent checks for you – then you still had to stop the car and use a land line, but they had made long-range contact between teams a damn sight easier.

The Liverpool crew were telling Gareth that Haase's bag man, Zulu 3, was travelling fast. He was driving a grey Saab saloon which had been given the designation X-Ray 23. (On an operation all persons have call-signs beginning Zulu and all vehicles have call-signs beginning X-Ray.) The really bad news was that Zulu 3 was accompanied by a second vehicle, driving a short distance behind, which was clearly there to spot any surveillance. The main question was how long was this minder cover was going to stay with them – was he just covering the early part of the journey or would he be going all the way to the meeting? No matter how far he went it was certainly going to make our job much harder. There was also the danger that the Liverpool team who had already followed him for several hours that morning wouldn't be able to remain undetected until they handed over to us.

Gareth decided to gamble. Once Zulu 3 was definitely on the M1 heading south, he told the Liverpool vehicles to break off their surveillance and let the target run. Our best guess was that the meeting would be somewhere in or around London and we would just have to hope that we were right. If Zulu 3 kept heading south we should pick him up somewhere on the motorway. It was just a matter of keeping our eyes open. Even so, it took balls to make a decision like this. If we missed him then the whole operation would be crippled and there would be hell to pay when we got back. But if it worked, the counter-surveillance vehicle would spend the next twenty minutes or so looking for a team that wasn't there.

As we continued to race north, Gareth began to call cars off of the motorway as he calculated the approximate area where we would intercept Zulu 3. Vehicles would turn left at each slip-road and 'plot up' wherever they could get a view of the motorway. The idea was that each junction would be covered if Zulu 3 turned off suddenly and, if not, the mobile could simply join the tail, disguised by traffic joining at that junction. Some vehicles would pass him and take up station ahead so that he was covered from in front and behind.

Jackie and I were about the third car to receive the order

to peel off. I drove up the motorway slip-road and at the round-about at the top we managed to find a position, just before the bridge which crossed the motorway, from which we would be able to see the target approaching in the distance, but made sure that we weren't where the minder might see us. We sat there listening as the radio calls of the other cars faded away until we were out of radio contact. Now it was a matter of waiting until they came back towards us – hopefully bringing Zulu 3 with them. Although it was cold, the sunlight was very bright. Jackie took her jacket off, put some sunglasses on and started chewing yet another stick of gum, all the while never taking her eyes off the road below.

There was no sound as we sat there, except the static of the radio in our earpieces and the rush of air as traffic passed beneath us. I was in quite a lot of pain, although I didn't want to say anything to Jackie. I had noticed over the last year with the Kilos that I was suffering a lot of pain in my stomach when out on a surveillance operation. I wondered if I was developing an ulcer. Certainly the greasy fast food we gulped down when working out on the streets, coupled with the stress and the long hours, made us all candidates, but once I was on the move I was fine. It was the long periods of waiting that caused the pain. I kept meaning to go to the doctor and get it checked out, but there never seemed to be the time and, secretly, I wasn't sure I wanted to know. Like a lot of men, I was hoping it would go away in its own time.

I tried to take my mind off of it by thinking about the job ahead. I had already given up talking to my new partner. While we were training in Bournemouth I had managed to have a quick word with Phil about her. He had warned me that the team knew Jackie as the 'Invisible Girl'. You can tell a lot about someone from the nickname the team gives them; they are often cruel, but none the less accurate for that.

'She just doesn't join in,' said Phil. 'I mean, you've seen her

– she's only five feet nothing, bottle blonde hair, never says anything – you just don't notice her. She's been on the team for a year, but you wouldn't know it. She hasn't got any particular friends, doesn't come down the pub after work. She's just a fucking non-entity. She's useful out on the ground because looking the way she does no one's going to pick her out from a crowd, but if John thinks you're going to turn her into an HEO you're going to have a pretty tough time. I've got Slapper and Greg as my EOs. Both of them could make HEO tomorrow given the chance. Then there's Rick, Mac, Natty. They've all got years of experience under their belts and are just waiting for a chance. Good luck with that one mate.'

I'd only known Phil a few days, but it seemed strange for him to be so harsh when talking about someone. Perhaps he thought he'd overdone too, it because the following day he came over and said:

'Look, I'm not sure it's all her fault. They always complain about men in the work place making it difficult, but women can be worse. When she turned up she was given a pretty hard time by some of the women on the team as soon as they sensed she was a quiet type. She was ribbed about . . . well just about everything really. I don't think they meant any harm, but they didn't exactly put out the welcome mat. Maybe she just needs a break.'

There was something else as well. In an overwhelmingly male dominated organisation such as the Division it seemed to me that female officers had two choices: either they could be like 'the coven', share in the gossip and risqué humour or they could refuse to stoop to such 'laddish' behaviour and remain detached and professional. Both approaches had their merits. It seemed that Jackie, like the Widow on the Kilos, had simply decided on the latter path. Sometimes this was interpreted as unfriendliness, but the Widow was one of the best officers on the Division and she knew what she was doing. In the same way, I didn't think Jackie's quietness was necessarily a black mark against her.

So I had tried hard to make conversation as we drove north. Maybe she just needed someone to break the ice. Even so, we had hardly exchanged two words on the way out of town, but then we had both been concentrating hard. Now she was simply sitting there chewing gum and watching the passing traffic. I could see why people were uncomfortable around her.

'I hope you don't mind me doing the driving today, I just wanted to get it out of my system, driving with a new team, you know?'

She didn't say anything. She just nodded and kept staring out of the window, the muscles in her jaw moving rhythmically.

'Next time out you drive, OK?'

'Sure.'

'How long have you been on the team?'

'A year,' she said quietly, without looking round.

'What do you think of it?'

'OK, I suppose.'

Blimey. Phil had been right, this was hard work. I didn't know if I could take three years of this. She reached over to the back seat and grabbed a pair of binoculars so she could watch for the target car.

'Where were you before?'

'Airport,' she murmured.

'Any particular airport?'

'Manchester.'

And so it went on. I wondered if John had deliberately landed me with the moodiest EO on the team as some sort of test. Despite the poor impression she made on me, her staff reports showed that she was a good officer. She was from a small industrial town in the north of England. She had done some time as a clerk in a local VAT office, then on a revenue fraud investigation team there. But she had always wanted to come south to one of the big drugs teams. So after a couple of years learning the ropes at the airport she had applied to the Division, which, as usual, was short of female employees, and they were only too glad to accept her. They were even more keen when they found that she wanted drugs work and didn't mind the long hours this entailed.

Phil had said she was ambitious. Perhaps she felt that having a brand new HEO as her manager wasn't going to help her case, not like having one of the established characters such as Gareth or Paddy, but there was nothing I could do about that. She and Ralph were the first two people I'd get to manage in the Division. I desperately wanted to get it right and I wanted to like her, but she wasn't making it easy. As I sat there, wondering what to say next, the radio crackled into life.

'Lima 3, Fox 12.' It was Slapper.

'Lima 3.'

'Relay from Fox 2: we are about three miles from your position. The sheepdog is all over us and we have several toasty mobiles. Fox 2 would like you to take the eyeball as he passes your position.'

'Lima 3 received.'

In surveillance terms, a vehicle or an officer can be described as 'warm', meaning that they have been close to the target a great deal, 'toasty', which means that they have been close to the target too much and should be pulled out for a while, or 'burned', which means that the target has definitely spotted them. 'Sheepdog' was the code-word for a minder vehicle and he was clearly giving them some problems.

Taking the eyeball position from a standing start was a tall order and would take careful timing to make it work. Jackie was still peering intently through the binoculars.

'As soon as you pick him out, let me know and I'll start rolling.'

She nodded and as she did so the radio crackled into life again.

'Lima 3, Fox 12: we are at blue four seven, centre lane. Sheepdog is about five hundred metres back.'

All surveillance maps are marked with coloured dots for ease of reference. Without even looking at the map I knew that blue four seven meant that he was at the half-mile warning post. Sure enough a few seconds later they were with us.

'OK, got him,' said Jackie adjusting the focus wheel on the binoculars.

I set off and started to move onto the roundabout. We couldn't enter the slip-road for joining the motorway until we were sure he had passed the slip-road for leaving the motorway – we were still responsible for covering the roundabout if he came up here. Jackie pressed the concealed radio transmission button on the side of her seat.

'Fox 12, Lima 3: Sierra please.'

'Sierra' was the code-word for the current speed of the target. Jackie knew that I would want to adjust our speed so that we could move smoothly into the eyeball position.

'Fox 12, Sierra 70, 75.'

'Lima 3 received.'

There was a momentary pause as we waited for the 'go' signal. We were both trying to calculate where Zulu 3 was. It seemed to be just a little too long before Slapper called:

'That's Fox 12 at blue four six and lifted. He's all yours, Lima 3.'

I accelerated down the on ramp and quickly reached 80 mph, watching for any sign of Zulu 3 moving past.

'FUCK!'

Something shot past us in the third lane like a grey streak. It was the Saab, and from the way he left us standing he was doing at least 100 mph. He was pulling the trick of suddenly accelerating to see what came with him; like a Grand Prix driver, he'd gone slow to allow everything to bunch up behind him then he'd suddenly made his move. Slapper hadn't called it and must have lost sight of him earlier than he claimed. Now we were in trouble. I dropped a gear, pushed my foot to the floor and swung across the nose of the car in the centre lane. The driver hit his horn in protest. I couldn't blame him. It was a dodgy manoeuvre but we had no choice; the two inside lanes were packed and, with the rest of the tail hanging back, if we didn't go with the Saab now we might lose him.

Jackie was as annoyed as I was. She shouted over the roar of the engine:

'Yeah, thanks a lot, Slapper! He's lifted off like a fucking rocket!' She leaned forward in her seat, trying desperately not to lose sight of the Saab.

'This is Lima 3, at one hundred, now one ten. All mobiles close up!' She glanced back over her shoulder. 'Someone give me an update on that fucking sheepdog, I've got nothing here.'

We were in the outside lane but a very long way back. He was already a dot in the distance. It meant that he couldn't spot us, but we had to close the gap or lose him. Then some fool pulled out in front of us and suddenly we were both thrown forward as I braked hard. The tyres squealed as I swerved into the middle lane and then accelerated to undertake him. I wasn't worried about Zulu 3 being able to see us, he was still too far away, but we needed to know where that minder was. There was no sign of him in my rear-view mirror.

'Fox 2, I have the sheepdog. At blue four six. Burning, burning.'

It was Gareth. 'Burning' meant that the minder was accelerating hard. He had probably realised he could no longer see his mate and was trying to catch up. That was bad news for us: he could come up behind us at any time.

'Lima 3, Fox 5: I'm your backup. I'll let you know when the sheepdog comes past. You're clear to go with Zulu 3.'

That was Jess. We might have known that he would be somewhere at the front. Meanwhile Zulu 3 was really pushing it.

Not only driving fast, but undertaking as well if he had to. The traffic on this section of the motorway was not too heavy, but it was spread over all three lanes with only the occasional gap to get through. It took everything I knew to plan ahead. For the next five minutes he maintained this sudden burst of acceleration, taking his car all over the road to keep moving forward through the traffic. The only blessing was that he couldn't have any time to keep a close watch behind. But even though I was doing my best to use other vehicles as cover, it could only be a matter of time before he caught sight of us. No one else was travelling as fast as we were.

'We need to hand this over soon. We are getting toastier by the moment,' said Jackie.

'Feel free,' I replied.

As soon as a car was in a position to take over from us, we should get a call of 'two three' over the radio to let us know, but so far not even Jess was there and we had to keep going.

There was a knot of traffic ahead. Zulu 3 had got past by undertaking down the inside lane, which was relatively empty. As Zulu 3 swerved back into the third lane I figured that I was out of his eyeline and tried to follow his course along the inside lane, but his manoeuvre must have irritated someone and as I tried to push through they suddenly swerved in front to prevent me.

'Shit!'

I stamped on the brakes to stop us disappearing into his boot. I changed down and the roar of the BMW's engine went up several octaves, There was nothing to do but swing onto the hard shoulder to go past this idiot; the other lanes were blocked. But even as we passed him he deliberately swerved towards us as if meaning to sideswipe us. In a moment it was over and we were gone, but where did these self-appointed guardians of the road come from? It wasn't the first time one of them had almost killed me. Jackie had been thrown forward by the sudden braking, but she just tightened her grip on the map book and concentrated on keeping sight of the target. She might be a sulky so-and-so at times, but there was nothing wrong with her nerve.

'I've lost him,' I said.

She was peering into the distance.

'Still got him. About a dozen up in the outside lane, just on the bend.'

She must have sharp eyes. I could just see a grey blob which I guessed must be what she was looking at. I managed to gain some ground using the second lane, which for some reason was fairly empty, and we were just preparing to move up much closer to him when his speed suddenly dropped right off and he moved back into the inside lane. I quickly let our speed fall off and fell in behind a heavy goods vehicle, easing over occasionally to make sure he was still there. The reason for his sudden change of pace became clear as we cruised past a police patrol car sitting on an observation hump by the side of the road.

A few minutes later I heard a car horn and glanced to my right. It was the prat who had tried to run us off the road. The drop in Zulu 3's speed had allowed him to catch us up. The balding, middle-aged driver was obviously still unhappy, mouthing obscenities and gesticulating. I pulled my ID wallet out of my top pocket while still keeping one eye on the road ahead. I held it open against the side window so that he could see the warrant card and metal badge. Over the top of it I mouthed the words 'fuck off' and glared at him. He probably had no idea what a Customs & Excise crest looked like, but must have thought it was a police badge. Anyway, it was enough. The driver held up a hand, mouthed 'sorry' and eased his car back.

'Charming man,' muttered Jackie sarcastically, before punching the transmit button for another radio call.

'Two three identify.'

In order to answer the call 'two three' you had to be in visual contact with the eyeball car, but I couldn't see anyone behind us.

'Two three, Fox 5,' said a triumphant voice.

It was Jess. We might have guessed he'd still be there.

'What about that sheepdog, Jess?' asked Jackie.

'No sign yet, mate.'

'Lima 3, Fox 2: I've still got the sheepdog, now passing blue three six.'

Jackie glanced at the map book on her lap.

'He's still about half a mile back,' she said.

'I'm not bloody surprised,' I replied. 'Let's pass it.'

Jackie nodded.

'Lima 3, Fox 5: X-Ray 23, five up in the inside lane, you have the eyeball.'

'Fox 5, yes, yes.'

Jess's anonymous blue Sierra eased out from behind an estate car about three hundred metres behind us and cruised past in the second lane. Donna, the leader of the coven, who was acting as Jess's navigator, gave us a little wave from the passenger seat as they cruised past. I gave her a grin and a good-natured two-fingered salute in reply. I let the speed fall off further.

'That's Fox 5, nine nine,' called Donna.

'Lima 3: lifted,' replied Jackie, sitting back in her seat with a sigh of relief. 'Nothing like a bit of excitement to start the day,' she said.

I smiled at her but she didn't smile back. Clearly the ice hadn't broken yet.

Zulu 3 pulled the same trick twice more as we headed towards London, once with the minder staying close to him and once with the minder hanging behind and watching for anyone coming from way back. We didn't know if they were still suspicious or just checking for the sake of it. It was interesting to watch an amateur conduct counter-surveillance. Whoever it was clearly knew the theory of what they were doing, but reading about it and doing it are two different things. Although he was a nuisance, we always knew where he was and were able to make sure that the manoeuvres of our vehicles fitted in with the surrounding traffic patterns.

By now we were getting close to the junction of the M1 and M25. I wondered if Zulu 3 would head all the way into central London. But at the junction Zulu 3 headed east and they separated, with the minder vehicle leaving the motorway and then heading back the way he had come. Slapper followed him for a few minutes more, but he was definitely headed back up north.

We continued to drive at a much more sedate pace around the M25. There were no more tricks. We still had to keep an eye open: just because the old minder had pulled away didn't mean they hadn't arranged for another vehicle to take over. But you could tell from the radio calls that everyone in the tail felt much more relaxed now that he had gone. Meanwhile, we kept expecting Zulu 3 to take an exit and head into central London, but he just kept heading steadily east and south.

'Why on earth would the Turks make him come so far south for a meeting? Wouldn't it make more sense to meet him halfway?' I asked.

'Bringing him down here makes a point. Let's the Liverpool crowd know who's in charge,' said Jackie. 'After all, the Turks have the drugs, they call the tune.'

We wondered if he was heading for Thurrock services just north of the River Thames — it was often used as a meeting place by smuggling gangs — but he kept going. He ignored the turning for the A13 leading into the East End of London and kept heading south for the Dartford River Crossing. Soon we were following him over the bridge. Where on earth was he going? He seemed to be skirting his way around London. This was well beyond the Turks' normal territory. From the radio traffic from the rest of the team it was clear that several of them thought that Paddy had made a mistake and that Zulu 3 was going to head all the way down to Dover and out of the country.

All this speculation was probably the reason that we relaxed and made a mistake. There was a row of tollbooths at the far end of the bridge. As the traffic bunched up in queues and waited for their chance to pay there was a perfect opportunity for the target to look around and study other vehicles. The standard pattern for tackling these booths was to spread the team out. Some would overtake the target and go through before he got there. The others would join as many different queues as possible. The beauty of the system was that no one was in the queue behind the target, which is where people always expect surveillance to be.

Jackie and I were in the eyeball position as we approached the booths. We took a lane about five away from the target. There was no danger of losing him. We could see him quite clearly through the traffic in the other queues. Jackie commentated on his progress towards the booths. As luck would have it we passed through our booth at exactly the same time and were able to pick him up again smoothly on the other side. Mentally, the entire team settled down for another long motorway drive when he suddenly caught us all out. The first exit from the motorway is almost immediately after the booths and Zulu 3 took it.

'It's an off, off, off, at blue one!' shouted Jackie.

There was a burst of cursing over the radio from various other call-signs and at least three mobiles were clearly detached from the tail because they had already driven past the exit. They would have to drive all the way to the next exit and come back. Jackie and I stayed with him and fortunately we had good cover from other traffic. Within a minute or so he drove into the car park of a large motel. Jackie glanced at me as if to say 'what now?' We had no backup, so the only thing to do was go with him. The Saab pulled into a parking space near the entrance to the motel. I drove past him, further into the crowded car park. We were out of his direct line of sight, but could still see the driver's door of the car.

'That's Lima 3 complete the car park. Still nine nine.'

Someone must have been close behind us because almost immediately Donna's voice came over the radio.

'That's Fox 5 complete the car park, Lima 13 going foxtrot.'

She was going into the motel ahead of Zulu 3. This is the secret of modern surveillance – wherever possible always be ahead of your target. Gareth acknowledged and called on other mobiles to hold short. He didn't want to expose any other mobiles in the car park until he was sure what sort of security the Turks had.

'Fox 2, Lima 3?'

'Lima 3.'

'Have you two got something smart to wear into that motel?'

I glanced at Jackie, who nodded.

'Lima 3: yes, yes.'

'OK, get changed and get ready. We'll call you in as soon as we get the all-clear from Donna.'

Zulu 3 climbed out of the Saab. He was an unshaven Caucasian man in his mid-thirties, with collar-length dark brown hair. He was dressed in a dark jacket, grey trousers and an open-necked checked shirt. He was carrying a small tan-coloured holdall. He walked straight through the entrance of the hotel. Jackie was busy changing her trainers for some smarter shoes with heels. She pressed the concealed transmit button.

'That's Zulu 3 complete the motel, towards you Lima 13.'

'Lima 13 received.'

I finished putting on a tie and grabbed my jacket from my kitbag on the backseat.

'Ready?' I asked.

'Yeah, let's go,' she said.

We climbed out of the BMW, locked it and strolled across the car park hoping that we looked like a smart young couple who had stopped for lunch. Not for the first time I cursed the size of the standard issue 'undercover' radio I used. It fitted in a shoulder holster under my right arm and fed a radio signal, via a loop of antennae under my shirt, to a tiny earpiece. That way there was no need for any wires running to the earpiece, such as you see bodyguards using around the US President. The earpiece was so small and sat so deeply in my ear that it was all but invisible. The radio set itself was a different matter. It was possible to make adjustments to the harness and the battery pack, but no matter what I did it always seemed to make an obvious lump under the arm of my jacket. Jackie didn't have the same problem; her radio was hidden in her shoulder bag.

She looked just right. She'd put her hair up and brushed her fringe back to change her appearance, but it was the little touches which made all the difference, like the strappy high heels and the long dangling earrings. She didn't look like a surveillance officer and if you saw her you might remember the earrings but you wouldn't remember her face.

We heard Donna's voice loud and clear through our earpieces:

'That's Zulu 3 through the lobby and straight into the bar.'

That was a surprise. They were having the meeting out in the open. We would normally have expected the meeting to take place in a hotel room, but perhaps the two sides didn't trust each other enough for that.

Jackie moved closer to me and put her hand in mine. Considering that she had hardly made an effort to speak to me all afternoon, I was a bit surprised. Then she pulled me closer, let go of my hand and slid her arm around my waist. Instinctively

I put my arm around hers. She smiled across at me, but under her breath murmured: 'Check the door.'

I had already spotted him. There was a dark-skinned man wearing a light grey suit, standing there, scanning the car park. He was a big guy, with close-cropped hair and a thin black moustache; he looked every inch the professional bodyguard. It couldn't have been less subtle if they had parked a tank outside the door. As we walked towards him I wondered if he was armed. It would fit the Turks' usual operating pattern. Clearly they were taking security for this meeting seriously.

Jackie switched into acting mode. She began chattering amiably about her friend and the problems she had buying a new car as we strolled towards the door. All I had to do was smile and to mutter 'uh-huh' and 'really'. The guard glanced in our direction but didn't appear to be interested in us. When we passed him my earpiece was on the far side from him. Jackie's was covered by her hair.

As we entered the motel we relaxed for a moment, but then realised that he had followed us in. We crossed the carpeted reception area towards the lounge with the guard a few paces behind. There were glass display cabinets to our right, exhibiting jewellery of some sort. The backs of the cases were mirrored and I could see his reflection in them. I pulled Jackie's arm and we stepped over to make a show of examining the jewellery. I watched the reflection of the guard as he turned and walked away down a corridor behind us. I had no idea where he was going, but for the moment he wasn't our problem.

I couldn't see Donna, but her voice came through loud and clear in my earpiece so she must have been close.

'Straight through the doors. They're at the third table on the left.'

I had one hand in my pocket where the transmission switch for my personal radio was located. It had two buttons, one for voice transmission and one to transmit a tone. I tapped out an acknowledgement. As we moved to another of the display cases I looked around. No one was near us so I decided I could risk a message.

'All mobiles be aware, there is a watcher circulating in the hotel. IC2, six-foot tall, thin black moustache, grey two-piece suit.'

'Fox 2.'

I turned to Jackie.

'OK let's go,' and we walked through the archway into the lounge.

As soon as we entered I was aware of them. The lounge had various low coffee tables scattered around, with a mixture of armchairs and sofas next to them. Some of the sofas were against the longest wall of the lounge and Zulu 3 was sitting on one of these, facing two dark-haired, Mediterranean-looking men in chairs on the other side of the table.

'Get us something to drink. I'll find us somewhere to sit,' said Jackie, smiling sweetly. If her heart was thumping as loudly in her ears as mine was, she didn't show it. I collected a couple of coffees from the bar at the far end of the room. When I turned round to look for her, my heart nearly stopped beating altogether. The hotel lounge was surprisingly busy for the middle of the afternoon and there weren't many free tables, but there was one right next to the targets. That was where Jackie was sitting. It made sense – we needed to see and, if possible, hear what was going on – but even so this seemed pretty bold. I made my way between the tables, trying not to spill too much of the coffee on to the saucers. I placed the cups on the table and sat down. Zulu 3 glanced up at me, but only for a moment. Oddly enough, that seemed to help. I concentrated on Jackie and half-turned so that I was facing her.

My earpiece was now in the ear facing the criminals. They probably wouldn't notice it but there was no sense in taking chances, so I reached up as if to brush my hair, palmed the earpiece and moved it to the other ear a moment later. Still half-listening to Jackie chat away, I pressed the signal button in my pocket three times. The team was waiting for the three tones to let them know that we were in place.

Gareth's voice came back loud and clear so there was a strong signal, which was a relief. Obviously Jackie and I couldn't talk this close to the targets, so Gareth now asked a series of 'yes/no' questions which I answered with one tone for 'yes' and nothing at all for 'no'. Of course, this meant that every question to which the answer was 'no' had to be repeated so that it could be answered in the affirmative, but experience had shown that any other system – especially where transmission was poor (that meant almost anywhere) and tones went unheard – led to answers being wrongly interpreted and suspects getting away.

'Do you have the target in sight?'

One tone.

'Has he met the contacts?'

One tone.

'How many contacts are there?'

Two tones.

'Two tones received. Does Zulu 3 still have the holdall?'

One tone and so on. It was laborious, but based on this information the team would plot up around the motel and Gareth would decide whether more footmen were required inside. It was a fine balance: you didn't want to put officers close to the target unless you had to, but use too few and there was always the chance of missing a vital contact or departure.

Gareth was an old hand at this and quickly determined what was happening. The only sticky moment came when he asked if we could hear what was being said. Annoyingly I couldn't. It was just too faint to make out, but Jackie was sitting closer. I leaned forward and murmured under my breath:

'Can you hear them?'

Jackie simply smiled and shook her head whilst continuing to gabble on about dresses or something. Once again I had to admire how good she was at this. I let Gareth know the situation.

'OK, Lima 3 and all mobiles, if they split we will stick with the new contacts and drop Zulu 3. We need to identify the new players. Confirm.'

I pressed the button once again. Outside Gareth was ordering a vehicle into position so that photographs could be taken. The two new contacts and the guard were quickly given target numbers: Zulus 26, 27 and 28. It would be our job to let them know when the Turks left. Meanwhile I could hear over the radio that Donna was monitoring the movements of the bodyguard, now Zulu 26. Apparently he was heading our way.

We sat and drank our coffees slowly, Jackie chattering away quite happily, me mostly smiling and nodding whilst keeping a view of the meeting within my peripheral vision. It was tantalising. Occasionally, when the level of background noise in the lounge dropped away, we could almost hear what was being said. It was clearly in English, not Turkish. There was an almost overwhelming temptation to move just a little closer to hear what they were saying. But although the information could have been invaluable we knew it would have been too risky.

The bodyguard walked through the entrance to the lounge and approached the table next to us. Zulu 3 looked up at him cautiously. The bodyguard leaned forward to murmur something in the ear of the older of the two Turks. As he did so his jacket bulged open slightly and I could quite clearly see the grip of what had to be a 9mm automatic under his left arm. I quickly looked away. Jackie was turned away from him and hadn't seen anything. I knew I had to tell the rest of the team.

It was exactly at that moment that I realised I was no longer hearing the gentle hiss of static in my earpiece. I gave the transmission button a push but heard nothing in reply. It was probably a dead battery; in those days they often gave false charge readings and would suddenly go dead when you most needed them. But it was vital that we got the link back to the team outside.

I leaned over to Jackie and murmured, 'Zulu 26 is armed.' Amidst the general level of noise in the lounge, no one but her was likely to hear me. Her eyes widened in surprise and a second later she glanced over her shoulder. I don't know if she could see the gun, but she nodded slowly.

'OK, that makes things interesting.'

'The worse news is I've just lost radio comms.'

She didn't look surprised; personal radio sets were notoriously unreliable.

She smiled and nodded again.

'No problem. I'll just go to the ladies', I'll be able to contact them with my set from there.' She stood up, gave me a peck on the cheek and wandered off through a doorway next to the bar.

Zulu 26, the bodyguard, had wandered off again. I sat there alone, drinking my coffee and sitting sideways-on to the three men at the next table. Without Jackie there I felt that I really stood out. I wished that I smoked; at least it would have given me something to do rather than just staring into space.

Zulu 3 picked up the tan holdall which was on the floor next to the sofa and placed it on the coffee table. The younger of the two Turks, Zulu 28, unzipped it, glanced inside and then put it on the ground beside him. It astonished me that no one else in the lounge paid any attention to what was happening. Here were men passing a bag to each other as if they were straight out of a spy film, accompanied by an armed guard patrolling the area who couldn't have been more obvious if he'd worn a neon sign on his head saying 'Gangster'. It was as if I was inhabiting some mysterious level of the world which other people couldn't see.

As I was puzzling over this I caught sight of the holdall. It was still unzipped. It probably contained money, but it would be nice to be sure – it would make a lot of difference to the evidence in court. Just seeing a holdall passed between them would mean almost nothing; being able to confirm there were bundles of cash in it could change everything.

Then I realised that the older of the two Turks was staring at me. He had noticed my eyes on the holdall and was immediately suspicious. I turned away; after all, I could be anyone sitting there. People often made eye contact in a restaurant, so what? I looked around the bar as if wondering when Jackie would return. Out of the corner of my eye I saw him say something to Zulu 3, gesturing towards me at the same time. Zulu 3 shook his head. Then the Turk was staring at me again. This time I didn't know where to look. I knew he couldn't see my earpiece as it was in the ear on the other side from him, and I had only given the bag a quick glance – what had upset him so much?

He gestured to the big Turk who was now standing at the archway. That was when I knew I was in trouble. It's not unknown for criminals to challenge people they suspect at these sorts of meetings. Innocent members of the public may get upset, but criminals often consider the aggravation worth it for the chance of catching out a surveillance officer. The big Turk was crossing the room towards us. At that moment Jackie returned, slumped onto the sofa next to me and grabbed my arm, giving me a kiss on the cheek. That changed everything and the next moment the bodyguard was being waved away and the Turk seemed to have lost interest in us.

I breathed a huge sigh of relief and said to Jackie, 'Darling, I think I want to marry you.'

'What?!' she exclaimed under her breath, and for a moment she gave me a mystified smile. It was the first time I had seen a genuine smile from her all day.

Less than five minutes later the meeting broke up. Now that

the action was over my radio set sprang back into life and I was able to give one long, continuous tone on the handset to alert the rest of the team. Gareth's voice immediately responded:

'Lima 3, is that the meeting breaking up?'

One tone.

'OK got that. Sit tight. All mobiles let Zulu 3 leave the area, we are staying with the new contacts.'

The Turks seemed in no hurry to move. Annoyingly, we could now hear snatches of what they were saying to each other, but it was in Turkish, which neither of us spoke. So much of the F/Ls' work was against Turkish gangs that the Division actually paid for some of the team, such as Jess, to have Turkish lessons. Pity he wasn't here.

It was imperative that Jackie and I stay in the bar. I went and fetched another cup of coffee. We had already made them suspicious once, following Zulu 3 out would have been too much. Eventually Gareth radioed that Zulu 3 had left the car park and had been seen heading north towards the river crossing. Shortly after that the Turks stood up and left. They hadn't given us a second glance so perhaps we had got away with it, but I certainly wouldn't be able to go close to the older one, Zulu 27, for the rest of the day and probably for a week or so if we could manage it. Meanwhile Zulu 26, the bodyguard, was in the car park, but he couldn't have been a very good lookout because Slapper was still able to get some excellent photographs of them using a telephoto lens.

Now that they were gone I was able to tell Gareth about the handover of the holdall whilst pretending to talk to Jackie.

'Received Lima 3. Fox 12 will stay behind at the lift-off. Have Lima 10 transfer to his mobile and you can drive one up for a while.'

Great. That meant I would spend the rest of the day doing my own map reading and radio work as well as driving. Now that the Turks had left and the adrenalin had stopped pumping

I suddenly felt really tired. Still, if I could stay quietly at the back of the tail it shouldn't be too bad.

Jackie and I listened on our earpieces as the team tracked the three Turks to a large Mercedes saloon and followed it as it left the area. As soon as they were well on their way, Slapper gave us the all-clear. We found him sitting in the car park in the war wagon, then we went to the BMW to get Jackie's kit and to change some of our clothes again. Back in the car she was quiet again, almost sullen. The smile and that moment of contact between us were long gone. It was like a switch she suddenly threw. As she sat on the edge of the open boot of the car and changed out of her high heels she said, 'Bet you any money you like we're going to Green Lanes.'

'Why? Do we do a lot of work around there?' I asked.

'Sometimes it feels like we bloody live there,' she replied with venom.

We left the car park at speed, determined to get back to the tail as soon as possible. Jackie was driving the other car and I let her take the lead as it would save any unnecessary fiddling with maps if we went deeper into London. She drove fast and wasn't afraid to take the slightest of gaps to overtake if the opportunity presented itself. The Widow would have approved.

The tail was heading for the Dartford Tunnel when we lost radio contact but, sure enough, as we emerged from the other side we picked up their signals again. We needn't have rushed. The Turks were driving very sedately, well under the speed limit, and the rest of the team was strung out a long way behind them, in contrast to our earlier frantic dash down the M1. I could only imagine that the Turks didn't want to be stopped by the police with a holdall full of money in the car. They turned off the M25 at junction 30 and then towards the centre of London. Before long we were on the North Circular Road. As we stopped at occasional sets of traffic lights I took off my tie and jacket. I had an old green parka and a grey baseball cap on the seat next to me, ready for if I suddenly had to go out on foot. It wasn't much of a change of look, but it would do. I didn't plan to get close to the targets again that day.

Jackie's prediction about Green Lanes turned out to be right. It is one of the main centres of the Turkish community in north London packed with halal butchers, kebab shops and sports clubs. It was like downtown Istanbul, with Arabic script everywhere, brightly coloured posters for Asian films in many of the windows and the faint strains of Middle Eastern music audible from almost every other shop. There were very few white faces in the street, which was going to make our job harder. I had never seen the sports clubs before. They had plain shop-fronts with the names of Turkish sporting teams emblazoned across them. For 'members only', they were like private clubs everywhere: the perfect cover for illegal dealings. A lot of white gangs liked to use private bars for the same reason.

The Mercedes (which now had the call-sign X-Ray 40) pulled up in the main road right outside one of these sports clubs. All three of the Turks climbed out and went inside. I pulled up in a side road and put on the baseball cap and coat. There was no way we could follow them in so we would have to sit and wait. In the meantime, we could only guess at what was going on inside. Our job was a long way from complete – saying that a club on Green Lanes was being used as a cover for smuggling was like saying there's tea in China; so what? It was possible that the club didn't even know what they were up to or this might be a one-off visit. For our day's work to be complete we had to wait until they left and follow them until they went home. Then we would be ready to work on them over the next few weeks. I pulled on the baseball cap and parka and settled in for a long wait. It was even colder now and it was getting dark.

Several hours passed. Even though we were all tired Gareth kept us on our toes, driving round the area to make sure that no one had parked in a location where they stood out and regularly rotating vehicles parked in the main road. He also kept a three-person foot-team out walking the streets, watching anyone else who went in and came out, getting descriptions, logging registration numbers. It was cold work but no one complained because it made a change from the monotony of sitting in a car. Everyone was expected to do a stint, even Jackie and me, and of course Sod's Law dictated that it was when we were on the street that the suspects came out again.

It wouldn't have mattered if they had simply driven off, but instead Zulus 26 and 28, the bodyguard and the young Turk, went to the boot of the Mercedes. Zulu 28 was carrying the tan holdall. I was in a delicatessen across the road with eyeball on the entrance of the club, and so it was my job to describe what was happening to the rest of the team.

'That's Zulus 26 and 28 at the rear of X-Ray 40 . . . boot open . . . They're both fiddling with something in the boot . . . looks like they are sorting something . . . I am unsighted.'

The microphones on personal radio sets could be concealed behind the collar of a coat and were extremely sensitive, so they could pick up my voice even though I was mumbling so that no one else in the shop could hear. Gareth's urgent tones cut into my commentary.

'Can you get in close for a look Lima 3?'

'Lima 3: I'm burned,' I reminded him.

'Fox 2 to all footmen, can anyone take this?'

'Lima 10: no, no.'

'Fox 8: no, no.'

Gareth must have still had his hand on the transmission switch because we all heard him say 'Fuck!' There was nothing for it.

'Lima 3, I'll get a look, wait one.'

I was on the ground, it was my call. After all, in the dark, how much of a risk could it be? I stepped out of the shop and went to the edge of the road, waiting for the heavy traffic to clear so I could get across. On the other side of the road I could see Zulus 26 and 28 still bent over at the boot of the car. Suddenly a voice I hadn't heard before burst over the radio net, very loud and very clear.

'Tanaaaa! Lima 9 is on plot and has the eyeball!'

A motorcycle roared up and swung in behind the Mercedes, its front wheel almost hitting Zulu 28 in the back of the legs. The rider climbed off and unbuckled his helmet. As he did so he leant forward quite blatantly so that he could see what was in the boot of the Mercedes. I couldn't believe that neither of the suspects noticed this, but they were so intent the boot's contents that they didn't even glance up at him. I ran my mind over the team list: Lima 9; this was Ralph, my other EO, the comedian. He was supposed to be in Liverpool today. I turned away from the side of the road and began to walk up the street.

'What's in the boot Lima 9?' asked Gareth.

Ralph had placed his helmet on the seat of the bike and was now fiddling with the panniers at the back.

'You're not going to believe this guys. It's groceries: tins, packets and all that kind of shit. It's got Turkish labels. Have you guys been working a deadly grocery smuggling ring while I've been away?!'

'Shut up Lima 9,' growled Gareth.

We didn't realise it at the time, but we were missing an important clue. All thoughts we might have had about what the Turks were doing with the groceries were immediately interrupted by the next call.

'Wait one: Zulu 28 has the holdall open . . . and we have a nice bundle of cash passed to Zulu 26.'

Bingo. That was what we wanted.

'That's Zulu 26 now with a box containing the groceries . . . Boot closed . . . Zulu 26 is back to the club . . . Zulu 28 carrying a tan holdall is now towards green one nine.'

Green one nine was south of the club. I looked across the

road and there was Zulu 28 walking briskly. There was no way Ralph could follow him but I could see that Billy Wright had now caught up with us and Jackie was not far behind.

'Fox 8 has the eyeball,' called Billy.

'Lima 3: two three.' I stayed on the opposite side of the road, so that we had him covered if he crossed.

We followed him down the road about two hundred yards until he turned right into a side-road. Billy kept going – you never follow a target if he makes a change of direction, that's why you work as a team. It was now my job to commentate from where I was standing, in a darkened shop doorway on the other side of the road. I also had to call Jackie through when it was safe. For once everything seemed to be running smoothly, all thoughts of tiredness forgotten.

'That's Fox 8 lifted.'

'Lima 3 has the eyeball. Lima 10 wait.'

'Lima 10: received.'

I could hear Gareth ordering more footmen on to the street to back us up, but it wasn't necessary. Zulu 28 only walked a short distance before unlocking a car and climbing in. I couldn't quite see what it was because of the other parked cars.

'That's Zulu 28 into an unknown X-Ray. Come through Lima 10.'

Jackie stepped out of the kebab shop where she had been queuing and quickly turned the corner. Gareth was manoeuvring vehicles to begin a mobile surveillance as soon as he drove away. As the car moved I could see that it was a black XR3i hatchback. Jackie called the registration as it pulled away and the mobile team picked him up as soon as he reached the end of the road. Soon their radio signals faded as they headed further south into London.

Meanwhile Gareth already had another foot-team out covering the club, waiting for either Zulus 26 or 27 to emerge. Jackie, Billy and I used the backstreets to return to our vehicles. Gareth had split the team by sending three vehicles with Zulu 28. We only had enough people to cover one more departure. Gareth announced that we would follow and house Zulu 27, the older of the two Turks who had been at the meeting. Zulu 26 only appeared to be hired muscle.

Zulu 26 left shortly afterwards in the Mercedes. It was another long, dull hour before Zulu 27 emerged. The foot-team followed him to an expensive-looking Jaguar saloon, another sign that we were on the right track, and we followed him away. It was another long and boring surveillance. There was no sign of any minder vehicles and Zulu 27 drove slowly and carefully. It was a real pain; in many ways a slow vehicle is harder to follow than one driven quickly because the team has to constantly loop past him and swap the eyeball position frequently. Eventually we took him to a prosperous-looking estate of detached houses in Kenton. He parked the Jaguar on the drive and went inside. That should have been our cue to go home but Gareth wasn't that easily satisfied. He kept the team on the ground for another two hours, waiting and watching. Zulu 28 had been followed to a flat just north of St Pancras station. Neither Zulu 28 nor Zulu 27 reappeared that evening and no one else arrived at their addresses. Finally, towards midnight, Gareth stood us all down to go home.

Even then we weren't finished. We all had to meet up at a point halfway between the two groups to sign the surveillance log. This is a book in which all the day's observations had to be written down as they happened by a 'logkeeper' – the most unpopular job on a surveillance team.

The system was unbelievably pedantic. Every sheet was numbered so that nothing could be removed. Every single move by the targets had to be individually witnessed and signed with time and date, which was a real pain. In court, the slightest error could allow a defence lawyer to cast doubts on the whole document and have it excluded from the case. So, even though it was a major nuisance at the end of a long surveillance when we were all really tired, most of us were prepared to stay for an extra half-hour or so to get the log signed rather than risk a jury never hearing what we had seen that day. We all knew of cases which had been lost because of this.

Finally the log was complete. Gareth wanted us all back out on the ground by seven the next morning. We were going to cover Zulu 27. As the older of the two, living in a better area and with a better car, the chances were that he was higher up the hierarchy than Zulu 28. I quickly did the calculations in my head: by the time I had dropped off Natty, who lived near me, got home and got to bed, I would have four hours before I had to get in the car and set off again.

4

Fiddler on the Roof

The alarm burst into life and I thumped the 'off' button with my fist. I tried to unglue my eyes and squinted at the face of the clock. 7.30 a.m. It was a late start today because we had only finished the previous day's work in the early hours. We had been working on Zulu 27 at his house for over a week now. He seemed determined to win the award for 'most boring target in the world'. He never went out, never saw anyone, never did anything. If he went to the supermarket for some shopping we almost went crazy with excitement because it meant that we could get out of the damn cars for a while. The previous day our intelligence team had a given us a tip that he was going to a restaurant in Tottenham and they believed it might be something to do with the drugs syndicate. He had been there until the early hours of the morning with his family, but no one else had turned up. I didn't mind working long hours, but when the effort seemed to be wasted it was a bit hard to take.

Somehow I found the energy to stumble into the kitchen and stood there, yawning while I waited for the kettle to boil. In the hall I could hear Nicky on the phone to the nanny, asking her to stay late the following day. When she came into the kitchen I asked, 'You need Jenny to stay late tomorrow?'

Nicky hesitated. She looked uncomfortable as if she hadn't

realised that I had heard her. As I waited for an answer I noticed that she looked smarter than usual; it looked to me as if she was wearing a new business suit.

'There's a party with some of the people from a neighbouring office. I knew you'd probably be working again so I was just asking her to cover for me.'

'I could get the evening off and we could go together. I think they owe me one by now.'

She was fiddling with the top of the coffee jar.

'You never enjoy these things. You know you don't. I just didn't think it was worth telling you about. Thought I'd avoid the aggravation.'

She was right. I always seemed to end up standing next to someone called Quentin who would ask me whether I had been at Cambridge and then lecture me about how the thing to do was get into the property market so that I could afford a Porsche. I couldn't talk about my work and didn't really understand theirs, which was highly technical. But I knew Nicky had been working really hard to cover for me while I started working on the F/Ls and I wanted to do something to show that I appreciated it.

'I'll let John know I need the night off. It'll be OK.'

She still wasn't meeting my gaze, preferring to put last night's washing-up away in cupboards and banging the doors closed.

'Don't be silly, you've only just started on the team, you know you won't get the time.'

'No, really, I'll go.'

'NO!'

She slammed the mug she was holding on to the worktop.

'You wouldn't like it and I don't want you there.'

I think she could see I was shocked that she had finally said it, because her face softened and she added, 'It's sweet of you to make the effort, but I know how much it means to you to make a good start with this team. If it was something important you know I'd want you there. But this is just a social thing, you wouldn't know anyone. Get the kids up. I'll see you tomorrow, I've got to rush.'

And with that she gave me a quick kiss and was out of the kitchen before I could say anything else. A few seconds later I heard the front door slam shut.

Of course I knew that this was bad. But as I got ready for work and made breakfast for the children, my mind started asking darker questions. Was she seeing someone else? Was there really a party at all? Eventually I told myself that I was being paranoid and that we were just going through a difficult patch as so many marriages do. Sadly, I didn't fully realise how bad things were.

After dealing with the kids I had phoned Control to see if I was needed out on the ground, but instead I was called into the office for a meeting with the rest of the team. We all knew it was something serious when we saw John waiting for us, as well as the intelligence officer for our team. Like all ID teams, the intelligence unit attached to the Limas was responsible for analysing leads from a variety of sources. Once we were all in, John kicked the meeting off.

'All right, Peter is going to give you all the latest picture on the Turkish syndicate, then I've got some other news for you.'

He signalled for Peter to come forward.

'We finally have some good news for you,' Peter began. 'As you know, Zulu 27 hasn't done anything since we started on him. However, we still believe he's a player in the organisation. From today we're going to ask you to look at Zulu 28, who we initially assumed to be working for Zulu 27 because he was younger, but we now believe that it may be the other way round. According to one of our sources, he's very active in the book trade.'

This comment brought some polite laughter from the team.

To avoid being understood by a passer-by when talking about drugs smugglers often spoke about dealing in another commodity. For some reason it often seemed to be books and it had become a sort of running joke on the team.

'But here's the best news of all,' continued Peter. 'We believe that the man at the head of the organisation is none other than Volkan.'

That made us all sit up and listen. Volkan was a name of the head of a major Turkish syndicate. I think the reason we all remembered him was because his name sounded as if it had been taken from some James Bond villain, despite the fact that it is a fairly common Turkish name. He dealt only in heroin and only in major consignments. He was known to be the mastermind behind several recent operations, but although British gangs importing from him had been taken out by ID teams, no one had been able to touch his syndicate. Only one Turk who was a member of the syndicate had been arrested and, although he had been offered a very lucrative deal, he was clearly too terrified of Volkan to talk. Zulu 28 sounded like our first definite lead.

'Up until now Volkan's organisation has only dealt with the London gangs using contacts through the Turkish community there. This deal up north seems to be a new venture for Volkan. One theory we've come up with is that Haase may have met Zulu 28 when he was last in prison. Certainly Zulu 28 appears to have been given the job of dealing with this new venture, but he also seems to be well-connected enough to deal with others in the organisation. If you stick with Zulu 28 we might be able to get a lead on these other smuggling gangs as well.'

This definitely sounded worthwhile. Peter was offering us the prospect of taking out not only Haase's gang, but also the syndicate supplying half of London. Add to that the possibility of taking out a major international player like Volkan and this was definitely a stake worth playing for.

'One thing that's puzzling us at the moment is where the money is going. We've done a very thorough check on all UK and foreign bank accounts controlled by Zulus 27 and 28, together with those of any of their contacts, but while both of them have more money than you would expect, it's nothing like the amount generated by these massive drugs deals. So, somehow the money must be getting back to Turkey. Keep your eyes open for any indication of what the route for the money might be: visits to bureaux de change, visits to people who might be connected with financial services, anything. If we can't show an evidential trail for the money then at the end of the day we may not have a case, so it's vital that we discover what they're doing with it.

'For those of you who haven't come across Volkan before I'll give you some brief details. His syndicate is big; we reckon he's doing in excess of 500 kilos of heroin a year. He's reputed to have considerable commercial interests in Turkey through which he launders the money – hotels, new housing developments, that sort of thing. We believe that he has good connections in the Turkish military and possibly in the government. For that reason we haven't been able to make any use of our own official Turkish connections. Security in the syndicate is very tight and that's why it's been so hard to get a lead on him. He only uses people from the old country or those who can be vouched for by people he knows well. We know that he's been into the UK to inspect his organisation at least twice, but no one has got a picture of him or even managed to see him. He always travels under a different alias. If he comes here he'll stay with a 'clean skin', someone with no connection to the organisation.'

John stepped forward, thanked Peter and ushered him out of the door. Once he'd gone, John firmly closed the door to the room behind him. One or two of us glanced at each other. This looked serious.

'All right, that was the good news, now here's the bad. This means the policy of running half the team in Liverpool and half the team in London is going to continue for the foreseeable future. All leave is suspended until further notice.'

There was a chorus of groans but, glancing around the room, you could see that they were mostly in jest. The truth was that most of us were excited at the prospect of finally taking out a major importation organisation for once.

'And while we're dealing with bad news there's some more, but, before I tell you, I want to emphasise that this absolutely does not go off this team, got it?' He took a moment to run his gaze over each of us to emphasise the point.

'You all know that Knowles's life has been threatened and that we are doing all we can to get a lead on whoever has picked up the contract. Some of you may also know that Knowles has been away from Liverpool and working in London where he should be safer. Well, the latest news is that whoever picked up the contract knows about this and has come down here to find him. Somehow they have managed to find out where he is.'

'It's got to be a leak from the Liverpool Old Bill, hasn't it?' said Slapper.

'That's what we thought after the contract was first put out,' said John, 'so we've been protecting news of his movements carefully this time. We didn't let the police know where he was. If we had to pass any information then we used another officer as a cut-off. Now it's possible there was a leak and that someone in the police found out, but if there wasn't,' he paused for a moment, 'then that means the information came from within the Division.'

Now there were murmurs of disagreement and several officers shook their heads. It was unthinkable that someone on the Division could ever give information about another officer to a drugs gang.

'Yes, I know. I can't believe it either. But until we know for sure, watch your backs. If anyone finds someone who is asking questions about what we're doing, report it to me, no matter how casual or friendly it seems. Maybe they're speaking to someone else and don't realise where the information is going, but we've got to find this leak because Knowles is in serious trouble. That's all.'

The meeting broke up and Gareth immediately gathered us together to talk about Zulu 28. He drew a quick sketch map on a whiteboard of the area around Zulu 28's home. It was important that we put him under physical surveillance. Although we might have tried a bugging or telephone tapping operation, none of the material if produced would have been admissible in court.

'Everyone seen the plot?' he asked.

Most of us had. Even though we weren't officially working on him yet, all the good officers had taken opportunities to drive round the area because we knew he was a major player in the syndicate and sooner or later we would be up against him.

'It's a bastard of a road isn't it?' said Gareth. 'I've considered all the options and I think our best chance is some sort of long-range camera to monitor the exit from Zulu 28's block of flats. That will allow the vehicles to park further away where they will be less suspicious. Harry, take Ralph and someone from photographic down there this morning and see if they can put in one of their remote video cameras for us. As for the next day or so, we'll use an obs van; you two will have the duty for today. Now, let's have a look at the tactical situation . . .'

For the next half-hour or so we discussed the various routes out of the area and how the team would cover them, the number of officers required at any one time, emergency drills and the really important stuff like where the nearest burger bars were located.

As soon as the meeting was over, the team went out to plot up on Zulu 28 while Ralph and I went down to the photographic unit. The unit was only comprised of three men but, in terms of evidence, photography was so important that they were involved in every single operation the Division conducted. Apart from all the various routine tasks they had to undertake, such as development of films and upkeep of equipment, the unit had to advise on covert photography: they were responsible for placing some of the hidden cameras or remote CCTV systems which were used on the most sensitive cases. And yet despite the fact there were only three of them, two old men and an 'apprentice', you could always pop down to see them, explain the problems of a location and they would take the time to advise you about camera types, speed of film and so forth. For really difficult or important operations they would even go out on the ground themselves to make sure the team captured the vital evidence. All in all, the photographic unit was another example of one of those small, dedicated groups in the Division who never got any praise – no one ever thought of giving them an award or honour – but without them the Division would have been nowhere.

The unit itself was like an alchemist's laboratory. It was oppressively hot, it always stank of the metallic tang of photographic chemicals and the staff were usually bent over benches, fiddling with bits of technical equipment or using magnifying glasses to examine negatives. The room was dominated by two massive machines for developing rolls of photographic film such as you see in large supermarkets these days; the 'kerchunk, kerchunk' sound, as they towed their lines of film through various trays of developing and fixing liquids, was a constant accompaniment to any visit there.

Ralph and I stood at the counter by the entrance to the photographic unit and hit the bell. Barry, one of the technicians appeared, drying his hands on a cloth. We explained the layout of the target area to him and the difficulty of getting a view on the entrance.

'Yeah,' he agreed, 'definitely sounds like a job for a remote. Trouble is I haven't got one lads. They've slashed the budget to the bone this year. We haven't even got the money to repair them when they go bust any more.'

'Oh come on', I protested. 'You must have kept something back for emergencies.'

'It's always a bloody emergency though isn't it?' said Barry, looking at us with a wry smile on his face. I had the feeling that he had the equipment, he just wanted to be convinced that the job was worth it. Ralph was way ahead of me.

'How about if we mentioned the name Volkan?' asked Ralph.

I gave Ralph a warning look.

'Look, if Barry is working for the other side we really are in trouble,' he said.

'Yeah, all right, I know the name,' Barry interjected. 'The Tangos just missed him last year didn't they? All right, I'll try and get down there later today and recce for a site. I'll give you a call this evening if it's possible.'

Ralph and I left and drove over to the Division's garage in the north of the city, where all the large operational vehicles were stored. We selected a Ford Escort obs van bearing the name of a fictional firm of builders on the side. An observation van is any vehicle in which an officer can be hidden so that he can watch and report on a particular location. They range from the large and very sophisticated to the tiny and hideously cramped. This van was at the lower end of the market. In the back was what appeared to be a pile of tools and other decorating equipment. This apparently random pile was hollow and could be slid out on rails so that an officer could climb into the back of the van. When the dummy load was replaced there was just enough space for the officer to sit inside and a small area through which he could get a view out of the rear window. It looked really uncomfortable, but there was very little choice left in the garage. The question now was, who would spend the next eight hours in it? Ralph had a resigned look on his face, but I couldn't help feeling that, as the new boy on the team, I probably ought to put myself forward. When I told him so he was very relieved. As I clambered into the back, clutching the camera equipment and a small rucksack in which I kept my essential kit, he said, 'Have I told you what an excellent line manager you are, Harry?'

'Piss off, Ralph,' I replied, trying to work out which position would be least likely to cause a thrombosis.

'Pissing off right now, sir!' he said, saluting smartly and sliding the dummy load back on its rails.

I heard him climbing into the front seat as I tried to sort out my kit by the light of a pocket torch. There was a socket by which I could connect my microphone to the van's concealed radio system and an emergency button which I could use to set off the car alarm if someone started tampering with the vehicle. In the rucksack I had a bottle of water, some chocolate bars, an empty plastic bottle – which I knew I'd have to use at some stage – and a roll of cling film, which I hoped I would never have to use. There were also other bits of kit such as a Swiss Army knife with about six different screwdrivers (because some piece of equipment was always likely to go wrong), a monocular, which is a kind of small telescope, and a small FM radio. The FM radio was one of the most important things: it was possible to listen to that on one earpiece with my personal radio earpiece in the other ear. It could always be switched off if something important happened, but in the meantime it was vital in helping to pass what was guaranteed to be a very long, very boring day. As the van rocked and bounced its way towards St Pancras station, I loaded and adjusted the camera and tried to get myself comfortable with all the equipment to hand. Once the van was in position there would be very little chance to move because of the risk of noise and because it might cause the 'empty' van to rock.

I couldn't see a lot out of the rear window, but I knew the streets well enough to know when we were approaching the plot. Ralph swung into the road containing Zulu 28's small block of flats and I could hear him on the radio, both in my earpiece and through the bulkhead of the van.

'Lima 9, Lima 9.'

'Lima 9, Fox 2, go ahead.'

'Lima 9 approaching with the vulture.' ('Vulture' was the code-word for an obs van.)

'Received. Fox 7 is in Tibet and will move as you arrive.'

All the cars had call-signs to help identify them quickly. Tibet was a dark blue Ford Sierra which Sarah had parked on the opposite side of the road from Zulu 28's flat. Ralph drove past her slightly and then, once she had pulled out of the way, he backed us into the vacant space. I gave him directions to make slight adjustments to the way the van was parked until I had an uninterrupted view of the entrance. Ralph then wished me luck, locked up the van and strolled away down the road to be picked up by another mobile.

'Lima 3, Fox 2: radio check.'

'Fox 2: strength five.'

In the ID radio signals are always rated between one and five, with five being the strongest. Now there was nothing to do but watch the doorway and wait. I switched on the radio. Steve Wright's show was playing. That would do for a start. I opened the first of many chocolate bars.

Placing a surveillance device, such as a concealed camera or microphone bug, isn't as simple as finding the right place and bolting it to a wall. Up until about 1990, you simply spoke to the property owners and the deal was done on a handshake. Many law-abiding people were happy to help and that was that. But now everything had to be done on paper in case someone threatened to sue the Division. The document we had to issue warned householders that, whilst the Division would do its utmost to protect them, they couldn't be guaranteed anonymity and might have to appear in court. Most householders got as far as that part and could immediately see themselves in the witness box, being grilled by an aggressive defence lawyer about all sorts of things, whilst being measured up for a good beating or worse by some thug in the dock who, until a few minutes ago, had no idea they lived just across the road from him. We were sure that clause lost us more OPs than threats by any criminal gang ever did, but with the arrival of the 'compensation culture' of the 1990s, it was all part of the game.

So Barry had some difficulty finding a place where he could install the camera. The ideal solution would have been to put in a camera right opposite the flat, and Barry found two locations which seemed possible, but of course life is never that simple. When we checked out the places he suggested we found that in one case we couldn't get permission from the owner and in the other there was a security concern about the occupant. Finally, on the third day, we found a building which was a long way away but which Barry thought would be OK. The best view was from an office in the building belonging to some 'business consultants' – I never found out exactly what they did, but they wouldn't allow us access to their offices. However, after some negotiation they did give us permission to install a camera on the roof. So, on the fourth day, Barry and I found ourselves standing in the hallway of the third floor of the building, leaning out of the window and wondering what we were going to do next.

We worked during the day, on the assumption that two men working on a roof isn't that suspicious during the day; at night the risk of being seen was less, but we would definitely be in trouble if we were spotted. What looked like a simple job from the ground, though, turned out to be a nightmare now that we were up there. We needed to bolt the camera firmly in place, but the building was very old and the roof was in such bad repair that we couldn't get a bolt to take purchase. So, after a bit of clambering around on the ledge outside, Barry decided that the best place to site the camera was at the base of a chimney stack. That meant crawling up a slate-roof incline. The only hook ladder we had with us wouldn't catch on the ridge where there was a flat roof. So Barry decided the best way to get up the slippery roof was for me to give him a boost whilst lying flat. It wasn't a ridiculous plan – the slope was quite gentle – but a steady drizzle had been falling for the past half-hour and the old, broken slates which made up the roof didn't look at all safe to me.

'It's a bit wet for clambering around on a rooftop isn't it? How about if we come back when the rain has stopped?' I asked.

'Ah, don't be silly,' he said. 'You just give me a lift up to the ridge and it'll only take a couple of minutes. Do you want this camera in or not?'

I tried one last weak excuse.

'It would look bloody suspicious wouldn't it?'

'Nah,' he shrugged. 'Who's going to be looking up here?'

He was right. None of the people passing on the street below even glanced in our direction.

Before I could have any more doubts he said, 'Come on then, let's get it done,' and was out of the window, swinging easily from the frame onto the narrow ledge outside. As soon as he was clear I gingerly clambered out after him, although, like all good vertigo sufferers, I made sure I had at least nine-teen of my fingers and toes in contact with the building at all times. Leaning on the slate roof I made a stirrup with my hands and boosted him up towards the ridge. It was further than it looked and by the time he was able to get a hold I was reaching far above my head.

'Got it,' he said and scrambled the rest of the way up.

'I thought we were supposed to have some sort of specialist team who installed these things,' I gasped.

'Yeah, so did I,' said Barry, looking back over his shoulder. 'If you ever meet them let me know. In the meantime, pass me that drill before I lose all feeling in my fingers.'

I passed various bits of equipment up to him as the rain continued to patter down. I remember thinking that the Divisional health and safety officer would have had a heart attack if he'd known. Finally, Barry was satisfied. He passed the various bits of equipment back down to me and then lay down and hung off the chimney himself. As I reached up and took the weight of his foot in one of my hands, my feet slipped on the rain-soaked ridge.

'Shit!'

I started to slide over the edge of the roof, watching Barry's horrified face disappear in the other direction as I slid away from him. I spread my arms out, my finger tips desperately scrabbling for any handhold, trying to press my body hard against the roof in an effort to stop myself. But it was only as my hips arrived at the edge of the roof that I stopped sliding, the lower half of me now hanging over the three-storey drop to the street. At the time I wasn't even aware that the freezing rainwater in the gutter was soaking through my shirt.

I didn't dare move my arms for fear that I would slip further and, with most of my weight then off the roof, I would be carried all the way over. My feet desperately kicked against the wall, hoping to find a ledge or gap in the brickwork so that I could get a hold. The thought kept running through my mind that, after years of worrying about being shot on an operation by either terrorists or drug smugglers, I was going to die by slipping off a wet roof because some crazed old photographer had talked me into it. It just didn't seem fair.

'Stop moving for God's sake,' called Barry. 'I'll try and work my way down to you.'

Blow that. If he came sliding down the roof the chances were that he would hit me and knock me off. I had one good hold on the window-frame with my left hand and I kept swinging my right leg up to try and get purchase on the ledge. I dislodged something from the wall and my mind conjured up the horrible image of someone being knocked unconscious in the street below. At the third attempt I finally managed it and had enough leverage to get my upper body through the window. I hauled myself in and collapsed in a soaking heap on the floor. Barry followed me in moments later. I felt dizzy and my heart was thumping so hard that my chest hurt. I just lay in the hallway, trying to stop my legs and hands from shaking. Barry slumped against the wall beside me and slapped me on the shoulder.

'Well, that's something to tell your grandchildren about,' he chuckled.

'There's just one thing,' I said.

'What's that?' he asked.

'When the time comes to get that thing down again . . .'

'Yes?' he said.

'If you ask for me, I'll kill you.'

'Fair enough,' he grinned.

At first, Zulu 28 turned out to be as dull as his older partner Zulu 27. He seemed to spend most of his mornings in bed, get up late, go out for lunch and spend the evening at nightclubs. But there was nothing which looked like drug dealing. This is the trouble with the gangs running importations – apart from the odd meeting here and there you sometimes have very little evidence of what they are doing. The surveillance team has to sit and wait for a very long time and, if their attention lapses, they can miss the crucial meeting they've been waiting for. If it hadn't been for the meeting with Zulu 3 we would never have known that these two Turks were members of the syndicate. However, Peter and his team insisted that we were on the right track and fortunately it wasn't too long before we were back on the scent again. It began with another early morning meeting called by John.

'As you all know, the next step in this case for the London team is finding out how Volkan's syndicate are bringing in the heroin. This may sound too good to be true but, according to an intelligence source, they have 'merchandise' coming in on a flight from Italy today. Estimated time of arrival at Heathrow is 18.25. Zulu 28 is going out to meet it. We have no more details than that so we're going to have to cover every possible smuggling method: baggage, freight, passengers, cabin crew and airframe. First the baggage handlers. You know what that's like: if we have a crooked individual or even a whole crew working amongst the baggage handlers then they know just how the airport works. Spread yourselves around the tarmac using as many different covers as possible. Jess, you're our Heathrow expert, I want you to take charge of that. Have a word with the commander of the Heathrow Investigation Unit, see whether they've got any current intelligence on stuff going through, particularly any hint of a Turkish or an Italian connection. Seeing as we're not letting them in on this you're probably going to get the run-around, but ask anyway.

'Next we've got the baggage itself, including cabin crew carry-on luggage. Slapper, you take that. Make sure no piece of luggage goes where it shouldn't, especially the cabin crew's. They're not going to like it, but they'll just have to be unhappy. Assuming we haven't had a baggage handling rip-off at the unloading, I want all the luggage opened before it goes into the terminal.'

There were groans all round the room. This was a massive job involving picking or busting the locks on every piece of luggage for the entire flight.

'If we pick up something in a passenger's baggage let the bag run, get someone into the channels and make sure the uniformed staff let it through without checking it. Then we'll pick up the mule with whoever meets him – almost certainly Zulu 28, but we might get lucky and they'll be someone else. Of course the bad news is that this is going to bring it on top early, but if we have gear we can't allow it to reach the streets. Harry, take three officers to follow Zulu 28 into the terminal and stay with him. But stay loose on him, the last thing we want to do is spook him. Mac, you'll need to go out this morning and plant a tracker on Zulu 28's car because we haven't got enough bodies to do a full-scale surveillance on him.

'Finally, if there is gear and I decide to knock it, I want him taken out on the road before he gets to Green Lanes or anywhere else. Once it goes into a building we lose control of it, and I don't want that happening. Understood? OK, get moving.'

So it was that we found ourselves staking out Heathrow airport. Although Peter's tips were usually reliable, we were a bit sceptical about whether this really was going to be an importation. Airport smuggling has gone out of fashion a bit in the past ten years or so. Terrorism has increased the levels of surveillance and security at airports so much that we now live in the age of the 'super smugglers' who send huge shipments in freight or by boat, knowing that they only have to get one or two consignments through to make enough profit to see them through the whole year. If you use the airport you can usually only smuggle a few kilos in one go. Of course, you still get a few amateurs who try this route, and there is enough profit in the powder for 'stuffers and swallowers' from poorer areas like Africa or the Caribbean to try it on, but with the amounts we expected Volkan to move, there was no chance of him using that method.

Jess placed as many of his team as possible in different locations out on the tarmac, using a variety of disguises – airport cleaners, maintenance workers, anything that might give some cover – but the baggage handlers were very watchful. He'd had a word with the Investigation Unit about who they thought the current players were on the baggage teams, and had already had to pull out one of his officers because he was attracting suspicion from members of one of the loading crews. The problem was that in those days some parts of the baggage-handling staff were like a little mafia. There were all sorts of dodges going on. There was always the chance to riffle through luggage and lift high-value items. Sometimes, to disguise the thefts, the whole item of baggage would just go missing. They were also well placed to lift out items of baggage and spirit them away before the luggage arrived for Customs inspection. Another dodge concerned items held in bond or storage, waiting for duty to be paid; items often went missing together with the paperwork so that the loss wasn't reported. Of course, the airport authorities were always trying to clamp down on it. Baggage handlers' cars were regularly searched as they left the airport, surveillance teams were used and the ID had even tried putting in undercover agents. The trouble was that these people worked at the airport all the time. They made sure that whenever a vacancy came up it was family members or close friends who applied for and got the job. Many of them lived locally and they had mates and relatives everywhere: in security, on the gates, office administration, cleaners, the lot. It was a private network with eyes everywhere. They were particularly good at monitoring what the local Unit were up to because they knew all their officers by sight. If members of a baggage team were involved it was going to be very hard to catch them, but we were as ready as we could be.

Thanks to the tracking device which Mac had planted on Zulu 28's car, we were able to pick him up on his approach to the airport and our two-car team followed him into the short-term parking complex. On foot, Jackie, Ralph and I followed him through the airport where he began wandering around the shopping area. So far Peter's information was good. But as I stood watching Zulu 28 I glanced up at the balcony above me. Zulu 26 was standing there.

He was wearing a brown leather jacket and dark trousers rather than a suit this time, but the photographs we had taken on the day of the meeting with Zulu 3 were so good that there was no doubt it was him. However, there was a moment of panic as I wondered why the hell we hadn't picked him up earlier and what he might have seen while we had been following Zulu 28. I picked up the holdall, which I was using as part of my cover, and wandered over to a shop-front where I was out of his sight. I hit the transmission button in my pocket.

'Lima 3 to all callsigns: we have Zulu 26 on the premises. He did not, repeat not, arrive, with Zulu 28. Be alert for possible minders.'

Gareth was up in Liverpool so John had come out on the ground with us. I could hear the radio chatter as he moved the team around from the Unit's radio room where he was monitoring the operation.

'Fox 6 and Fox 8 reinforce the team in the terminal building.'

'Fox 6.'

'Fox 8.'

We now had to keep an eye on them both and, within five minutes, Zulu 26 had made contact with two other Turkish men who were wandering around the terminal. John promptly labelled them Zulus 34 and 35. Ideally we would have had a couple of officers on each of them, but we just didn't have that much manpower. There was nothing we could do but assume that we could be in their line of sight at any time and act accordingly. Zulu 28 was now watching the arrivals board intently. He was definitely waiting for something.

We listened as the Air Italia flight landed and taxied towards the terminal. We were getting constant updates from Jess over the covert radio. That's one good thing about working at the airport: they have plenty of booster stations for the radios and you rarely have the transmission problems you get in other built-up areas.

'Aircraft hold doors open,' said Jess.

'Baggage unloading.'

There was silence on the radio for several minutes. Zulu 28 got tired of watching the boards and wandered off. We stayed with him. He looked as if he was just browsing around the shops again, but at one stage he and Zulu 26 passed each other as Ralph was watching them.

'From Lima 9: I've just seen a very clear OK signal from Zulu 26 to 28. There's definitely something going down.'

Apparently they hadn't talked, but Ralph had seen Zulu 26 give a very definite nod, as if to say all clear, which Zulu 28 clearly acknowledged. If you hadn't known what they were up to you wouldn't have given it a second thought. Two armed police wandered past, as Ralph was standing there, and never saw a thing.

Zulu 28 returned to the arrivals board and the radios crackled into life again.

'Stand by, stand by,' said Jess. He must have been near some heavy machinery because the roar of it in the background was almost drowning out his voice.

'One of the security cars has pulled alongside the aircraft. We have one IC1 male out and talking to the two baggage handlers. Wait one.' There was a short pause then: 'Bingo. We have three bags off the baggage trailer and into the back of the vehicle. Wait. And that's the security vehicle away towards the terminal buildings. Towards you Lima 8.'

IC1 meant Caucasian, not Mediterranean, but it still sounded promising. The question now was, where was Zulu 28 going to make the collection? Jess's team commentated on the vehicle's progress across the airport from their various vantage points. The individual in the car eventually parked up and made his way to the lost-luggage counter, where he deposited the bags. This was a crucial moment. Jess needed a decision from John as the SIO.

'Fox 5, Lima 1?'

'Fox 1.'

'Do you want him lifted boss? We can do it out of the way of the other Zulus.'

'Have you got photographs?'

'Yes, yes and I'd know this bugger if I ever saw him again.'

'OK Fox 5, let him run. He may have an all-clear message to give to a cut-out. If he's on the airport staff he's not going anywhere.'

'Fox 5 acknowledged.'

Jess kept his team watching the counter closely. It was possible, indeed likely, that the pick-up was being done by some lowly mule whom we hadn't yet seen and that Zulu 28 was just here to oversee the operation. For the moment the bags were the key. They held the drugs and nothing else was as important as retaining control of them.

My team stayed on Zulu 28. We were watching his every move in case he signalled to someone else on the concourse to go and pick up the bags. Seeing that signal could be the difference between putting him in prison for ten years and letting him walk free from court because he claimed he was nothing to do with it. But he seemed to be in no hurry. He just stood there waiting, watching the flight boards.

Slapper's team had finished the mammoth task of searching the rest of the incoming luggage and cleared it to be placed on the baggage reclaim conveyor belt. As they collected their bags and headed for the Customs channels, most people probably had no idea that their bags had already been thoroughly searched.

'Fox 12, Fox 1. All clear here,' he said. 'We've done the lot. It's clean. Looks like your bags are the ones, Jess.'

'Fox 5. All covered here,' replied Jess. This was going way too smoothly.

Ralph decided to ruin the mood. 'Lima 9, Fox 1: I don't think it's the bags, boss,' he said. 'From the way he's watching these boards he must be a bloody good actor. I think he's waiting for someone.'

'Let's hope not,' said Jess. 'I don't want to be stuck watching these bags for the next six hours.'

'Fox 1, Fox 12: are you sure those bags are clean?'

'Clean as a whistle boss, unless they're bringing in a teaspoonful we'd have found it.'

Slapper had been recruited from Heathrow and he had plenty of years' work there under his belt. He'd seen most of the ways that drugs could be brought through the airport, including obscure methods such as soaking the linings of suitcases in solutions containing cocaine so that the linings could later be treated and the drugs reclaimed. But Volkan's syndicate were major players; they wouldn't be dealing in a few kilos of the drug. If Slapper said the bags were clean then they almost certainly were.

Our hopes were dashed as soon as the passengers began clearing Customs. Zulu 28 was away and stood waiting alongside the railings at arrivals. Before long a tall, overweight but distinguished-looking Turk emerged, pushing a trolley laden with suitcases. He greeted him with a smile.

There was general cursing over the radios as this was relayed. John was clearly worried about the bags.

'Fox 12?' growled John. He didn't need to say what he was thinking.

'I swear to you boss, the bags are as clean as a whistle.'

'Could be Volkan himself, boss,' said Ralph.

'He looks like Zulu 28's bloody granddad,' muttered someone.

'All call-signs, clear the air,' ordered John. 'I don't care who it is, we stay with this guy until we house him. I want two footmen on Zulu 28 and the new arrival; I want two on Zulu 26 and two on Zulus 34 and 35. All other mobiles plot up to cover the exits from short-term parking. Move it.'

The radio was alive with chatter as people moved to follow targets or take up positions. Zulu 26 and his two friends weren't hard to find. They fell into place at a discreet distance from Zulu 28 and the new arrival as they headed for the car park, looking around for surveillance. It kept us on our toes, but we did this sort of thing every day and they weren't a major problem for us. I didn't think this was Volkan. Zulu 28 left him to push the heavily laden baggage trolley and, knowing the power Volkan had, I didn't think he would have done so if this were him. But judging from the security they had put out, whoever this was, he was clearly important.

Over the radio I could hear John ordering Jess to get one of his team to open up the bags at left luggage. Shortly afterwards a call came through confirming that they were clean. It took several days to clear up what had happened, but eventually we found that there was a perfectly innocent explanation as to why the bags had been taken straight to the lost-luggage office, and the hole in security procedures was sewn up. It freed Jess's team to join what was going to be a very complex mobile surveillance.

We took Zulu 26 and his charge to the short-term car park and discovered which vehicles the minders were driving. Zulu 26 was in his Mercedes and Zulus 34 and 35 in an anonymous green Honda saloon. After some difficulty cramming the visitor's luggage into his car, Zulu 28 drove slowly out of the car park, followed by his minders. Drugs F/L fell into place around them.

5

The Money Man

Following the Turks on foot at the airport had been easy, but once they were in their cars it was murderous. Zulu 28 seemed to take a very long way round as they headed across London in the direction of what we assumed must be Green Lanes, and the two minder vehicles were all over the place trying to see if he was being followed. It made our lives hell. We had the advantage that it was dark, so there wasn't much chance of the minders recognising people in cars, but we had to keep changing number plates in case they were noting them and by the end of the first hour every vehicle in the tail had been through its collection of ghost plates. To complicate matters, Zulu 28 also kept throwing in 'phantom stops': he would pull in to a side-road or forecourt of a building. Neither he nor his passenger would get out, but the minder vehicles would circle the area to see if they could spot any surveillance vehicles. Peter had warned us that the people working for Volkan's syndicate were good and it was clear to us that at least some of these people had undergone some sort of professional training.

Ralph and I were in one of the vehicles. There had been several good opportunities for Zulu 28 to spot us in the past ten minutes and we were probably 'toasty'. As Zulu 28 pulled into the side of the road yet again, I glanced across at Ralph to see who was our backup. He just shrugged and said, 'Still nothing. We're spread all over the place at the moment mate.'

I didn't want to go past Zulu 28, but we had to find a way to keep the eyeball position in case this stop was the final, important one. So, muttering curses under my breath, I swung our car into the gravelled drive of a large house on the opposite side of the road, slightly short of Zulu 28's position. There was a parking area in front of the house with about a dozen cars parked around it. We pulled up by a hedge which bordered the road. By standing on the door sill and using the binoculars Ralph could just see over the top of it to where Zulu 28 was waiting. As I was sitting there, listening to the radio as the other mobiles struggled to get into position, I looked at the building. There were lights on in many of the windows and, although it may have been a family house at one time, I wondered if it was some sort of college now.

There was no point in knocking on the door and asking for permission to park there. We didn't plan to be there long and explanations might only draw attention to us. Anyway, there were so many cars in the car park that one more didn't seem to make any difference. If the occupants saw us and wanted to ask questions they could simply come out and ask.

'Zulu 28 is out of the vehicle. It looks like he's going up to the door of that house,' called Ralph. 'Pass me the camera. I probably won't get anything, but there's a light on in the porch and you never know.'

I reached over and grabbed the camera off the back seat, passing it across the front seat towards him. Ralph used the telephoto lens to keep sight of Zulu 28. I had the driver's window down and was vaguely aware of the crunching of gravel as footsteps approached the car. I looked up.

'What you do here?'

The voice was hostile and had a distinctly foreign accent. It sounded East European. There was a man in a white shirt buttoned up to the neck standing behind me. I quickly climbed out of the car and pulled out the leather wallet holding my warrant card. I held it out to him. He snatched the wallet and peered at it closely.

Ignoring his rudeness, I said, 'Sorry about this, sir, Customs and Excise. Is it OK if we park in your car park for a couple of minutes?'

'You must go away,' he said.

Then, before I had a chance to say anything, he again snapped: 'What are you doing here?'

'We're part of an undercover team working on a case in the area. It's necessary for us to stop here for a few minutes because we are waiting for a car to pass by, it will only take a minute and would be a tremendous help.'

He rubbed at the warrant card as if he thought it was a fake and peered intently at it again.

'You cannot stay here. No police here.' His manners hadn't improved any.

Over his shoulder I could see the curtains at the windows being held back and a lot of people watching what was going on. Two more rather large individuals were now walking towards us. They were dressed in similar style to Mr Charming.

'You must go – now.' This was accompanied by a shove to my shoulder so forceful that it almost knocked me back into the car.

'OK no problem, we're going. Just give me a minute,' I said, then I reached for the radio. I used the handset so that they would be able to see that this was some sort of official vehicle.

'Lima 5, Lima 3: have we got anyone who can take this? I'm going to have to leave this position. I've got some very hostile civilians here.'

'Wait one Lima 3, I'll see if I can move someone in.'

'Never mind, wait a minute Phil, we've walked into something here – either get us out or send me some backup.'

The other two had arrived now. One of them had gone

round to the far side of the car and was standing behind Ralph, who glanced over his shoulder.

'You leave now,' demanded the leader, his face about four inches from mine, just begging to be butted.

On the other side of the car there was a scuffle. The newcomer had taken a swing at Ralph as he turned to face him. Ralph avoided the punch and put the guy into a wrist lock. He dropped him to the floor and put his foot in the small of the man's back.

'You are fucking nicked mate,' he said, and I could see him reaching to the back of his belt for his handcuffs. He looked over at me as if to say 'what the hell is going on?'

Now there were rather a large number of similarly dressed men pouring out of the building. There must have been fifteen to twenty of them and some appeared to be carrying sticks. I couldn't believe how quickly this had escalated. It was like a nightmare.

'That's it Phil, Lima 3 is lifted,' I shouted into the radio, and chucked the handset back into the car. 'Ralph, we're leaving NOW.'

I had the car in gear and moving backwards as the crowd loomed towards us. Ralph threw himself in through the passenger door. None of the crowd ran, they just kept walking steadily and menacingly towards the car. It was like something out of a bad zombie movie. As we manoeuvred, the guy who had been thrown to the ground by Ralph scrambled to his feet and threw one of the car park's sizeable gravel chips at us. It bounced off the boot with a loud thump. As we roared away, half a dozen more lumps of rock hurtled after us. Thankfully most of them missed and then we were away down the road.

In all my time on the Division I never saw an incident like it. Perhaps they had recently suffered vandalism or a racist attack, but even so . . . Ralph was absolutely furious.

'What the fuck was that about!' he shouted, punching the

dashboard. 'Let's get the rest of the team, go back there and fucking nick the lot of them! Who the heck were they?' He followed this with a string of obscenities as he worked out his anger on the fixtures in the car.

The following day we checked with the local police and found that the house was rented by some sort of new age cult. We decided not to make a formal complaint – it wasn't worth the paperwork – although we did warn the local police to watch out if they ever had to visit there.

What really mattered was that we had lost our opportunity to see what Zulu 28 was doing at the address. Whether he had spoken to someone or delivered something we just didn't know, but he was soon on his way again and before long we were plotted up around the sports club in Green Lanes. The two men were barely in the club for half an hour before we were off again, driving towards central London.

The minders remained at the club, probably feeling that their job was done. Even so, we had our work cut out to stay with Zulu 28. He loved to drive fast, clipping red lights and forcing his way out into the traffic at junctions, regardless of the angry reactions of other drivers. Altogether it had been a very long and tiring day for the team and, by the time Zulu 28 reached his destination, we had lost one vehicle in a minor accident and the rest of the drivers were dropping with fatigue.

As we had headed into central London, we had thought that Zulu 28 must be taking his visitor back to his flat. But in fact they headed to Park Lane, where Zulu 28 lodged his visitor in one of the more expensive hotels. This was good news for us, as we usually had excellent co-operation from the heads of security at the big hotel chains. Most security staff love the excitement of being involved in a big investigation and the companies owning the hotels didn't want these people in their establishments any more than we did. Phil had worked with the security officer at this hotel before so, as soon as Zulu 28 and the new man had checked in, Phil and I showed our cards at the reception desk and were directed to his office. He was a heavy-set man with a ready laugh and I liked him immediately. He remembered Phil and listened to our story with interest. Obviously we couldn't give him too much detail, but we felt he was on our side and we let him know enough to make it clear that this was a major operation. He took us to the room from which hotel security monitored the building. Officers on foot were still stationed around the hotel, and both Phil and I knew from the radio transmissions that they had gone to the restaurant. The head of security tracked through the various cameras until we found where they were sitting. He studied the image for a while and then pressed a button and printed out a copy.

'Do you want me to circulate this to my boys on the security team?' he asked.

'No thanks,' said Phil. 'We don't want anyone else aware of our interest.'

'Fair enough. I suppose you'll need evidence to show the two of them together, copies of credit card details and all that?' he said.

'Every little helps,' grinned Phil.

'Right, I'll make sure we hang on to the CCTV footage of the reception area, showing him checking in.'

'While they're out of the way we'd like to get a look at his room,' ventured Phil.

The head of security sat back in his chair with a slight smile on his face.

'Oh yes? Will I be seeing a search warrant?' he asked.

'Writ of Assistance,' replied Phil. 'We'll sort the paperwork later.'

The Writ of Assistance is a Customs and Excise power dating back to the reign of Elizabeth I. It allows officers to search any premises at any time if they believe there may be 'items liable to seizure' there. The officer doesn't have to apply to a court and it can be used immediately. It is an incredibly powerful weapon and one of the things which gave us an edge over the police. Defence lawyers have been trying to get rid of it for years and the Commissioners of Customs and Excise have had to fight fiercely to retain it.

'All right, I'll get you a pass key. I'll watch them from down here. If they start to head back I'll give two rings on the internal phone.'

We dashed up to the visitors' room and let ourselves in. From the look of the room, he had simply dumped his bags and then gone downstairs with Zulu 28. We knew we didn't have much time, so Phil went through the luggage once more and I searched the room. If he was carrying something incriminating it was possible that he would have taken it out of his luggage and secreted it somewhere.

Phil had a difficult job getting past the locks on the suitcases, and it didn't help knowing that the phone might ring at any time. Slapper's team would already have been through the bags, but they would only have seen them as a few amongst the whole plane load; besides, they were looking for bulky drugs. Now we knew that this was our man, we could be more careful. But after ten minutes we had both come up with nothing.

'I don't get it,' said Phil. 'Who is he and what is he doing here? He's obviously something to do with the organisation.'

'Do you think he is Volkan?'

'I doubt it. Volkan is supposed to be ultra-careful about his security, so why would he hang around Zulu 28?'

Suddenly it struck me.

'Count the bags,' I said.

'Six,' said Phil, then a few seconds later he hung his head. 'Shit.'

There had been seven bags when the visitor arrived at the

airport. At some stage during the drive from the airport one bag had gone missing. It must have been at the stop we'd been unable to cover, but we couldn't be sure. The phone rang twice as we were trying to work this out, so after one last quick look around, to make sure that we hadn't left any trace of our presence, we left.

One question remained: what had happened to the missing bag? Phil and I puzzled over this as we left the hotel, but overall we thought that we were doing well with the job so far. As we stood down for the night and went home to prepare for an early start the next morning, none of us knew of the devastating blow which was about to hit the team.

It was 6.00 a.m. the next day when I yawned my way into the office for the early morning briefing. I thought that we were simply preparing to go out for another day's surveillance on Zulu 28's mysterious new elderly companion, but as soon as I walked through the door I could see that most of the team were sitting in small groups, looking fed up. I threw my kitbag on to my desk and went over to Ralph, who was standing at a table with a soldering iron, trying to fix his bike's radio system.

'What's happening?'

Ralph glanced up at me and then looked round.

'It's been a right massacre,' he said. 'They're moving about half a dozen of us to other teams. And worst of all, we're losing Gareth.'

Ralph had no love for Gareth, who hadn't always appreciated his happy-go-lucky attitude towards the discipline of being in a close surveillance team, but he knew how serious it was to lose a major figure like this. Even on a team like Drugs F/L, which was packed with star players, there is always one dominant character who defines the character of the team and acts as its driving force. I wondered if he'd fight the move. He'd certainly have the support of every person on the team.

'He must be as mad as hell,' I said.

'Nah. He's effectively been promoted,' sighed Ralph. 'They gave him a choice of practically anywhere he wanted to go, and he's set himself up with a nice little number running a brand new unit. They're going to specialise in running under-cover officers on long-term operations. Sounds bloody dangerous to me.'

The moves weren't supposed to be officially released for several days, but one of the AOs had already got the news from his contacts in the personnel unit. All together we were losing six officers; not a crippling number out of a team of thirty, but every one of them was a big name. We were losing Derek to a local unit in Birmingham; the coven was being broken up, with both Sarah and Natty going to senior posts on other teams; Gareth was taking his deputy, Marcus, to the new under-cover unit; and Terry Banks was moving to a regional ID unit nearer his home, although he would be hanging around for a few weeks longer to assist Paddy. Most of these people had been working up in Liverpool. What was going to happen up there now with most of the experienced crew, who knew the area, leaving? As Ralph had said, it was a massacre.

John arrived with Peter shortly afterwards. As soon as he stepped through the door several people called out, demanding to know what was going on. To John's credit he didn't waste time trying to fob us off with excuses.

'All right, all right,' he shouted above the noise. 'Everyone can back off and stop moaning right now. It's a done deal so we live with it.'

Once the protests had died down, he continued: 'Apparently there's been a lot of pressure on management from the Treasury to increase the effectiveness of revenue-collecting teams, especially on the VAT, tobacco and alcohol duty-evasion teams or something. Anyway, we've just drawn the wrong end of the stick.'

'Given up on drugs then, have we boss?' called Ralph.

John shot him a look which said 'you're not funny and shut up.'

'I don't like it any more than you do and I've done all I can to stop it, but there it is. This is not fucking nursery school so you *will* work around this. In the meantime, I'm doing my best to make sure that we get some good people in exchange, so just wait and see what I can do before you all start throwing your toys out of the pram. Peter?'

The intelligence officer looked slightly embarrassed to be given the job of motivating a group of very disgruntled officers who made it clear they felt they were being stabbed in the back. He cleared his throat and held his notes defensively in front of him.

'We've managed to confirm the identity of your mysterious visitor,' he began. 'He's not Volkan nor is he someone who's been connected with Volkan's organisation before, so it looks like he could be a new lead.'

Peter paused to put a blown-up copy of a passport photograph on the whiteboard behind him.

'He's a retired Turkish military officer. We couldn't risk checking him out through the usual channels in Turkey, but we've managed to get some details from the Americans. They have no traces on him drug-wise, but we have been able to get some basic information.'

'Does he sell books?' asked Mac, and there was quiet laughter from the rest of us.

'General import and export is all the paperwork says,' replied Peter. 'He's been in and out of the UK regularly over the past two years. No criminal record at all as far as we are aware. That would make him perfect as a courier. Anyway, whatever he's up to, this is only a short trip; he's booked out on the 16.00 flight to Ankara.'

'What about the missing suitcase?' asked Jess.

'Could be some sort of equipment. The rummage team were

looking for drugs so it's possible they would have missed it if it was, say, a radio scrambler. The other possibility is that there was paperwork, possibly with coded instructions or a message of some sort about where to meet the next importation. If they are varying the route and method each time they bring the gear in that would explain why we've never been able to get close to Volkan's importations. The good thing is that we've got him now. So every time he comes back into the country, we'll be able to monitor him even if he doesn't go near Zulu 28 again. We know from his records that he travels a great deal within Europe, especially to Italy, which we believe is another of Volkan's major distribution areas. At the moment we're considering sharing the identity of this contact with the Italian police but, as you know, every agency we give this information to increases the risk of a leak.'

'So what do you want from us today?' asked Phil.

'We need to confirm his role, if any, in the organisation. If he is a courier then they may be using word of mouth, seeing as that's the most secure way of passing information. It's unlikely that he'll say anything important but there's always a chance, so stick with him this morning and get your Turkish speakers up front whenever possible.'

That concluded Peter's part of the briefing and it only remained for John to warn us to stay on our toes as usual. There wasn't great deal of time for analysis as we had to get up to Park Lane in case our visitor made an early departure. Officially this new target was Zulu 33 but, as we raced to the hotel, Ralph started referring to him as 'the General'. The name stuck.

We needn't have rushed. The General didn't appear for breakfast until well past nine and then he took a leisurely trip through the West End, shopping. He picked up a lot of small, high-value items, such as jewellery and electrical gadgets, so whatever business he was in he was clearly doing very well. He had lunch in an expensive brasserie while we sat in cars in the surrounding area munching our McDonalds and other junk food. The Turkish speakers on the team were kept available, but the General didn't meet anyone and they were never called forward. All the time we had our eyes open for more minders – not just Zulus 26, 34 and 35, but also ones we might not have seen before. We knew that Volkan's syndicate had a large pool of goons to call on. Something like a shopping trip is perfect for setting up a counter-surveillance route and we were on guard all morning. But there was something about the General's relaxed wanderings around the shops that made us think that this was a trap. Soon he was back to the hotel where Zulu 28 duly arrived to pick him up thirty minutes later, driving a Range Rover we hadn't seen before. We added the registration number and description to the ever-growing list of target vehicles.

There then followed an easy surveillance out to Heathrow. Zulu 28 drove as fast as he always did, but much of the journey was motorway driving and caused us no great problem. All our well rehearsed changes and clipping moves worked as smoothly as if it had been an exercise. In fact, by the time we reached the airport most of the team were starting to lose interest; it seemed that whatever the General had come here to do had already been done and we had missed it. It was only when Zulu 28 began helping the General unload his bags in the car park that things suddenly became interesting again. It was Jackie who spotted it. She was parked just a few spaces away from them and was in the middle of unpacking a pushchair from the boot of her car, but she still managed to murmur under her breath.

'From Lima 10: we have seven cases again, repeat seven.'

That made us all sit up and take notice. The missing bag had reappeared. Either that or a new one had been added; only six had left the hotel with the General, so this must be a new one which Zulu 28 had brought with him. I had deliberately chosen to share a car with Slapper that morning, figuring that, since he was our expert on the airport, if there was a chance of getting involved, the best place to be was with him.

I was right.

'From Lima 5: Lima 3 and Fox 12 can you get into position to receive those cases on the other side of the check-in?'

We were parked on the level above the targets.

'Lima 12 yes, yes,' radioed Slapper, grabbing the camera from the back seat. 'Come on Harry, I'll show you how it's done.'

We walked briskly through the terminal. We had to be aware that there could be minders about: running figures at the airport attract attention not only from villains but also from wandering armed police who can be a right pain in the neck if you have to explain yourself to them. We went to one of the control points and showed British Airport Authority passes to get access to the airside part of the airport. This was another bit of bureaucratic nonsense which had developed in the last few years. Theoretically our warrant cards should have been enough to get us airside, but since the ports and airports had been privatised they insisted on their own security systems. This meant that officers had to carry wallets stuffed full of electronic passes for ports and airports around the country, as well as dealing with all the accompanying hassles of keeping them up to date. Like all passcard systems you could bet on it letting you down at the most awkward moment and, sure enough, that's what happened now. As Slapper swiped his card through the scanner there was a warning buzz and the attendant looked up.

'Sorry sir, your card isn't valid,' he said.

Slapper passed it through two or three more times and the buzzer sounded each time.

'I'm sorry, but you'll have to go to the administration office to get the card re-authorised,' said the attendant. We tried reasoning with him, but he wasn't in a mood to be helpful and kept insisting that he was only doing his job. The administration office was miles away and getting the card re-authorised could take hours.

'Fook this,' said Slapper in his broad Yorkshire accent. He produced his warrant card and held it in front of the attendant's face. 'Investigation Division. This is an emergency. If you want me, you'll have to fooking chase me. Come on, Harry.'

We charged off down the corridor. There was a faint cry of 'Oi! You can't do that!' behind us, but he didn't sound very determined and we kept going. All the time we could hear relays from the foot-team in our earpieces as the General and Zulu 28 heaved their laden baggage trolley closer to the check-in. Even with Zulu 28's manic driving they had still left their arrival very late and were having to rush to get to the check-in before the gate closed. We weren't going to have much time to examine the luggage before the plane left.

Slapper and I seemed to run for miles around corridors at the rear of the airport and I knew that I would never be able to find my way back again. Eventually we came to a conveyor belt and at the far end I could see the plastic strips which guarded the access hatch for the belt to the check-in desks. Occasionally these would be slapped aside as another collection of bags were sent through. There were several baggage handlers working around us, but despite the fact that we were in plain clothes no one gave us a second glance.

'It'll be one of these three, Harry. Keep your eyes peeled,' said Slapper, tossing the camera to me as he pulled a Swiss Army knife from his pocket. I had no idea how he could tell from back here which conveyor belt was which; it was simply the knowledge gained from years of working here. I checked the settings on the camera. The relays over the radio let us know when the cases were being passed through and, sure enough, they were soon rolling down the belt towards us.

'What happens if he's taking the extra bag as carry-on luggage?' I asked.

Slapper grinned.

'Then we're fooked mate, aren't we?' He pulled all the bags off the belt and dumped them on the ground. 'You were in his hotel room, which one do you think it is?'

I quickly ran my eye over the bags. They were a matching set in different sizes so it was hard to tell which was the odd one out, but it seemed that there was an extra suitcase.

'One of these,' I said, and Slapper immediately set about popping the locks with his knife. The first one only contained clothes and when Slapper opened the second one we were greeted by the sight of even more clothes, which didn't look too promising. But as we lifted these out we found dozens of packets of cereal and coffee jars packed in the layer underneath.

'What the . . .' said Slapper, and as he picked up one of the boxes it practically fell to pieces in his hands. Roll after roll of fifty-pound notes fell out. I picked up one of the coffee jars. It was filled with instant coffee granules, but as I shook it I could clearly see that it was mainly stuffed with rolls of money; the coffee had been added afterwards in the hope of disguising them. These were probably the groceries from the boot of the Mercedes.

'There must be hundreds of thousands here,' said Slapper. 'But it's a right fooking mess. Look.'

Every box he pulled from the suitcase was so torn and crushed that the money just fell out. Some of the coffee jars barely contained any coffee at all and the rolls of banknotes could quite clearly be seen through the glass. How the hell did they expect to get through Turkish customs? It was one of the worst concealment jobs we had ever seen. Then in our earpieces we heard Phil.

'From Lima 5: that's Zulu 33 through controls. They're putting him straight on the plane.'

'We haven't got time to muck about,' said Slapper. 'I'll lay it all out on the ground here and you get as many shots as you can.'

There was no time to count all the money. We simply had to count the number of rolls, make a note of the denominations and estimate the value. It came to well over £400,000. The pictures were going to be crucial evidence. I wished Barry was there as I tried to gauge the light conditions and shutter speeds. I took photographs of the boxes packed in the cases and then laid them out on the ground with some of the contents showing. Then I took shots of the luggage with close-ups of the luggage tags which would clearly identify these pieces as belonging to the General.

'Are you guys finished or what?' said a voice behind us.

It was one of the baggage handlers, waiting to take the last few pieces of luggage out to the plane. We hastily replaced boxes and jars, piling the clothes on top and hoping that we had left it all looking more or less untouched. If there was some sort of 'tell' in the case it couldn't be too subtle because the case would get knocked all over the place during loading and unloading. Slapper snapped the locks back into place and tossed the last case to the handler, who threw it on to the transporter and drove off across the tarmac. It broke our hearts to let all that money go out of the country and back to the syndicate, but there was nothing we could do. If we had sprung the job right there, we would have only nabbed the General and he could have come up with almost any story about the origin of the money. Volkan would certainly arrange for some sort of cover story. We'd probably have a hard time even proving that it was an offence. In the meantime, the Turks would know we were on to them and we'd lose Volkan, Haase, Bennett, the lot.

We radioed our discovery to the rest of the team and then wandered back into the terminal, where we stood with Phil at one of the windows, watching the airliner take off.

'Bastard,' muttered Slapper as he watched it go. 'Still, at least we know how the money's getting out.'

'Don't worry,' muttered Phil grimly. 'Next time he comes back here, we'll have him.'

Over the next few days we mainly sat in the office, conducting routine surveillance on our targets and waiting for the phone to ring. The first phase of the operation was over. From all the recent activity it was clear that Haase's gang must have recently received a delivery of heroin in Liverpool. They had handed over the money to their Turkish connection and now Volkan's bag man had flown the money out of the country. But the amount in the General's suitcase had been far more than the proceeds of one deal; it certainly looked like more than could have been in the holdall which I'd seen Zulu 3 pass at the motel. And the money in the case just represented part of the profit going back to Turkey. Our intelligence team estimated that at least half the money would have been spent in the UK, paying off people like Zulu 28 and the security teams. Other money would have been invested or salted away in bank accounts in small amounts so as not to arouse suspicion. So where had all the extra cash come from?

It must have come from Volkan's rumoured London operation. Somehow we had to get a lead on that. That was Peter's job. From all the various intelligence sources at his disposal, there had to be some lead which would give us a name or a place or a time and then we could move. In the meantime, there was nothing to do but kill time in the office until John decided what our best chance was.

The pause also gave us a chance to solve another problem: who could take Gareth's place? It's strange how the process of electing a new leader works on a team. It was generally agreed that no single officer could replace a figure like Gareth – none of the HEOs had been on the team long enough – but, as we sat around talking, there seemed to be a growing consensus that two officers working together might. Phil was one of them. Next to Gareth, he had served longest on the team and his heavy-set looks and casual manner masked a quick mind and years of operational experience. His hand would be strengthened by one of the other HEOs on the team. Chris Barron had been there almost as long as Phil. I hadn't seen much of him since he had been almost permanently posted up in Liverpool. The two of them were firm friends with a passion for golf when they could find the time. There was a sort of golf 'mafia' in the Division which provided them with some useful contacts on other teams. Although their careers had followed separate paths they had both done their apprenticeships as EOs on a rummage crew down in Dover, which is about as good an introduction to the patterns and trends of drug smuggling in Britain as you can get.

Like all experienced officers they had kept their heads down whilst Gareth was in charge. It had been Gareth's team and they had let it run that way. But now there seemed to be a general feeling that they had done their time and, with Paddy away so much, they had earned their chance. You could already feel the team looking at the two of them for guidance as we talked about how the job might run next. I liked Phil. He had been the officer who had welcomed me on my first morning. I could already see he was a top-class investigator, but he didn't have any of the self-important attitude that often went with it.

So when the phone finally did ring, just as we were all leaving for the end of a day, all eyes – including mine – turned towards Phil. Paddy, Terry and John were away and Gareth was already working with his new team. Someone had to answer it. Phil paused for a moment, glanced around the room at the rest of us and then picked it up. He spoke once or twice and scribbled some notes on a scrap of paper which Ripper passed to him. The call took less than a minute.

'Right. Paddy says Zulu 28 is on the move. He's heading for a meet with an important contact. As we know from whenever our Turkish speakers have got close to them, they've been talking about the drugs as paintings as well as books recently. Well, Zulu 28 is supposed to be on the way to see the "picture framer". It could be the man in charge of the heroin concealments. The OP crew will try and stay with him as long as possible, but we need a team out on the ground now, so wave goodbye to your plans for the evening. We have no precise time when the meeting is supposed to take place, but it's this evening and he could move at any moment, so get over there fast. Ralph, you'll be there fastest on the bike – if he sets off, stay with him until the cavalry arrives.'

But Ralph was an experienced biker and was already grabbing his leathers and heading for the door as Phil was speaking.

'On my way chief!'

Chief. It was said mockingly, but without malice. Another sign of acceptance of Phil's new role.

'Well,' he sighed. 'Get going. I'll track down John and get this cleared with Control.'

Always just before home time. Bloody typical. I grabbed my kitbag and a set of keys as I headed for the door. Jackie was just a few steps behind me, as quiet as ever. Within three minutes we were roaring out of the gates of Custom House and into the evening traffic, car horns blaring.

It was a terrible evening. The pouring rain killed visibility and made high-speed surveillance driving even more hair-raising than usual. Despite that, we had driven like fury to get across London to Zulu 28's address behind St Pancras station. We hadn't quite made it to the plot in time and Zulu 28 had left, so Ralph and the two officers manning the OP had tried to follow Zulu 28 and relay reports of his position. The rest of the team had worked desperately to catch up as he drove westwards across London at his usual manic speed. By using a few illegal shortcuts and busting a few red traffic lights the team had gradually fallen into place. There were no minder vehicles that night as far as anyone could tell and, thinking that the hard work was done, we had all relaxed a little.

And that was when we blew it.

One moment Zulu 28 was there, the next he wasn't. He was seen to turn right at a junction where another mobile was positioned to pick him up, but he never arrived. Either they missed him in the heavy traffic and the darkness or someone made a wrong call at the junction. Either way we lost him. The team conducted a 'starburst', a technique in which all mobiles search outwards in every possible direction from the last known sighting, but he was gone. It was gutting for the team. Just when we thought we had made a significant break-through we were knocked back again. If this was a meeting with the man in charge of the drug concealments then we had just missed a major lead. The team had taken some hard knocks, but then we couldn't expect to win them all and there was still a chance that Peter would come up with some more details on this new contact.

There was nothing for it but to head home, get some rest and start again tomorrow.

6

The Brixton Connection

Unfortunately the next day didn't help. Nor the next. In fact, for the next few weeks it seemed as if the job had ground to a complete halt. In both London and Liverpool we continued to keep the main targets under surveillance, but they just didn't seem to do anything. They spent a lot of money, visited a lot of nightclubs and casinos, but there was nothing which suggested another consignment of heroin was imminent. Old hands knew that it was just a matter of being patient and waiting it out – every long-term surveillance operation goes through periods like this – but in the meantime the stress was telling on some members of the team. We had all been working long hours for many weeks now and the end of the job still didn't appear to be any closer. There were various petty arguments over trivial things – a classic sign that everyone's nerves were overstretched. It's the difficult periods during an investigation, like this, that they don't show in the films. People get lazy, mistakes are made and the whole job is at risk of stalling. John did his best to send as many people as possible on leave, but what the team really needed was a breakthrough against Volkan's syndicate.

These weeks marked an especially low point for me. Nicky and I finally agreed to a trial separation. It had been on the cards for some time that our marriage would become yet another of the Division's long list of casualties. We had barely seen each other recently and when we did we usually argued. Neither of us really understood what the other was doing with their life any longer. But we didn't want to slam the door just yet. Neither of us was seeing anyone else – we were too busy and too tired – but we couldn't go on like this either. My health had been getting worse, her job was suffering and we had to do something before we really flew at each other and the children suffered. We agreed to split looking after the children so that we could both see them as much as possible, and both sets of grandparents were a massive help, offering to cover the gaps and helping to make the arrangement work. There was still a small chance it would all work out all right. It was just that neither of us could see how.

And then, after about three weeks of nothing but gloomy news, the operation finally began to come into life again.

Zulu 28 was having breakfast at a café not far from his flat, as he sometimes did on the mornings when he managed to get up. He would spend an hour or so reading the Turkish papers and drinking small cups of thick black coffee. We followed him as usual, some on foot, some in cars, and settled down for the usual wait. This morning Mac had drawn the duty of sitting elsewhere in the café and keeping an eye on him. We had only been in place for about fifteen minutes when Mac's voice came whispering over the radio.

'From Lima 11 to all mobiles: heads up guys, something's going on.'

'Fox 3: what is it, has he moved out of the shop?' This was Chris, Phil's friend who was down from Liverpool for a week. He was acting as plot commander for the day.

'Nah, he's still sitting there, but something's wrong. He's looking all about, he's not reading his paper today. He's either waiting for someone or we're all going on a little trip.'

'Oh piss off, Mac!' said Chris. 'Let us know when he moves and stop fantasising.'

I was sharing a car with Sid that morning. Sid was a new HEO on the team, but he was a very experienced officer and had worked with many of the team before. He was married with kids of his own and, although I had only known him a few weeks, he had been a great help, covering for me if I missed a shift or giving friendly advice. We were becoming firm friends. He looked over at me and I could tell he was thinking the same thing I was.

'Mac's not often wrong, is he?' said Sid. I smiled and shook my head. Sid started up the car.

'Get us somewhere close, eh,' I suggested. Then, activating the covert radio switch, I said, 'Lima 3, we're just adjusting our plot. Wait one for new location.'

It appeared that we weren't the only ones with the same thought.

'Fox 14, we're rolling, just getting a better position on the south side.'

'Lima 3, Fox 14, received.'

In five little words you could tell that Chris was peeved, but we were right. Sid and I had hardly pulled into our new position, just at the rear of the coffee shop, when the call came through.

'Stand by, stand by. Red Honda minicab to the front of the café. Registration number follows. Zulu 28 has got up, he's into cab and that's away north and out of my sight.'

There was a brief pause and then:

'Fox 12: I have the eyeball.'

'Lima 10 is backup.'

Twenty seconds later Sid and I pulled up in front of the café and Mac jumped in the back.

'I bloody knew he was up to something,' said Mac, triumphantly, as we pulled away. As Sid battled to get us through the traffic, I pressed the transmission switch.

'Lima 3, Fox 3: that's footman collected. He'd like to be

awarded a medal by you personally at the next stop.' Mac thumped me on the arm.

'From Fox 3: don't you worry. I've got something for the footman and when we have the next stop he's really going to get it!'

'Lima 3: received.'

It was all good-natured. After weeks and weeks of nothing, Zulu 28 had finally broken his pattern. It looked promising. Billy Wright was already in touch with Control, who had instant access to all the computerised databases.

'From Fox 8: we have a trace on the Mike Charlie, that's a known vehicle, X-Ray 16.'

'Fox 3: received.'

One of the UK businesses in which Volkan's syndicate was investing was a minicab firm in north London. The intelligence team were still trying to work out how many of the staff there knew where the money behind the firm came from, but at least two or three of the cabs were regularly used by the syndicate and this was one of them.

We stayed with the minicab. There were no minder vehicles that we could detect but, despite the fact that this was a fairly routine surveillance run for us, the tension was almost unbearable. We couldn't afford to lose this after so many weeks with no leads at all. You could hear in people's voices over the radio that they were anxious not to blow it.

'Fox 14, can I get some backup here? It's getting a bit warm.'

'Fox 14, Fox 10: we called the backup five minutes ago. Are you going to hand the eyeball over or what?'

'Fox 14: I can't see you. Where the fuck are you?'

'Lima 7: we'll take it, if you're baulked Fox 10.'

'Back off Lima 7!'

'Clear the air, clear the air. Take it easy guys.' Chris did his best to maintain a semblance of order, but it was a scrappy and bad-tempered run. We were soon heading north-west on the

A5 and just north of Hendon the cab pulled into a residential area. We had no known addresses for the area. This looked like something new. But the cab dropped Zulu 28 at the entrance to a large park and drove off.

'Lima 7: that's X-Ray 16 lifted. Zulu 28 into the park on foot.'

Chris had already worked it all out:

'Lima 7 deploy footman and then ensure that X-Ray 16 leaves the plot. Fox 5 backup. As soon as he's clear both rejoin the team. All other mobiles deploy footmen and plot up on the park.'

The radio transmission turned to heavy breathing for a moment as whoever was Lima 7's footman climbed out and followed Zulu 28 into the park. It was one of the new people, Gabi. She was going to need help. We raced to other entrances to the park to get footmen out. Sid pulled up in a side-road. I grabbed a camera and stuffed it into a sportsbag for cover. If he met anyone it would be important to get evidence of the meeting. I climbed out of the car and Sid moved off almost as soon as my feet hit the pavement. Through my earpiece I could hear Gabi following Zulu 28. There was a constant low rumbling noise which you always got if some piece of clothing was constantly rubbing against the microphone, and whenever she transmitted another message there was the sound of a lot of breathing. Gabi was a large woman and she was hurrying to keep him in sight. We already knew that she had a habit of getting too close to the target. It was a beginner's mistake and we couldn't afford to risk that here.

'From Fox 3: stay well back from the target Lima 13. Watch out for minders.'

'Lima 13, yes, yes.'

From Gabi's descriptions I tried to work out where Zulu 28 was in relation to me. I could hear that Billy and Jackie were also somewhere in the park. They must have parked their vehicle somewhere so that they could get out as a couple. It was better cover for wandering around in a park. For me, getting pictures wasn't going to be easy without being noticed by the target.

'From Lima 13: Zulu 28 has made contact with an unknown IC2 male. Description follows.' IC codes are a standard way of classifying different surveillance suspects. There are six types: IC1 is Caucasian, IC3 is Afro-Caribbean and so on. IC2 meant that the man was of Mediterranean appearance.

Jackie and Billy had now caught up with Gabi.

'From Lima 10: we see you Lima 13. We can take this now. Keep walking past them and lift.'

'Lima 13: yes, yes.'

Clearly Jackie thought Gabi was in danger of being spotted by the targets. By telling her to 'lift' Jackie was suggesting she returned to her vehicle. There was no problem with this. We all made suggestions constantly to each other during a surveillance. It was a team effort. Meanwhile I had problems of my own. The park wasn't that big but I was blowed if I could work out where Zulu 28 was. It was important we got shots of this meeting. I was trying not to run in case I suddenly came into their view, but at the same time I needed to hurry – there was no telling how long this meeting would last.

'New contact is designated Zulu 44,' said Chris. 'Lima 7 back up Lima 10 and Fox 8.'

'Lima 7 received.'

I was really beginning to sweat now, as much from the pressure as from the effort of walking briskly through the park. Then I saw Billy and Jackie walking along a path through the trees. Zulu 28 and his new contact were about fifty metres ahead of them. Zulu 44 was smartly dressed and wearing a heavy coat. He was clean-shaven, had the typical dark colouring of a Turk and appeared to be in his-mid forties. He was certainly not a target we had seen before. I looked around. The park was pretty empty and I had reasonably good cover where I was. Pulling out a camera and taking shots is a very showy thing to do, but sometimes you just have to go for it. If anyone else was in a better position than me they would have said so by now.

'Lima 3: going for haulage.'

'Fox 3: received.'

'Haulage' was the code-word for photography. I pulled the camera from the bag. It had a long telephoto lens. I stood with my shoulder resting against a tree to steady the heavy camera and zoomed in on Zulu 28.

'Got you,' I murmured as I focused on him and Zulu 44. The pictures had to be good enough to show recognisable faces or they were worthless as evidence. This shot looked good.

I pressed the shutter button and the motorwind whirred into action for about a second. Then nothing happened.

Film jam.

Muttering every curse I could think of I tried to clear the jam, but my cold fingers couldn't even open the catch for the back of the camera. I stood fiddling with it for about a minute, but there was nothing I could do. This was Sid's camera and there was clearly some trick to opening it which I didn't know.

'From Lima 3: that's a negative on that haulage.'

'Fox 3 received,' replied Chris, in a voice dripping with anger. 'Any other footman in a position to get haulage?'

No one was. The meeting was breaking up.

'All footmen drop Zulu 28. Stay with Zulu 44. All mobiles, stand by, stand by,' ordered Chris.

I shoved the camera back into the sportsbag and took up position to back up Jackie and Billy, walking through the park as casually as I could. Zulu 28 passed me going the other way and didn't give me a second glance. The meeting in the motel was a long time ago now. As usual, Jackie was doing well out on the ground. She and Billy kept Zulu 44 in sight as he left the park and were never in danger of showing out.

'Fox 3, relay from Lima 9: that's Zulu 28 complete X-Ray 16 and lifted.'

So the minicab had come back to pick him up. I later found out that Ralph had followed the minicab to a nearby newsagents. Zulu 28 had sent the driver to buy cigarettes to keep him out of the way during the meeting.

Eventually Zulu 44 was out of Jackie's sight and I took over. He made no attempt to get into a car but kept walking. I passed the eyeball to Big George, another of the new officers. George took up the surveillance. He was a Geordie and stood well over six feet tall, hence his nickname. But he wasn't just big, he was also smart and had already proved to be a valuable addition to the team. Shortly afterwards Zulu 44 went into a house. Bingo. We were up and running again.

The house was so ordinary and our observations over the next two days showed Zulu 44's life to be so unremarkable that, at first, we all worried that this new target wasn't even involved in the syndicate. But, after some research, Peter arrived at a team meeting tremendously excited and told us that he was sure that this man was a 'cut-out', one of the numerous word-of-mouth contacts whom Volkan used to maintain security within his organisation. On the third day we set up observation on Zulu 44's house very early. Peter's analysis of the gang's operating habits convinced him that an important meeting was coming up. We decided we would believe it when we saw it. I felt even more sceptical, stuffed as I was in the back of an observation van, just down the road from his house.

But Peter turned out to be absolutely right and my time in the van was mercifully short. A black cab arrived at the house and, smartly dressed, as ever, Zulu 44 set off. We followed, with me bouncing around in the back of the white

Transit, which was the observation van, and Ralph singing loudly in the front. He was in the middle of writing the sketches and comic songs for the ID annual dinner and he loved to try out new material on a captive audience. I'll never forget one particular song about a certain member of senior management renowned for his determination to advance up the career ladder. To the tune of 'Maria' from the musical *West Side Story*, Ralph bellowed:

'The most beautiful sound I ever heard . . .

Promotion, Promotion, Promotion, PROMOTION!'

'Shut up you daft bastard!' I yelled, hammering on the bulkhead as we hurtled around yet another corner, causing all the camera equipment in the back of the van to collapse on top of me. All I could hear above the roar of the engine was Ralph chuckling his head off.

'And now . . . verse two!' he shouted.

The cab took Zulu 44 to yet another coffee shop, this time near the Cromwell Road. The members of Volkan's syndicate always seemed to like to use these places for their meetings. I think it was because white faces stood out so easily amongst the regular customers. It made them feel safe. This time there was a smaller, dapper man, almost certainly another Turk from his dark colouring, waiting for him there. Another short meeting took place, covered by Mac, who was simply able to park across the road and watch them through the café window. The new target was designated Zulu 45, but he was immediately christened 'Sammy' because Mac reckoned he looked like Sammy Davis Jr, and that's how he was known ever after. The meeting took no longer than ten minutes and then we easily tailed Sammy back to his basement flat near Earls Court.

The target list was beginning to get so long that we wondered if we were ever going to find out who the significant players were. But it soon turned out that Sammy was the genuine article. Astonishingly, he had already done a long stretch in prison for heroin smuggling and he appeared to have gone straight back into it. Peter and his team were cock-a-hoop. Their sources confirmed that this was Volkan's London contact. All we had to do now was follow him to the gang which was distributing the merchandise – one of Volkan's best customers and the pillar of his drugs empire.

We soon established an OP on Sammy's flat. He lived in a side-road off a busy high street, on the other side of which we were able to get a room above a shop, directly opposite the entrance to the road. The line of sight on the steps down to the flat was very oblique, but then no OP is perfect and we could just about manage. Besides, the room gave us an excellent view down the length of the side-road. We now discontinued our surveillance on Zulu 28 and kept a full surveillance team plotted up in the area around Sammy's flat twenty-four hours a day. Discovering the identity of the London dealers now became priority number one for the southern team.

However, events were continuing to develop up north and John called everyone back to the F/Ls' office for a meeting a few days into the surveillance on Sammy. We knew it had to be important to leave Sammy without any cover. Peter and his team would be checking all possible intelligence sources and we could always be called back at short notice, but we really hoped it wasn't going to turn into another frantic dash across London through heavy traffic.

Sure enough, John was waiting for us in the office, looking grim.

'We've discovered the source of the leak on Knowles,' he announced. 'You'll be pleased to know that it didn't come from the Division. Our belief is that it came from the local police and that our operation in Liverpool is compromised. To protect Knowles and the progress which we've made in the job to date, I'm pulling the team out of Liverpool temporarily. The local intelligence unit have several indications that Haase has been made suspicious by one or two recent incidents up there and we need to give it time for the situation to cool down. When we do re-establish the team we will be avoiding all contact of any kind with the local police. We haven't yet traced the leak to a particular officer or civilian worker and until we do we can't take any risks. Obviously this information is particularly sensitive and if it got out it could have a particularly negative effect on our relations with other police forces, so it's vital that this news doesn't go out of this room.'

'Well, at least we'll have some more bodies to help down here,' said Ralph.

'I'm afraid that's the second piece of bad news,' said John. 'The Liverpool team have large amounts of leave owing and we'll still be running some operations up there even though we're pulling out of direct surveillance on Haase and Bennett. Furthermore, because we are loosening our hold in Liverpool, we have to maintain surveillance on Zulu 28 here as well as the new target, Zulu 45.'

There was a chorus of groans around the room. This sounded impossible. We could barely spread ourselves to cover one target. Two was ridiculous. John held up a hand for silence. Gradually we quietened down, although Ralph had climbed out on to the window-ledge and was threatening to jump if John pushed us any harder. It was a pity we were on the ground floor, really. John just shook his head and ignored him.

'Yes, I know, we're stretched pretty thin. But Peter and his team are convinced that Sammy is the London organiser for Volkan. Apparently both he and Zulu 28 appear to be senior lieutenants in the syndicate. Zulu 28 handles the northern contacts, Sammy does London. If we get them both we can take Volkan's heroin supplies to both London and Liverpool simultaneously. It will bring down the whole organisation.'

There were various murmurs of disagreement from the team.

What an intelligence unit predicted and what actually happened were often two different things. To get us out on the ground they were always telling us that this was going to be the important meeting or that the next contact was going to be the big break: just one more effort. Six weeks later you found that you were still working against the same target and the intelligence unit, sitting back in their comfy chairs in their air-conditioned offices, still promising that the breakthrough was just one more meeting away.

'Well, like it or not, we're going to do it. This is potentially too big for us to pass up. We'll run reduced teams on both targets. If we get a significant tip one team will reinforce the other. In the meantime I'll see what can be done about getting reinforcement from the Yankees and Novembers. Sort them out, Phil.'

Another chorus of grumbling followed John out of the room. Phil didn't look any more happy than the rest of us, but he went up to one of the whiteboards and started writing out a duty roster. As we prepared to go out again there was a lot of talk about what 'recent incidents' in Liverpool meant. According to the gossip there had been a couple of suspected show-outs. Haase and Bennett were known to be thorough in their counter-surveillance measures, even more so than Volkan's gang. It seemed that there was also a shortage of 'clean' surveillance vehicles, ones which weren't listed as possibly spotted by Haase's gang. Some swaps would have to be done with other teams in order to get some new vehicles in.

'I want to talk to you two about this surveillance on Sammy. I want to give it to Mac as operational commander. I'd like you and Sid to oversee it. You know that technically Paddy is his HEO, but Paddy is always up in Liverpool and Mac is never going to get a break. He's due for a move in a year; if he doesn't get a job as case officer now he never will.'

'Can we really let Mac head up an operation as serious as this?' said Sid, doubtfully.

'Well, you know what this is going to be like. This operation's going to be a matter of graft, not brains. It's a case of sit on Sammy until the deal goes through and then nab the lot. There's nothing complicated about it. It's just a matter of staying with him until the job breaks. Mac's calmed down a lot over the past couple of years; his wife's had a kid and the whole experience has really changed him. John thinks if we give him the responsibility he'll take it really seriously, no licence to piss about. But you two have the seniority. So it's up to you.'

I looked at Sid. It was fine by me, I hadn't been in the team five minutes; Mac had been there four years. He'd earned his shot at being case officer and there was plenty of time for me. I didn't realise there would be a problem until a few days later, when Jackie seemed to be in a worse strop than usual. It wasn't until we were in the office, preparing to go out on surveillance, that I had a chance to ask her what was wrong.

'I hear that Mac's heading up the operation against Sammy,' she said.

'So?'

'I've got one year left on this team as well. I'm only junior to him by three fucking months! How many chances do you think there are going to be for an EO to be case officer in the next year? None, that's how many. Did you even suggest that I run it instead of Mac? It's just Paddy trying to make up for the fact that he's never here. It's fucking jobs for the fucking boys!'

She stormed off to the ladies' toilets to put on her personal radio kit. As I watched her go I could see why she was sore, but I didn't think she was right. Mac had done his time and earned his chance. He might be slow sometimes, but he was reliable as a rock and, when he had a mind to be, thorough. In this job that counted for a lot. Besides, three months' seniority didn't sound like much, but it was important.

Ralph was fixing a piece of kit from his motorbike at the next desk.

'She's got a point you know,' he said quietly.

'Maybe. But what about you? You're due a case officer post as well.'

He smiled.

'Nah. I'm having too much fun. The last thing I want is responsibility. I mean, blimey, just imagine all that paperwork. Mac's welcome to it.'

At least he was happy, but Jackie and I were no closer.

We manned the OPs on Sammy and Zulu 28 around the clock. Because my parents were looking after the children, I tended to take a lot of the nightshifts so that I could see the children for at least part of the day. Sammy never stirred until at least twelve, but the evenings were different. Almost from the very first night, Sammy went out. Jackie and I were watching from the OP as he left. We had only just come on duty and there had barely been time to get settled in before he was off.

'He looks smart this evening,' murmured Jackie and I looked up from the other side of the room where I was reading a book, wrapped up in a sleeping bag, trying to keep warm because the heating in the room was turned off.

'Stand by, stand by, that's Zulu 45 from his flat foxtrot. Towards you Fox 12.'

'Fox 12 received.'

'No consideration, some people,' muttered Jackie as we hastily packed the cameras away and prepared to race outside to follow him. She had only just finished setting them up.

Sammy headed straight for his car, a flash Audi coupé, and set off into the evening with a weakened surveillance team of three vehicles following. Jackie and I rushed to get all the OP gear downstairs and into our car, then Jackie drove like a maniac to catch up. But we needn't have bothered; he hadn't gone far. He drove into Knightsbridge and parked his car illegally in one of the backstreets. I hoped he might get a ticket, not because

I was vindictive, but because it would be good evidence. I joined the foot-team, which quickly deployed to follow him. He made his way back through the narrow streets and disappeared through a doorway. I looked at the name above the door.

'From Lima 3: You guys are never going to believe this: it's a bloody casino.'

Mac was straight onto the radio.

'Put fifty pounds on red for me Harry. I'll pay you back tomorrow.'

Well, I was in charge of the evening shift and putting Sammy under surveillance meant going where he went, so we would just have to put some people into the casino with him. After all, he could be in there for a meeting. There was a dress code for entry and, after a brief discussion over the radio about who had the neatest clothes, I eventually went in with a young Asian girl called Gita, who was on loan from the Yankees. It was going to be tricky going in with covert radios. Obviously casino security would be on the lookout for fraudsters trying to cheat the tables. I took my earpiece out and agreed that Gita would act as the communications link with the team outside. Her earpiece was concealed by her long hair.

Gita and I went in and toured the gaming rooms, looking for Sammy. She was fairly new to the Division and really nervous, which, oddly enough, helped me to forget my own nerves as I murmured reassurances to her. We eventually found him. He was playing poker in one of the side-rooms. In fact, from the speed with which he had found a table and the banter going on, it looked as though he was a regular, so at least he didn't seem to be here for a meeting. But now there was another problem. If we tried to remain undercover in the casino it was likely that sooner or later we would attract attention from casino security. There are strict rules against undercover officers gambling on duty, even for cover purposes, and I didn't like the thought of trying to reclaim the expenses the following day if we lost.

The easiest thing to do would be to approach the casino directly, but that raised other issues: most of the casinos in London were moderately straight if we approached them for help. It wasn't that they were that much more honest than anybody else – the kind of people who run casinos are not choirboys – it's simply that it was not worth their while to stick their neck out for anybody else: one word from us to the police and they were likely to lose their licence. On the other hand some of the staff could be decidedly dodgy and might tip off a suspect if they thought they could get away with it just because they hated investigators. I had asked Sid to contact John and let him know what was happening. He would be checking with Control to find out if the casino owners could be trusted. I just hoped it wasn't going to take too long.

I took Gita to the bar and we ordered drinks. Straight tonic water is best if you can get away with it, because a casual observer will assume it's gin or vodka. We wandered around, sipping our drinks and watching the tables. Fortunately there were all sorts there so we blended right in. As far as possible we kept an eye on Sammy – his spending habits might be used as evidence against him in court one day. He certainly seemed to be having a good time, betting in what looked like one-hundred-pound chips. He was a high roller and was treated like one; complimentary drinks and the women loved him. He was a generous man – it was almost like he was giving it away. So intent was he on his game that we actually went and stood behind him for quite a while and then wandered away again, so as not to attract attention.

Finally Gita touched my arm and said, 'There's a message from John: we're clear to talk to security.'

Looking around you could tell which people were working for casino security. I picked one who was well out of Sammy's eyeline and went over to him. I showed him my warrant card, taking care that the badge wasn't visible to anyone but him.

'Customs and Excise. We need to have a quiet word with whoever is in charge,' I said.

He took one look at the badge and nodded.

'No problem,' he said, and then spoke into his own radio set.

I left Gita to keep an eye on Sammy. The security officer led me through a door into the private part of the casino. No one took any notice. I met the head of casino security, a grey-haired man in his late fifties who seemed pretty decent. He said he was ex-CID. I explained that we were there to keep an eye on a suspect. We wanted to use the casino's CCTV to keep an eye on him. He nodded and showed me to a room where the gambling tables were being constantly monitored by several men on a bank of video screens.

I pointed to Sammy on one of them. The security officer peered at the screen for a moment.

'Oh yes, we know him. You're right, he's in here quite a lot. Never any trouble is he, Jack?'

One of the other men shook his head without looking up, clearly not interested.

'Does he win?' I asked.

'Of course. Here everyone wins,' smiled the security officer.

'How long has he been coming?'

'We'll check his records, but I would say on and off for about two years.'

Two years. That was a lot of cash if he was a regular customer.

'Do you want us to save the tapes?' he asked.

'If you could save the tape for this evening that would be great. But if he's going to be coming here regularly we're more interested in how much money he lays out. Do you think you could provide us with figures?'

'Sure. I will have a word and we will track it.'

'Will it arouse any suspicion amongst the staff? I'd like to keep this as quiet as possible.'

'No problem. We often do this for the police and sometimes as part of our business. It won't look out of place.'

We went back to his office before I asked my last question:

'On nights when he is here, we may want to put an officer in to watch those screens and keep an eye on him. Can the guys in there be trusted?'

He smiled. 'Sure. I'll vouch for them personally. They're all good lads.'

It was probably wasted breath on my part. If an employee at the casino wanted Sammy to know then he would know. The head of security kept asking what sort of case we were working on and which office we were from, constantly stressing that he was ex-police. Why was he so interested? I wondered if I was just being over cautious. At the end of the day, we had to trust him – if we didn't take some chances we'd never catch Sammy.

When I was satisfied that the arrangements were clear I went back to the monitoring room and watched Sammy on the screens. I asked what sort of time Sammy normally left, but the goon I spoke to just shrugged and muttered, 'Depends if he's winning.'

I settled down for a long wait and took some more painkillers. I'd been to the doctor and the new prescription was definitely doing the job. They were so powerful that I not only had no pain, but I even felt pretty happy most of the time. If this was what taking drugs was like maybe I would join the opposition.

Sammy eventually left at about two in the morning. We followed him home, housed him and then the team had to get together to sign the observation log. And that was how Sammy spent a great many of his evenings. He certainly enjoyed his life and we soon got used to it. He liked well-cut Italian suits and was always smartly turned out. Whenever we followed him on shopping expeditions he always seemed to have plenty of cash to spend on anything he fancied. It was all evidence that would one day count against him.

Some time during the third week I was on the early shift in the OP at Sammy's address. I was working with Sid. We took the observation in turns, an hour on and an hour off. The other officer was supposed to note down everything on the log sheet, including the number of photographs taken of each visitor, so that the log could be matched up later with the right prints. Sammy's daily life had now fallen into a predictable pattern and we were starting to get a little sloppy. Working two targets at the same time was beginning to get to us and everyone was strung out. It was my turn at the window with the camera and I glanced across at Sid, who had just nodded off for the umpteenth time and was snoring away happily. There were no warnings from Peter of any unusual activity, so the team was expecting a quiet day. Sammy never did anything in the mornings anyway. I was wrapped up warmly in my little corner of the room and was having trouble keeping my eyes open. I looked at my wristwatch: it was just before ten o'clock. Only another couple of hours before I could get in the car and head home.

I had just turned away from the window, so that I could kick Sid awake, when I sensed movement out of the corner of my eye. Sammy had dashed up the steps from his flat, was around the corner of the building and gone. If I had turned away a couple of inches more I would have missed him completely and we would never have known he had left. I grabbed the radio handset.

'Stand by, stand by!' I shouted, so loudly that Sid nearly fell off his chair.

'Lima 3, Fox 5: Zulu 45 out of the magic box. Gone three one foxtrot like a whippet. Move fast or you'll miss him.'

'Fox 5 received. Be careful with that volume button Harry, you nearly blew my bloody ears off!'

I knew they would put a footman out to pick Sammy up at the end of the road. He was heading away from the main road and towards the backstreets where he often parked his car, but why was he going so quickly?

Sid was now wide awake and sitting forward, waiting for the call which would let us know that Jess had got the eyeball. Seconds passed, but there was nothing except static on the air.

'Fox 5: we've got nothing here. You sure about this one Lima 3?'

'Yes, yes. All mobiles be aware we have Zulu 45 foxtrot and loose. Keep your eyes open.'

'From Lima 9: I've got eyeball on the X-Ray. No change here.'

So wherever he was, he hadn't picked up his car. Both Sid and I were now standing at the windows, watching the streets in case Sammy had doubled back. I tried to rub some of the tiredness out of my eyes and as I did so I glanced down. I caught a brief glimpse of the top of a head as he passed beneath us.

'Lima 3: I have a possible sighting towards green five seven. Can anyone take this?'

But I knew the answer even before it came: all the mobiles were watching the perimeter of the 'box', the surveillance area which contained Sammy's flat. It would only be a matter of seconds but, by the time one of the footmen got here, he would be lost amongst the crowds. There was nothing for it. I'd have to go down there myself and check out the sighting. I dashed for the door, shoving in my earpiece and switching on my personal radio as I grabbed my jacket.

'I'm going,' I shouted at Sid. 'You OK?'

'Sure,' he called as I wrenched the door open. 'Go for it.'

As I took the stairs down to the front door three at a time

I heard Sid calling through my earpiece: 'That's Lima 3 deployed foxtrot.'

I burst through the doorway, all thoughts of minders forgotten. I looked up the street in the direction I had seen him walking. The entrance to the tube station was only about fifty metres away. I slid through the crowd and, just as I got to the entrance, I saw Sammy's back as he disappeared down the steps to the platform. I heard the rumble of an approaching train and could only hope that it was going the wrong way.

'From Lima 3: that's Zulu 45 confirmed at the ukelele.'

'Ukelele' was the code-word for tube station. The only person who overheard me was the vendor at the news-stand. I only hoped that the signal from my set was strong enough to reach one of the mobiles. You could never be sure with all the electronics and metal in an Underground station.

No one acknowledged, but there wasn't time to worry about that now. Mercifully there was no line at the ticket machine. I bought an all-zones ticket and practically vaulted over the barrier. Then I had to make my way slowly and apparently casually down the stairs, in case Sammy was looking my way. There were only half a dozen people on the platform. He was one of them, looking back towards me. There was nothing for it but to keep walking past him further down the platform, being careful not to make eye contact.

I glanced at the indicator board. The train I had heard pulling in had indeed been on the other line. It had bought us some time. But the next train was due on this platform in one minute. I still didn't know if anyone had heard my call. Then my heart leapt as I saw Jackie coming down the stairs. Not three paces behind her was Slapper with a baseball cap pulled well down, the brim hiding most of his face as he slouched along. Jackie walked past me, further down the platform; Slapper stayed near the stairs at the other end.

The problem now was that we had no idea where he was

going. He never normally took the tube and we knew his car wasn't off the road, so what was he up to? A successful surveillance on the Underground is one of the trickiest things for a team to achieve. Even with a full team it is difficult; a small team such as ours probably had no chance. According to the training manual, the mobiles should move to the next station and wait to see if the target and the foot-team emerge. Obviously the cars couldn't race a tube train from station to station, so other mobiles would leap-frog ahead to the station beyond that and so on. Even so, the chances of a loss were considerable because they couldn't be sure where the footmen were, and personal radios weren't powerful enough to transmit to the surface.

Right now the team needed to know which direction we were heading in. I was too close to Sammy to say anything safely, but through my earpiece I could hear Jackie, a few carriages down, trying to get a message through on her set. There was no response. As the rumble of the train was heard in the distance, I saw Slapper disappear back up the stairs to try and get a message out from the lobby.

The train pulled in. It was fairly full, which was good as it gave us plenty of cover. I got in the carriage next to Sammy's and saw Jackie get on a few carriages further down. Although I waited for as long as possible I couldn't see if Slapper had made it back down the stairs in time. Either way, I knew that above us the rest of the team would be driving like maniacs and the call would have gone out from Control for all available mobiles on the route to assist. I clung on to a handrail and watched Sammy through the connecting door as he sat in the other carriage. It seemed to me he was clocking the other passengers, looking for us.

'Harry?'

I looked over my shoulder. It was a guy I hadn't seen since I was at school. Lord knows how he recognised me; I barely recognised him. For a moment I thought this was going to be a lucky break. Unfortunately, he had changed from the quiet kid I'd known at school into the sort of person who could only have a conversation loud enough for the whole carriage to hear.

'So, what are you doing these days?'

I really wanted to tell him the truth. I mean, what's the point in doing an exciting job if you can't boast about it? I wanted to say 'I was a spy and now I'm an undercover drugs officer, and you're about ten feet from one of the biggest heroin suppliers in London.' But now probably wasn't the time, with several of the passengers listening to us whilst pretending not to.

'I'm a teacher,' I said, saying the first thing that came into my head.

'Ah, I always thought that was what you would end up doing,' he said, knowingly. 'Not working today then?'

'Supply teacher,' I said, hoping that explained it.

He decided to tell me what a successful missionary he was or something like that. The truth is that I wasn't really listening. All my concentration was on my peripheral vision and keeping an eye on what Sammy was doing. We pulled into the next station. Sammy didn't move. Through my earpiece I could hear Jackie a few carriages down, trying to get a message to any mobile outside the station above. There was no sound at all from Slapper.

At the next station Sammy did suddenly get off. Despite the fact that my old 'friend' was still chatting away just inches from me, I had no choice but to call it.

'Lima 3: that's an off, off, off.'

'Lima 10: Got it,' replied Jackie.

According to the rule book I was supposed to stay on the train until the last possible moment, in case the move was a bluff. It's a good thing I did because Sammy looked both ways along the platform, possibly clocking Jackie as he did so, and simply walked a short distance along the platform before stepping into my carriage. I wondered if this was a deliberate move to get a better look at me or whether he just didn't like the look of someone in the other carriage. Whether he'd seen Jackie or not she had to get back on the train as the doors closed as it seemed that there were only two of us down here. We would just have to pray that she wasn't burned.

The train moved off again. Sammy walked past but didn't glance at me. My friend was still talking. I hardly had to say a word, just keep smiling and nodding as if I understood what he was going on about. Sammy didn't move for the next few stations but then, as we pulled into Victoria station, he stood up again. He was too close to me for me to say anything, but I frantically pressed the tone button in my pocket to alert Jackie that he was on the move.

Sammy got off and began walking quickly down the platform. It didn't look like a bluff this time, and, anyway, he was out of my sight so I followed, apologising to my mate and saying that I had a meeting. To my horror he followed me.

'It's OK, this is my stop. I'll walk with you. Whereabouts are you going?' He even grabbed my arm to slow me down. Ye gods, he was persistent.

It was no good. I didn't want to be cruel, but I couldn't have him cramping my style any longer. I couldn't see Jackie anywhere, Sammy was fast disappearing along the platform and the last thing I wanted to do was lose him in the maze of tunnels beyond.

'Slapper are you receiving me?' I said.

'What?' he asked, thinking that I was talking to him.

Nothing. Bugger.

'Look,' I said, gently but firmly removing his hand from my arm. 'I'm really sorry to do this to you, but I'm not a teacher, I'm a . . .' It suddenly occurred to me that he wouldn't have a clue what an undercover Customs officer was, '. . . a policeman and I'm working undercover at the moment, so please, you have to piss off right now, OK?'

I left him standing open-mouthed on the platform. Fortunately, I've never met him since at Old Boys' Day, which is probably just as well. Sammy was well ahead of me. I walked quickly to get closer to him. I had no idea where either Slapper or Jackie were and we couldn't afford to lose Sammy now.

Sammy changed lines and was soon on another train. There was no time for niceties. This time I went and sat down alongside him. He never even looked at me, although once again he did seem to be clocking everyone else in the carriage. It was as I'd been told by a very experienced officer early in my career – stick really close to the target and they look past you, they never even know you're there.

We travelled south of the river. There weren't many stops left. I only hoped that one of the other two had managed to get a message to the mobiles or this was going to get very difficult. At Brixton I followed Sammy off the train. It was the end of the line and the station was so busy that following him wasn't a problem. Then, just as we were walking along the platform, my earpiece sprang back into life and I could hear both Slapper and Jackie. The next moment I saw her as well. I pressed the transmission button and murmured, 'Lima 3: I lost comms for a while there. Boy am I glad to see you two. I have the eyeball.'

'Fox 12: no problem Harry, we thought you were hogging it all to yourself there for a minute. Who was your boyfriend?' asked Slapper.

'Piss off, Fox 12,' I said jovially.

Sammy continued to make his way out of the station. At one point he stopped to buy a paper and used this as an excuse to turn round and have a look behind him. It was a pretty clumsy counter-surveillance move and I simply kept walking past him. As usual on surveillance, the important thing was not to do anything that made you stand out. I stopped a little way ahead of him to look at the tube map and, sure enough, he walked right past me again. He walked quickly up the steps and on to Brixton Road.

This was well off his home turf. Was it a shopping expedition or was this Sammy's big drugs connection which we had waited so long for? Neither thing seemed quite right. If he was shopping he would surely have taken his car – he generally drove everywhere. But the idea of people in Brixton buying heroin from the Turks was all wrong. There must be plenty of sources within the Afro-Caribbean community who could keep them supplied. And this was Yardie territory. Did Volkan have the sort of strength to muscle in here?

Sammy stood looking around for a considerable time and then wandered off down the street. The mobiles still hadn't arrived and our little three-person team had to stay with him. It wasn't hard to keep him in sight; he wasn't going anywhere, just window-shopping apparently. The problem was staying with him without showing out. Being a white face wasn't a problem: Brixton is pretty racially mixed – I've worked in areas of Leicester and Birmingham that were more racially segregated – but finding a reason to hang around and watch him was difficult. He kept going to and fro along the street and then up sidestreets and back again. This was not 'standard' Sammy behaviour.

I stood in a charity shop, pretending to flick through a second-hand book but watching him through the window. There was no one else in the shop, just two old ladies behind the counter, sorting through some clothes. I called Slapper.

'Fox 12, Lima 3?'

'Fox 12: go ahead Harry.'

'What do you reckon? Anything feel wrong to you?'

'Yeah. I've got a real itchy feeling on the back of my neck,' agreed Mac. 'Do you think we're being set up?'

I had no idea. Sammy had come straight here as though he had a reason, but now he was hovering. It wasn't that he was waiting to meet someone, because he kept moving around from place to place. It simply felt wrong, but I couldn't see anything out on the street. The trouble was that these people weren't the KGB or Mossad, they didn't play by a rule book; they made it up as they went along.

'Lima 10, do you see anything odd?'

'No, no. Still just Sammy mucking about,' said Jackie.

Sammy doubled back down the street for a third time to look in the window of Dixons again. Since when had he been interested in electrical goods? And why come all the way down here to do it? Yet he wasn't looking all around as if trying to spot us, so what was he up to?

Slapper cut in again: 'Well what do you think Harry? Should we pull out? I'll back you. He's definitely up to something.'

'Let's stay with him,' I said, 'but keep your eyes open. Call if you spot anything unusual.'

'Fox 12.'

'Lima 10.'

'What's that, dear?'

I nearly jumped out of my skin. One of the old ladies had crept up behind me and must have heard me talking into the hidden microphone in my lapel.

'Just talking to myself,' I grinned, then went to the counter and bought the book. Sammy had wandered out of my sight and was now being covered by Jackie. Anyway, it helped to have some bags in your hand if you were going to wander around under the cover that you had been shopping.

We followed Sammy for another five minutes. Then he went into a phone box. We were so spooked that we didn't dare go close enough to get the number, but just stayed back and waited. It was probably the smartest move we made all day. The call only took a moment and then Sammy came back out on to the street and began walking much more deliberately. Then Jackie spotted what we had been missing.

'From Lima 10: I've got an IC3 male, first-floor window of the record shop on the corner opposite your position Lima 3, can't get the road name. He's been there quite a while and . . . wait one . . . now he's taking shots of the street with a tele-photo lens.'

No sooner had she spoken than Slapper was back on the air.

'I've got two more IC3s on the corner opposite the tube exit. One of them has got a scanner. The bastards are not even hiding it. Do you reckon they're looking for us?'

'Could be. Watch your backs but we're staying with him,' I replied.

There was a large group of Afro-Caribbean youths hanging around a low-level brick wall. Many of them had hoods up. Sammy stopped to talk to one of them. I just kept my head down and walked past, but neither Slapper nor Jackie could take the eyeball.

I looked around. There was no cover in the street. Not even a bus-stop. There was nothing to do but chance it. I stood on the corner of the road, pulled out a packet of cigarettes and took some time lighting one up. I had started carrying half a packet around in case of emergencies like this. The youths were looking down the street, watching me. It seemed that I was well and truly 'burned'.

And then the cavalry arrived.

First came the crackling call-signs of the arriving mobiles over our earpieces and, within moments, I could hear Slapper relaying the situation. Four mobiles arrived practically together and soon new footmen were being deployed all along the Brixton Road. Sammy and the youth finished their conversation. With the youth leading they walked a short way back up the road and disappeared around the corner. I heard Jackie's call that they had entered the record shop there. I was just wondering whether one of us ought to follow them in when Phil's voice came over the air.

'All footmen hold back.'

Then: 'OK, that's a stand down to home.'

I didn't know what was happening, but I was glad it was all over. I radioed for a pick-up and Phil and his navigator soon pulled alongside me.

'You get something good then?' grinned Phil, nodding towards the bag in my hand.

I realised that I was still holding the brown paper bag containing the book I had bought in the charity shop. I had been too distracted even to notice what I was buying. I chucked it in the bin next to me and climbed into the back of the car.

John had taken a big gamble in keeping us on both Sammy and Zulu 28 at the same time, but it had paid off. As soon as the address of the record shop had been radioed back to Control, Peter started running checks. According to the local police, the shop was known to be the headquarters of a particular local dealer. He had a long criminal record and they had his name and every other detail. Now it was a matter of finding out exactly which members of his crew were working on the link with the Turks.

Meanwhile John wanted us back in the office for another meeting. This time many members of the Liverpool team were there, as well as the London team. John stood up at the front of the room.

'I have some bad news, I'm afraid. According to police intelligence, Haase's gang brought in a delivery two days ago. A big one.'

There were groans all round the room.

'We don't know at the moment whether this is just luck or whether he knew that close surveillance had been lifted and that it was safe to bring something in. We also saw no movement from Zulu 28 so we can't be sure yet that Volkan was the supplier, although it's quite likely. Senior management have decided we have to re-impose close surveillance in Liverpool or risk losing the job to a police team. I've put up a list of the team I'll be sending up there for the next few weeks. I've tried to include as many new faces as possible. You'll travel up tomorrow.'

Even as I walked towards the whiteboard with several of the others, I knew that my name was going to be there. Haase was a Division One villain and I'd never even been to Liverpool before. Now I was going to find out how tough close surveillance could really be.

7

Liverpool

'Bloo-oody hell!' Chris exclaimed, and then yelped as he spilled scalding coffee into his lap.

We were sitting in the team's black BMW near a Liverpool nightclub. It was late on a Saturday evening and, as usual when there was a quiet moment in an operation, we were watching girls pass by and wishing we didn't have to work.

As we sat there, nursing our styrofoam cups of coffee, yet another group of revellers walked round the corner. There was one particular girl in the middle of the group. Even today I can see her coming round that corner as clearly as if it was happening now. She was about seventeen years old and gorgeous, squeezed into a short, strapless black dress which left almost nothing to the imagination. As she passed the car, without even giving us a glance, both our heads turned to watch her, all thoughts of surveillance forgotten.

Suddenly she shouted at someone further up the street with a voice that could have etched glass.

'OI! GOBSHITE! GERRUS A PACKET OF CHIPS WILL YER, YER FAT WANKER!'

Chris turned to look at me. There was a moment of stunned silence and then we both doubled over, helpless with laughter.

'Welcome to Liverpool, Harry,' Chris gasped when he had finally recovered his breath. 'The city with some of the most beautiful girls on the face of the Earth – leastways until they open their mouths.'

Chris had been born and bred in Liverpool so he could get away with it. As a southerner, he would have probably thumped me if I had said it. He had been my guide for the surveillance operation so far. For security reasons, every officer from London had been paired with an officer from Liverpool whenever possible. They knew the city, they knew the villains and, if we were ever stopped or challenged, they did the talking. The locals on most of the estates where we were working could not only spot a stranger easily, but they were likely to raise the alarm with the local criminals. We couldn't afford to take any chances.

The streets were full of people out posing on a Saturday night. In fact, it was almost the early hours of Sunday morning so we'd passed the posing stage and were rapidly approaching the fighting-and-throwing-up-stage that seems to typify a traditional British Saturday night out these days. We were following one of Haase's lieutenants, Zulu 9, who had been touring the city visiting the clubs and dealing with some of the door security teams. Many of these bouncers were linked to the drugs gangs. Their job was not to stop dealers getting in, but to control which dealers got in. It was easy for the gangs to control door security – if you didn't do what they said, they paid hoods to make trouble – serious trouble – and, tired of the aggro, the club would hire a company owned by the gang. Most gangs had 'their' clubs and the bouncers were an important part of the drug-dealing system. We had to be especially careful of them. They had little to do except stand, chew gum and watch the streets. They could easily spot us if we hung about too long because they were used to watching the streets, so most of the time we stayed mobile. The surveillance technique most used in Liverpool was 'the glance': using multiple vehicles to drive past areas we were watching, constantly changing the profile of the team. You couldn't do something as simple as a straightforward surveillance in Liverpool. In the areas where they controlled the distribution, the drugs gangs owned the streets.

Today, when people hear that I've worked there, they sometimes ask me what I thought of Liverpool – the Mersey, the cathedral, the nightlife. But the truth is that, despite working there on and off for several months, I hardly saw the city centre. I think I only went through the Mersey Tunnel twice and that was when I was following targets. Most of my time was spent on run-down estates around Everton, Toxteth and Walton, where Haase's gang operated. I don't even remember the street names any more. I recognised places by their dot references on the surveillance maps – green one nine, red two four, amber three three and so on. A lot of my time was spent with my head down over a map book, in a speeding car, carefully plotting the progress of a villain's vehicle and shouting into a radio, or stuck in an anonymous OP on an industrial estate watching a flickering black-and-white picture being relayed from a hidden surveillance camera. Even when we were stood down from duty we didn't go into the city. We needed to avoid detection by the police as well as the heroin smugglers because of the fear that there was a police informer, so we were based in a hotel in Chester, practically on the Welsh border and twenty miles away from the area in which we were really working.

The nature of this close surveillance meant that I rarely saw John Haase up close either. His reputation was as one of the most violent criminals in Liverpool. He certainly looked the part: he wasn't overweight or unkempt like a lot of the drug smugglers I had worked against; although he was well on the way to fifty he kept himself in shape, didn't have a trace of grey hair and was usually immaculately turned out. The most striking thing about him was his stare. I heard someone on the team refer to is as a 'thousand-watt' stare, and they were right. It was something which struck you in almost all the surveillance photographs or if you happened to pass him in the streets.

I don't know if it was something he had practised to increase his reputation, but when he locked that stare on to you, you knew that his reputation for sudden and devastating violence wasn't just idle talk. You could see why he was leading Liverpool's most successful heroin-smuggling gang.

The case had been long and involved because Haase was a particularly difficult target. There were several reasons for this. The first was that he was a professional criminal. He knew how police and Customs undercover teams worked and how to combat us. Furthermore, not only did he appear to have sources in the local police, but also the intelligence team still feared that he might have a source in the local Customs office as well. However, it was his apparent source in the police which really gave him an edge; I think if Customs hadn't taken him down at that time, the police would have found it hard to stop him.

The second thing that made him a difficult target was that he had money, lots of money. During the time we had his gang under surveillance he passed more than £2 million in cash to Volkan's couriers, and that was nothing compared to the money he kept to spend in Liverpool. It seemed that he really could buy anything and anyone at that time. Drugs smuggling produces cash like you wouldn't believe – people talk about the 'profits of drugs crime', but you don't realise how staggering the amounts involved are unless you see the lifestyle it buys – and Haase knew how to spend his money: on security, on counter-surveillance, on paying for people on the estates to watch out for us and our equipment. It didn't matter what he needed; whether mobile phones, cars or premises, he could afford to change them all at will, anything to give himself some slight advantage.

The final advantage he had was that he was a loner. He trusted no one completely, not even his nephew, Bennett. He had seen earlier in his career the damage informers could do, and he didn't intend to be caught that way again. So penetration of his gang by undercover officers was practically impossible. The only way he was going to be brought down was by the traditional and painstaking art of day-by-day close surveillance and that takes time, lots and lots of time, before a successful case can be compiled.

There was only one bright spot. With a lot of the international smuggling gangs, any suspicion that the authorities are working on them will lead them to close down operations for a few months and change their routes. Then you've effectively lost the job, because you can't afford to wait around until the operation starts up again, and you have to move on to something else. But Haase was a career criminal. The lure of money and the gang he had to support would be too much for him. He didn't fear us, we were just a business risk. And for someone like him who had done plenty of time inside, the rewards were well worth the small chance that we might catch him. Besides, what else did he know how to do? He would keep going no matter what. That meant that we could keep working on the gang and, sooner or later, we'd nail them.

Successful surveillance in a place like Liverpool demands preparation. People think that surveillance means jumping in a car and following the target. In some cases that is right, but a team using only that method wouldn't last five minutes in Liverpool. For example, take the clubs and pubs which were favourite meeting places for gangs to organise runs and see to the distribution of the drugs to local dealers. It's no good simply turning up on the night of an important meeting, because the gang's minders will be looking for strangers. If you know that a particular pub is used regularly by a gang, then you have to start sending one or two undercover officers there regularly. They don't have to be there long, they just have to make an impression and chat to the bar staff or some of the regulars. Anything so that people remember them as a face they've seen before. When you send them you have to be aware of the level of interrogation they will face. It may be necessary to fix them up with a cover story or an address where they can claim they're staying. We had one officer who was spotted and taken away for questioning for over an hour. If they had cracked his cover story there is no doubt he would have been killed. Fortunately his story stood up when the gang sent people to check it out, but that's how dangerous the job could be. At that sort of level drugs investigation comes close to espionage.

But the opposition made mistakes as well. Haase or his representatives almost always used to meet Zulu 28 or his people in the same pub. That was very poor security and you would have thought that Haase would know better. We could only imagine it was because the Turks wanted somewhere they felt safe and that if Haase had kept changing the meeting place they might have feared they would be ambushed and robbed of the money one day. For us it became a goldmine for evidence.

Having been forced out of Liverpool once before, we needed a new strategy. After some thought John and Paddy decided that they were going to ease up on Haase and Bennett and concentrate on the lieutenants. The reason for this was that Haase and Bennett weren't going to get their hands dirty any more than they had to. If we were really going to learn how the syndicate worked then we had to follow the men who handled the drugs and the money from day to day: the couriers, the security men, the dealers. But that approach was going to produce another problem: as an experienced criminal like Haase wasn't going to let any one person know more than they had to, so surveillance became very bitty and disjointed as we followed first one crook then another.

Sometimes it became hard to remember who we were following and what they were supposed to be doing. Although there was an operational bible listing all these targets, complete with photographs and associated details such as addresses and cars, you can't take a copy of that out on the ground – if a copy were lost, that would be the end of the operation. So officers were expected to memorise the details of all the targets. It sounds like a tall order, but working every day against the same criminals really helped. Even so, I remember being really tired during a dawn watch on one particular address. For once, the idea of pairing southern officers with Liverpool officers had broken down. Having missed the previous evening's briefing I asked Sid which villain we were expecting to turn up as we sat in the car.

'Zulu 51,' replied Sid, settling deeper into the warmth of his coat.

I considered this for a while and then asked, 'Which one is Zulu 51?'

Now Sid thought for a moment and then looked at me with a bemused smile on his face.

'I have absolutely no idea. Give me the damned radio.'

Highly trained officers? Well, sometimes it could get confusing.

One of the more surprising things was that being out on surveillance every day meant that I rarely saw Paddy. He was the case officer and this was supposed to be his patch, but he always seemed to be away on some mission or other, usually to do with gathering intelligence. Whenever he could, Paddy would come out on surveillance, where his knowledge of the local area and the habits of the main criminals was invaluable, but otherwise he was always away somewhere. As a result of his absences a lot of the administration fell to Terry, his deputy, who sometimes seemed overburdened by all the paperwork which a major investigation produces. But it was a vital job: the big worry for all of us was that errors in the paperwork might give defence lawyers a field day when this finally went to court. It wouldn't be the first case where the drug smugglers were caught red-handed, only to walk away on a technicality.

Every night, once we were stood down, we had to drive all the way to Chester, where we had one floor of a local hotel booked out solid. The hotel were told that we were part of a specialist engineering group working on a project in North Wales. I don't know if they believed it and I don't think they cared. They must have been raking the money in. We also had to take steps to protect the specialist vehicles we used, such as observation vans; we didn't dare risk using police facilities, so most of them had to be garaged on an industrial estate well outside Liverpool. Obviously we had to use our own surveillance cars to travel between the hotel and Liverpool every day, but we did our best to make them secure and, although they contained covert radio systems, we always went to the trouble of unscrewing and removing the part of the system which encrypted the radio signals. This was a complete pain in the neck as it involved fiddling with a lot of miniscule little screws and bolts in a small recess at the back of the car. It was the last thing you wanted to mess with at the end of the day, when it was pitch black and you were tired out, and again at the start of the day, when it was so cold that there was still frost on the ground and your fingers were numb.

But it was just as well that all these precautions were taken, because one morning we discovered that one of our vehicles had been stolen. Nothing else in the hotel car park had been touched. Our worst fears were confirmed when the car was found burnt-out in Toxteth a day later. If it had been Manchester or anywhere else there would have been little risk of an association with Haase's gang, but Toxteth was right on his patch. When we sent a team from the local Customs office to examine the wreck, it seemed clear from the state of it that someone had been stripping it for parts when they had found the wiring for the concealed radios and realised what they had got. They had then dumped what remained of the car in a backstreet and set it alight. Of course, all the most vital parts of the encrypted radio system had been removed by us before it was left for the night – if they hadn't it would have been a disaster and all our communications would have been compromised. Even so, other parts were missing and there was some worry that if this was Haase's gang then he would have technical experts working to try and set up an intercept unit. They shouldn't be able to understand our messages because of the military-level encryption, but there was a danger that they would be able to find out which channels we were transmitting on, and activity in those channels would let them know when we were operating in the area. None of us quite trusted the radios in Liverpool after that.

But we weren't the only ones getting jumpy. A few days later we heard from the local intelligence unit that drugs gangs in the area were aware that the level of surveillance activity in the town had gone up, but no one was sure who the target was. One gang in Toxteth assumed it must be them. A gang member had seen a couple of British Telecom engineers working in the street outside his house, but had noticed that the fluorescent jackets they wore weren't the usual type. He immediately put in a call and a crew drove round at the double, piled out of the car and beat the two engineers senseless, telling the 'bizzies' that next time they should get their disguises better. They also turned over the BT van, looking for police radios or bugging equipment. The attack was so sudden and brutal that no one came to the men's aid. In fact they *were* genuine BT engineers; the reason for the difference in their uniform was that a new type of reflective jacket had just been brought in.

Sometimes it really was one of us who was in the wrong place at the wrong time. Slapper once pulled into a car park at the base of a group of two or three blocks of low-rise flats during a surveillance. It seemed like a safe enough area, nowhere near the target we were really watching. Suddenly he looked up to see three black men emerge from a stairwell and walk over to his car. One of them demanded to know what he was doing there. He told them that he was a salesman on his break, eating his lunch. Two of the black men then left. The other one just stood staring at him. Slapper began to get nervous.

'Where have they gone then?' he asked.

'They gone to get machetes. When they come back, if you still here, we gonna cut you up bad.'

Slapper was a big guy and not averse to having a punch up with the opposition, but he had also been around long enough to know when he was dealing with someone serious.

'That's OK mate, you don't need to tell me twice,' he said, and simply drove away – fast.

We never did find out what that was about but sometime later, after the job was knocked, a police officer I told about the incident almost fell off his chair laughing. Apparently the neighbourhood was reckoned to be one of the most dangerous areas in Liverpool and practically a no-go area even for them. But then if we had marked off on our maps all the areas of Liverpool which were considered dangerous for surveillance teams to work in, we might just as well have covered half the city red. That was how it was in Liverpool in the early nineties. It was a war zone. The drugs gangs were experiencing expansion like never before. They were becoming more vicious in their dealings with each other and more sophisticated in their dealings with us. They owned the streets and we operated like a guerrilla band. I hadn't known anything like it since training for work behind the Iron Curtain with MI6 – you had to treat all civilians as potentially hostile. The opposition had seemingly unlimited resources and, worst of all, if you were caught you could expect no mercy.

★   ★   ★

One of the advantages of being in Liverpool was that it took me away from all the problems with Nicky. We hadn't spoken much since the start of the separation, so I was surprised to get a message at the hotel one day after work, asking me to call her. I was worried that it was bad news, but what she told me was a complete surprise. She told me that the kids were OK and then said, 'A woman came to the house yesterday.'

'What about?' I asked, suspiciously.

'She said she was from the local chemist, something about you having a new prescription?'

That was right. The doctor had prescribed some stronger painkillers when I had told him about the increasingly bad stomach cramps I was having. I had picked up a big bottle of the tablets just before I left.

'She was worried that although it doesn't say anything on the bottle, you might try and drive after taking them. She said you musn't, in fact, it's positively dangerous. She said it only occurred to her after she served you because you said something about having to drive for your work. She seemed pretty serious. Have you taken any yet?'

'One or two,' I replied guiltily. Actually, I'd been taking quite a lot.

'Yes, well, you'd better get them to take you off driving duties for a while.'

And with that she put the phone down.

I went up to my room and read the label on the bottle. The tablets were dihydrocodeine. I knew that codeine was a painkiller, but the name of this particular drug rang a bell for some reason. After thinking about it for a while I looked it up in the lists of proscribed drugs in the Misuse of Drugs Act and there, under 'prohibited Class B drugs', was dihydrocodeine, right alongside cannabis. Great. I was a Customs officer taking a hallucinogenic drug. It certainly explained a few things: I had been strangely happy all day taking these pills, and they certainly dealt with the pain. They had also made me feel rather detached from everything and only that morning I had cut through three sets of red traffic lights on a surveillance run in a manoeuvre that even I thought was dodgy, looking back on it. It had certainly scared the heck out of my navigator . . .

So what was I going to do? All surveillance officers have to be able to drive because everyone has to take a turn behind the wheel. After thinking about it, I decided that normal painkillers and putting up with the discomfort seemed like the best bet. But I also knew there would be a temptation to take the tablets as long as they were around because they worked so well. After a few moments of regret, I went into the toilet and flushed most of them away, saving just a few for 'emergencies'.

That same evening John had called a meeting in one of the hotel rooms. The whole Liverpool team were there.

'As you know, we've pinpointed the pub where they're likely to receive the gear from the Turks. What we don't know is the house where they're taking it to cut it and prepare it before moving it on to the dealers. We believe that Haase is going there tomorrow. There won't be any drugs on the run tomorrow, but it's important to see him visiting the place and it's almost certainly the location where we will knock the job when it happens. Now, you know we can't stick too close to him in case he has a counter team out again, so that is going to mean lumping him.'

'Lumping' him meant attaching a tracking device to his car. It was a technique we used against some targets because it allowed the surveillance team to hang further back, where we were less likely to be spotted. It wasn't always reliable, but it was a big help. But lumping Haase's vehicle was about as dangerous as the job could get. Haase tended to park his car right outside his flat where he could see it and he liked to check on it at irregular intervals. He was a well known 'player' in the area and no one would interfere with his car unless they either had a death wish or were police or Customs. At the very least you could expect a slicing-up if he got near you because he usually carried a knife, even if he didn't have a gun. The trouble was that we couldn't afford to put a whole team out on this job. Lumping was an unpopular duty because of the danger involved and because it meant missing most of a night's sleep, but it was something John called for only when he absolutely had to. It required two people, one as lookout and one to plant the device. Jess and I knew that our turn had come round, and when he asked for volunteers we raised our hands to ironic cheers from the rest of the team.

There are very sophisticated devices, no bigger than your thumbnail, available to surveillance teams these days, but the 'lumps' we were using back then were huge by comparison – about the size of a box of cigars – hence the name. There were only a limited number of places on the underside of a vehicle where the device could be placed. Jess and I went out into the hotel car park and found the same model of car as Haase was currently driving and then climbed underneath to find out where best to hide the device. We had tossed a coin and Jess was going to actually place the lump, but both of us had to know what to do just in case there was a change of plan.

We went to bed early and got what sleep we could before meeting up again in the hotel reception at about one o'clock and setting off for the long drive back to Liverpool. We drove carefully. As we got nearer and nearer to Haase's address not only did we have our eyes out for the opposition but we also watched for the police. If we were stopped we could hardly say that we were Customs officers on an undercover mission, seeing as they weren't supposed to know anything about it. Driving around at that sort of hour is a risk as it attracts atten-tion from anyone of the opposition who's about, but the risk would have been even greater if we had arrived early and then just sat around somewhere, waiting for the right time. We drove past Haase's flat. His car was where it always was, right outside the flat, where it was well-lit by the street lamps. No one ever seemed to take his parking place . . .

We parked a couple of roads away and then set off on a circuitous route towards the street where the car was parked. We looked for signs of anything suspicious but saw nothing. In fact, the streets were unusually quiet: almost no traffic, no other people at all. In some ways that made things worse. There was always that little voice of doubt in your mind telling you that you had missed something, that they were out watching you and that you were going to get caught.

Finally, we arrived at the road where Haase was living. We split up. I walked on the side of the road opposite the flat and slid into the deep shadows of a doorway, from where I could watch the windows and see either way up and down the road. Jess was on the other side, walking close to the buildings. Haase's flat was on the first floor and Jess was less likely to be seen that way. When he was level with Haase's car he stopped and waited for a signal from me.

It was still very quiet. Only very occasionally was there the sound of a passing car on the distant main road. I was concentrating all my attention on Haase's window. He was an experienced operator. If he was watching he'd be standing back from the window where it would be harder to see him, not twitching the net curtains like an amateur. I waited to see if there was any movement, no matter how slight, or some reflection of light in the window that didn't make sense. I was well aware that it wasn't just my safety I protecting, it was Jess's as well. He would be the one stuck under the car if something kicked off. Of course I'd race across the road to back him up, but a lot could happen even in the short time that would take. The first we would know would be when he came bursting out of the door. All these thoughts were in mind as I watched the windows and the street in the other direction. I still saw nothing. Sooner or later you just have to go for it.

I nodded to Jess, who took three quick steps across the pavement, crouched down, and then was straight under the car. Unless Haase had actually been watching there was little chance of Jess being seen now. In some ways he was safer while he was under there. It was when he came out again that there would be another moment of danger. In the still night air, every tiny movement Jess made sounded deafening. The lump was attached with magnets, but to get a good fix it was often necessary to scrape away some of the road muck to get a clean surface. The noises seemed to get louder and I thought that someone must surely wake up. We had timed the operation on the vehicle in the car park. Allowing for working in the dark and clearing grime from the underside it should take no more than ninety seconds. But these things never went smoothly. The car you worked on in the car park was never the same as the one you encountered in the street.

The door to Haase's flat opened. There was no warning. No time to give a signal to Jess.

A man stepped out and my stomach tightened. I hissed 'Freeze!' into the concealed microphone of my radio set, desperately hoping that Jess's radio had caught the transmission. One noise from him now and we were done for. This was just what we had dreaded. But as I stood there watching I realised that this wasn't Haase. It was another man; similar build, with short-cropped hair, but not our man. For a moment I thought I'd got the wrong door, and I quickly counted them along the street again. No, definitely right. So who the heck was this? He lit a cigarette and just stood there in the darkness, silently smoking, looking up and down the street. A car went past and I shrank back into the doorway. Surely he could see me? He was only ten metres away. But no, he just stood there smoking. Jess must have been going nuts – if the guy had actually looked down and ahead about three feet he would have been able to see that there was something under the car. But, either because the bright street lights had ruined his night vision or because he simply wasn't looking, he didn't appear to see either me or Jess. He didn't even smoke the whole cigarette, but after a dozen or so drags simply trod it underfoot, turned and went inside. My stomach was so knotted with tension that it had given me a stitch in the side which began to hurt like hell. I looked back at Haase's window again. No light. Nothing.

'All clear,' I whispered into the radio.

There were a few more seconds of fumbling from under the car, which now sounded louder than ever, and then Jess slid out and walked away down the street. I followed on my side of the road, heart thumping. When I crossed the road and rejoined him for the short walk back to the car his first words were: 'Was that him?'

'Fuck knows who it was, but it wasn't our man,' I replied.

Jess shook his head and grinned with relief.

'I've done about thirty lumping jobs and that's the first time that's ever happened to me. I was having trouble getting one of the magnets to attach and I'm still not sure the lump is going to stay on, but if they want a new magnet brought along they can get someone else. I haven't brought enough pairs of trousers to go through that again,' he said.

We got back to the car without incident and drove home in silence, both tired out now that the adrenalin had stopped pumping. The difference between success and tragedy is just one tiny piece of luck, and we'd definitely had ours. By the time we got back to the hotel the stomach cramps had me in agony. Jess asked me what was wrong and I told him it was dodgy food at the hotel. I took some of the 'emergency' pills, which I had sworn to give up only a few hours earlier, and went to bed.

*   *   *

Just a few hours later we were plotted up in the area around Haase's flat. I was driving a small van and sitting alongside Phil, who had the tracking device on the floor between his feet. Despite Jess's worries about the magnet, the lump seemed to be transmitting well and we were getting a good, strong signal. Modern tracking systems can transmit to a standard computer on which the position of the target car can be shown against a street map or an aerial photograph of the area. Twelve years ago the system was far more primitive. Our tracking unit consisted of a small circle of red lights mounted on a box the size of a hardback book. The edge of the circle in the direction of the target would flash. That was it. Quite often you would get more than one light flashing, caused by something called 'signal bounce', and that was when it took an experienced operator to know which were the false readings. At other times it wouldn't work at all; it might flash into life for a few minutes and then die again. Tracking systems were a law unto themselves.

Because of the stomach cramps I hadn't been able to get a wink of sleep. I must have looked pretty washed-out because at one stage Phil looked at me and said, 'Blimey, you look rough. Are you feeling OK?'

'Yeah, I'm fine, just not sleeping too well,' I said heroically.

'It bloomin' looks like it,' said Phil. 'It's a good thing we're not sitting here on a date because you definitely wouldn't get a snog.' He waggled his eyebrows knowingly and, despite the fact that I was feeling so bad, I couldn't help but laugh.

We followed Haase at a discreet distance as he went about his usual routine that morning. But shortly after midday he headed for the one estate which we had definitely labelled 'bandit country'. Strangers were easily spotted and Haase had several associates there. But we had to know where the target house was. Paddy decided to put two footmen in. Phil and Mac were the two selected. They were dropped off at the edge of the estate and made their way through back alleys and foot-paths, looking for any sign of Haase's car. The signal from the lump was no use in this; it could only give a very general idea of the direction. We knew he was in there somewhere, but not exactly where. It was Phil who saw the car first. He came out of an alleyway opposite some shops and could see Haase's car parked further down the road to his left. The driver was sitting there, talking on a mobile. Phil didn't know if Haase was outside the right house or if was this a temporary stop because he was suspicious. He needed to keep Haase in sight for the moment.

There was a phone box across the road, outside a small parade of shops. Most of the glass in the sides had been kicked in, but it was the best cover there was if he was going to watch Haase. Phil radioed his position to Mac and then went over and picked up the receiver. There were plenty of people milling around, including a group of kids aged about ten who were kicking a ball around. The only thing Phil thought about them was to wonder why they weren't in school. Just in case anyone was actually watching, he dialled a number, put in money and started talking. He could still see the driver sitting in his car.

'You're the jack ain't yer?'

(Like 'bizzie' and some other less printable terms, 'the jack' meant the police or anyone like them). One of the ten-year-olds was standing right behind him at the open door of the phone box. Two others were backing him up.

'Piss off out of it!' snarled Phil.

The three of them watched him in silence for a while before the ten-year-old said it again.

'Yer are, yer the jack.'

Phil ignored him and carried on with his conversation on the phone.

'I know you're the jack 'cos you got a fucking earpiece in your ear for yer fucking radio.'

'Haven't you ever seen a bloody hearing aid?' said Phil.

The kid merely repeated 'yer the jack' and the three of them ran off down the road towards Haase's car. Phil's heart must have been in his mouth but the kids disappeared down the garden path of a row of terraced houses before they got to the vehicle.

He knew it was time to move. He tried to find out if Mac could take over from him.

'Lima 11, Lima 5?'

'Lima 11 go ahead.'

'Are you in a position to take this yet Lima 11?' Phil asked.

'No, no, I'm a bit lost, just trying to find you now.'

It was a maze of little roads and, of course, the footmen couldn't wander around with a street map in their hands. Mac might be another five minutes away. The kids had reappeared at the end of the garden path with a middle-aged man who was staring down the road at the phone box. One of the kids was pointing.

Phil was on the point of simply giving up, but he felt sure that if he could just tough it out for a little longer than Haase would drive away or move into a house and the job would be done. The man who'd been called by the kids was starting to walk slowly down the road towards him. Phil had run out of time and was just about to leave when Haase finally got out of his car and walked up to the door of one of the houses and was let straight in.

'That's Zulu 1 housed and address noted. Lima 5 lifted,' said Phil hurriedly.

He started to walk away down the street, hitting the button on his radio which signalled that he wanted an immediate pick-up. He glanced back and saw that the kids and the man were now walking briskly after him. Phil kept walking, knowing that if he ran he would really have blown it, but then there was a cry of 'Oi!' and the sound of running feet. Several other people in the street turned to look at what was happening. This is it, thought Phil, but just as he was about to make a run for it there was a screech of brakes, a car pulled alongside him and the passenger door was thrown open. For one terrible moment Phil thought it belonged to the opposition, but then he saw Slapper's cheerful face grinning up at him.

'Heard you needed a lift,' said Slapper.

'Just drive!' shouted Phil. He leapt in and the car swept away. The man – whoever he was – chased it down the road for a long way.

When news of this little incident got back to us we were sure that we had blown it. Even if this wasn't a member of Haase's gang, word would soon get round the estate. We briefed the local intelligence unit, who listened out on their sources for any mention of the incident, but nothing was heard and after three or four days we concluded that we must be in the clear. We never did find out who the man or the kid were but we got rid of the car, swapping it for one belonging to one of the other London teams, and kept Phil well off the estate for the next few weeks. We now had another vital piece of the puzzle. We were almost ready to move in.

It may have taken nerve for Phil to go into that estate, but it wasn't the bravest thing I saw while I was working with the team in Liverpool. That happened just a few days after Phil had his run-in with angry locals. The word from Peter was that Haase was going to fetch a weapon from a stash of firearms. As before we followed his car, and this time Bennett was with him. It was a difficult surveillance, but there didn't appear to be any minders out, probably because he didn't want people knowing where he was going. By chance I was teamed with Paddy that day, one of the few times it ever happened. At one point on the surveillance our mobile had the eyeball. Paddy and I watched Haase's car turned into the entrance of a cemetery. We pulled up in the entrance to a garden centre further down the road. I started to get out of the car to go out on foot, but Paddy put a hand on my arm.

'Stay here, Harry, I'll take this.'

'You must be joking,' I replied. 'These guys know what you look like and they're going for their weapons stash. You can't do it!'

Paddy had done several jobs in Liverpool and Peter's team had told us that Haase's gang had somehow got a description of him.

He thought for a while and then said, 'You ever been into this cemetery?'

'No,' I admitted.

'Yeah, well, I know it like the back of my hand. Besides, I have a good idea of which area of the cemetery they are heading for. If they challenge you, you don't even sound local and then it's all over. I can pass for local. They won't recognise me. It'll be fine.'

'They won't challenge me . . .' I began.

'Sorry Harry, I'm pulling rank on you, case officer and all that. Hold everyone else back. If we put anyone else in we could spook them. This close to the stash they'll really be on the lookout. I'll let you know if I want anyone else in.'

And with that he was gone, jogging across the road and ducking through a gap in the wall of evergreen trees which surrounded the cemetery.

The radio burst into life.

'Lima 3, Lima 5: do you need someone out to cover this?'

'Lima 3: foxtrot deployed,' I replied, letting them know that someone was already out on foot. They could work out for themselves who it was.

There was nothing else to say. I was just stunned by Paddy's courage. Even though we believed that those guys had a description of him, he was still putting himself up front because he knew how vital this morning's evidence might be to closing the case. It was also brave because there was no way we could put more footmen in there to back him up. This time in the morning, mid-week, there was no one else about and several people wandering around the cemetery would almost certainly show out. I tried raising Paddy on the radio to make sure that he was OK.

'Lima 2, Lima 3.'

Nothing. Just static.

I waited sixty seconds then tried again.

'Lima 2, Lima 3: acknowledge.'

Still nothing. He could already be in trouble.

'Lima 3 to all mobiles, we have lost comms with Lima 2 foxtrot. Attempt relay.'

I listened as the other mobiles all tried to raise him in case they were in a better position. No one could get a response from him. A car roared up alongside me. It was Phil and Chris. Chris wound down his window and leant out.

'Still nothing?'

I shook my head.

'What's the silly fucker playing at?' he demanded. 'All they've got to do is get one look at him and he's blown the whole thing. Why didn't he wait and call someone else through?'

'Beats me,' I admitted. 'All I know is that it's his job and he insisted on going.'

We sat there waiting. Every sixty seconds I would try and raise him. Seven minutes had now passed. How long should we allow him to get into position? It was a big graveyard.

'Fuck it, we're going into the cemetery car park to see what we can see,' said Chris. Just as he started to pull away we all heard a faint tone on our radios. I immediately hit the transmit button.

'Lima 2, Lima 3 confirm.'

A faint tone came through.

'Do you require backup?'

Nothing. That meant no.

'Confirm that you do not require backup.'

One tone. Yes.

'Do you have the targets in sight?'

One tone.

'Are they at the stash?'

One tone again.

Chris pressed the transmit button in his car.

'Lima 2, Fox 3: get out of it Paddy. We've got what we came for.'

One tone came back in reply. A short while later a grinning Paddy forced his way back through the hedge and jogged across the road.

'There's a sort of brick-built workman's hut or something in there. That's where they went. That must be what we're looking for,' he said triumphantly. 'Let's get out of the way and stand everyone down. That'll do for today I reckon.'

Paddy going into the cemetery was one of the bravest moves I ever saw during my time on the Division. But once was enough. We made sure he didn't get the opportunity to do it again.

We were always so busy with our troubles out on the streets that we tended to forget the man with responsibility for running it all. When I went down to breakfast a few days later, John was the only other person sitting in the restaurant. I was up earlier than everyone else because the stomach pains were now waking me up about four o'clock in the morning. Once I was awake there was no way I could get back to sleep so I would toss and turn for a while or listen to the radio, eventually just giving up and waiting until breakfast was served. There was no point going back to the doctors. I'd already been given just about every test available, including a barium meal. They had found nothing obviously wrong and just advised me to avoid stress – which was a joke. Besides, things were getting so bad that I was a little scared about what they might find if I did go back. For the moment I decided to hang on. I would go back to the doctor as soon as we were finished in Liverpool.

I carried a plate of bacon and eggs over and sat down across the table from John. We ate in silence for a while. He looked drawn and tired. After some small talk I asked him, 'How much longer do you think this will go on?'

He shrugged.

'Hard to say. It depends on when the Turks are ready to supply the next batch. We've got just about everything else ready, enough evidence to put both gangs away if we can get a chance. All I know is we can't do this much longer. We came straight off the back of another target job to do this. People have got leave backed up until God knows when and you can see for yourself that people are getting tired and making mistakes. If it goes on like this someone is going to have an accident or, God forbid, hit a pedestrian. We've raided just about every other team on the Division for replacements . . .' he sighed. 'Just between you and me, we're running out of offi-cers. If the importation doesn't happen soon we may really have to pull out of this and hand it over to the Old Bill. We can't just watch Haase's gang distribute drugs around Merseyside for ever and a day.'

He wasn't usually this downbeat in his assessments. It was his job to keep the rest of us going, but I guess that even he was entitled to an off-day. He needed the constant strain of this job to be over as much as the rest of us.

'It's got to happen soon,' I said.

'Let's hope so. Just one clear shot at them, that's all I want.'

We were all working hard out on the streets but he was under considerable stress too, it was just that we never saw it. He had to oversee all the operational matters in both London and Liverpool as well as co-ordinating all the intelligence analysis and liaison with other agencies. And at the end of the day he was responsible for the success or failure of this operation: this was one of the biggest targets the Division had ever taken on and an awful lot was resting on his handling of the case, possibly including Knowles's life.

But we were about to get the piece of luck which all that effort deserved. Just a few days after I had this conversation with John we heard the news from Peter that we had been waiting for.

Volkan was coming to London.

8

Volkan

As soon as we heard that Volkan was coming to London, John immediately moved to strengthen the southern team. For the first time ever there was a definite lead on the head of one of Europe's biggest heroin-smuggling syndicates and he was coming right to our backyard. I was one of the officers who packed my bags and headed for London. We had just a few days to get ourselves organised. We could be sure that the Turkish syndicate would put out their best people to protect their boss and, if the rumours were true, he would probably bring some of his own security people with him – the ones who the intelligence unit claimed had received specialist training from the Turkish intelligence services. In fact, the chances were that they were already in the country. Like the Secret Service's advance guard for the US President, they would be checking everything before the arrival of the main man because he was taking a massive risk. In Turkey his money and political influence kept him safe. But now he was leaving his fortress. He didn't travel often and he would be very aware of the threat of arrest in another jurisdiction where his money couldn't save him. All our thoughts of tiredness and stress were forgotten. This was what we had been waiting for.

At the time I couldn't understand why Volkan was leaving the security of Turkey to travel across Europe inspecting his organisation. Why take the risk? The simple answer is that running his drugs empire wasn't easy for Volkan: the larger and more successful a criminal organisation is, the harder it is to control. You can never really trust the lieutenants who are working for you, can never be sure that one of them isn't cheating you or even about to break away and form their own organisation. How do you know whether they are plotting against you? How can you be sure that the contacts they are making for transporting the drugs are really safe? Long-established criminal organisations such as the Italian Mafia, the Chinese Triads or the Japanese Yakusa rely on codes of honour and family tradition, reinforced with horrific brutality. Cartels such as the Medellin of Colombia are primarily producers and can forget about the product once it leaves their shores and becomes the importers' problem. But Volkan had none of these advantages. He was in charge of a complex organisation trans-porting heroin from Afghanistan, through Turkey and right across Western Europe. Criminals are notably disloyal, always looking for the chance to take over from the man above them. Volkan had to be able to visit all the various parts of the network to ensure that it was holding together and that he wasn't about to be replaced.

But there was something else to it. I think that an even bigger reason for Volkan to make the journey was the thrill. According to intelligence he didn't travel often, but, when he had to visit one of his satellite organisations, he travelled under an alias and apparently he also loved to travel in disguise. Having done that myself as a spy, I suspected that he enjoyed the buzz of knowing that he was one of the most powerful drugs barons in the world and that he could slip unnoticed through airport security systems and immigration controls, sticking two fingers up to every European police and Customs force as he did so. No matter how pampered his lifestyle was in Turkey, no matter how much money he was making (and according to the intelligence he was a millionaire many times over), nothing would be able to replace that feeling of actually being out there and seeing the respect and fear of those who worked for him right across Europe.

On the afternoon of the day before Volkan was expected, John called every available officer to a meeting in Custom House. The intelligence team were there and we had borrowed troops from every other team which owed us a favour. But everything was done under conditions of strict secrecy. We didn't think that Volkan had a source within the Division but we couldn't take the risk, and none of those who weren't a member of Drugs F/L found out who the target was until they arrived at the briefing. As usual, Peter from the intelligence unit summed up what they had been able to gather.

'We know from Interpol that he is flying in to London Heathrow tomorrow. Unfortunately, that's all we know. We don't know which name or even which nationality he'll be travelling under. We don't know which country he'll be flying in from nor what he looks like. Even if we did, it probably wouldn't help too much because he probably changes his look every time he travels.'

'What about meeters and greeters?' asked Phil. 'Can't we get a lead from one of our other targets and see which one goes to the airport?'

Peter shook his head.

'Volkan is notoriously careful. He won't use members of the UK organisation and he'll be staying with a "clean skin", not only someone who doesn't work for the organisation, but possibly someone who doesn't even know what he's up to. He will be determined to have as little contact with the UK organisation as possible because he knows that's our best chance of nailing him.'

'It all sounds a bit thin,' said Slapper. 'How do we know this isn't all just a wild goose chase?'

'Well, we have been watching all parts of the organisation and each leading target shows a marked increase in activity. The level of activity suggests that something important is going to happen in the next few days and that, coupled with the one piece of hard intelligence we have, is unusual enough for us to call it. Of course we could be wrong . . .'

There was a series of jeers and catcalls. We all knew about getting alerts from the intelligence unit for things which never happened.

'But I've looked at the evidence this time personally and I don't think so.'

That quietened us all down a bit. Peter was a shy and rather serious officer who might not last five minutes on a surveillance team, but when it came to intelligence analysis he was generally right.

'So this is the real thing and I hope you're ready for him. But we are not completely in the dark. Our strongest card is knowing that he is travelling tomorrow; this means we can narrow down the list of possible suspects quite a lot. Firstly, we can exclude all women. We know he likes disguise, but we don't think he's into cross-dressing yet.'

'I don't know, Peter,' said Mac, to much laughter. 'We should still frisk a selection of good-looking women coming through Heathrow tomorrow just in case.'

Sarah threw a shoe at his head. Peter smiled and pushed his glasses back up his nose.

'Then we can say that he must be within a certain age range and that he is a Turk. Now, he may be able to disguise those two factors to a certain extent but not completely, in my opinion. Thirdly, we are co-ordinating with the intelligence unit at Heathrow and analysing all ticketing arrangements for tomorrow, ruling out regular travellers, certain large corporate purchases and so forth. This means that we have reduced the list of suspects to just a few hundred . . .'

There were more jeers. It was still a needle-in-a-haystack job. Mac threw the shoe at Peter, who ducked.

'All right, all right,' called John, holding up his hand for a bit of quiet. 'Peter's team are going to draw up a list of the target flights. We can't hit them all, but he's going to give us the best chance he can.'

'What I don't understand is, why bother?' said Jess. 'After all, we don't know what he looks like. Are we hoping that his name is going to be printed inside his suitcase or something?'

Peter stepped forward again.

'That brings me to the one piece of luck we've had. The information suggests that Volkan will be carrying something particular – some technical drawings for a water filtration plant. Now this may be something to do with his cover. We can't be sure, but it's such a particular item that if we find those drawings then we've almost certainly found Volkan.'

'It's still pretty damned thin,' said Slapper.

'Yes, well, perhaps,' replied Peter, 'but on the other hand it's the only lead anyone's ever had.'

All eyes turned to John.

'Our first line of defence will be the airport,' said John. 'On the target flights one team will go through incoming baggage, looking for those documents, before it gets to baggage reclaim. We will also have uniformed officers on the benches who will pull in possible suspects for a light search, in case he's carrying the documents in hand luggage. We'll have a full surveillance team plotted up to take him away from the airport if we find him. The second line of defence will be the organisation, principally Zulu 28 and Sammy. We will also retain one team at HQ as a reserve, in case we get a late piece of information indicating that one of the other suspects is going to meet him. If any of them travel, we stick with them until they lead us to Volkan.'

'What about security, Peter?' asked Sarah. 'Any truth that he's got these ex-spies working for him?'

'Well, a lot of what we hear about the organisation is rumour, but it's certainly the case that several members of the syndicate are ex-military. That probably means that whoever it is has been trained in counter-surveillance techniques by the CIA. The two countries have a very strong liaison. Doubtless he's passed the information on to the rest of their security people.'

'CIA?' said Big George with emphasis, before turning right round in his seat to give me a knowing look.

'They're highly over-rated,' I replied. Several people laughed.

'So what's the third line of defence, boss?' asked Mac.

'The third line of defence is that I've got a bottle of twenty-five-year-old malt whisky in my desk for any officer who spots this bastard,' said John. 'We won't get another chance like this, so let's make it stick. Team lists will be posted before close of play today. Check your cars and equipment tonight. Be on plot at 0600 tomorrow.'

That night I wheeled a Z-bed through the darkened corridors of Custom House towards the F/L office. The wheels screeched from years of rust and it refused to steer in a straight line no matter what I did. Someone had said they were left over from World War II and I think they were right. I was never sure if these collapsible monstrosities were called Z-beds because of the way they folded or because of the course you had to steer to move them anywhere. Come to think of it, it was probably more to do with the position you had to lie in if you were to stand any chance of getting to sleep. Control had a store of them which officers could sign out if they had to stay overnight when working on a particularly difficult case. I had been signing one out regularly whenever it was Nicky's turn to be at the house and the guys who worked in Control (which was manned twenty-four hours a day) were terribly impressed with my dedication to duty. I didn't have the heart to tell them why I was really sleeping in the office. The trial separation didn't seem to be leading anywhere. There was no talk of divorce, but then she hadn't mentioned getting back together again either. We were still very civil whenever we met, but also very wary of each other.

I had spent some time in Control that evening talking to the officers who worked there and listening to the radio calls of teams who were out on the ground, working through the night. Despite the fact that it was the operational nerve centre of the organisation, Control was the most peaceful place in the building. There were always two officers on duty, the room was always nice and warm because of all the computers and other machines in there, and the coffee was always plentiful and hot. It was strange to hear the call-signs of mobiles from other teams as they hurtled through the streets miles away on jobs which meant nothing to me, or to hear the occasional check-in calls from OPs which were being manned overnight: watching some high-profile target or perhaps a warehouse where a drugs concealment was being built into a vehicle.

The Kilos were out in south London and listening to them work it almost seemed like old times again. Occasionally a call would come in from a team requesting a check on the Police National Computer or the Driver and Vehicle Licensing database and the two officers would move quickly to one of the machines where they would type, check screens and get a reply back to the team within minutes. Occasionally they would have to ring ports or airports requesting flight or sailing details, but most of the time they just sat there keeping a watchful eye on the progress of various operations. I had often spoken to Control over the radio – every time a mobile goes out on the ground the first thing the navigator does is run a radio check with Control – but I had never bothered to visit it before. I suspected that a lot of officers were in the same situation.

I finally dragged my protesting burden into the office and

set it up in the only clear piece of floor near my desk. The Z-bed was like a giant piece of metal origami and several times I nearly lost a finger in the vicious springs which held the bed together. At last I climbed into a sleeping bag and lay there, watching the reflections of the lights from the riverside flicker across the ceiling. I wondered if I was going to turn into one of those officers I had once half-admired – divorced, married to the job, sleeping in the office because I wasn't welcome at home. It wouldn't take much now. And yet once I had been a spy, rubbing shoulders with the public school élite, zooming around the world on glamorous assignments – well, they seemed glamorous now. Where had it all gone wrong?

Feeling depression and insomnia settling in, I took two more of the dihydrocodeine from the small number I had saved in my washbag for 'emergencies'. I told myself that the effects would wear off by the morning, as the delicious warm feeling rose up slowly from my toes until it enveloped my whole body and I drifted off to sleep.

'I don't fooking understand this,' said Slapper. 'If I do a surveillance that takes me from Fulham to Watford and then all the way down to Southampton and I have bought a sandwich at the motorway services, which I eat while I'm driving 'cos the target's on the move and I haven't had breakfast 'cos of plotting up early, does that mean that I claim the "within fifty kilometre" meal allowance, or do I get a breakfast allowance plus a distressed hours allowance at time and a half?'

'Dunno,' said Mac from the other side of the table. He had his feet up and was trying to work out which way up to hold a Hungarian bestiality magazine which had been seized from a passenger's luggage. 'What type of sandwich was it?'

'Don't be fooking daft,' said Slapper angrily.

Mac lowered the magazine.

'No, I'm serious. If it was a toasted sandwich it counts as

part of your meal allowance, but if it was a cold sandwich it comes under sundries.'

'Oh right,' Slapper said, and started to scrawl something in one of the columns on the form in front of him. Mac watched him and waited until Slapper had carefully copied out the cost of the meal.

'Unless of course you had a drink with it,' he said.

'You fat bastard!' shouted Slapper, screwing the form up into a ball and throwing it at him. Mac raised the magazine in self-defence and the paper bounced off a picture of a man doing something unusual with a chicken.

All this confusion was caused by a bold new government initiative designed to get 'value for money' from public servants. Apparently some bright spark at the Inland Revenue had decided that driving around in government cars and being given an allowance to buy food when we were out on surveillance meant that we were receiving 'perks', which should be taxed. The Inland Revenue had demanded that a whole load of complicated paperwork be filled out each day by every officer, detailing their expenditure and which section of the volumin-ous office regulations it was being claimed under. When the management had protested that operational officers couldn't just stop in the middle of a drugs surveillance and note this sort of thing down, the Revenue had threatened to simply slap a huge tax bill on the entire Division. The trouble was that not only did we not have time to fill the forms in, but also they were so complicated that none of us understood them anyway. I had a degree from Oxford and I couldn't make head or tail of them. In the end a lot of officers just put down whatever figure they thought would keep everyone happy and as a result most of them were out of pocket. No wonder the drug smug-glers thought they were the smart ones.

We had been at the airport all morning, checking the suspect flights which the intelligence teams thought looked promising, but so far there was no sign of Volkan and no sign of the architect's plans he was supposed to be carrying. All across London the targets who were part of the syndicate had also been strangely inactive. It was as though they were all waiting for something. Either that or Peter's information had been wrong again. Anyway, there had been a lull of several hours during which there were no suspect flights and the airport team was holed up in the Investigation Unit's offices, napping with their feet up, filling in their expenses sheets or playing three-card brag. I was winning rather a lot at three-card brag.

Slapper glanced at his watch and grabbed the small rucksack in which he kept his operational kit.

'I've run out of fooking time, anyway,' he said. 'Come on, Harry. The one o'clock flight from Rome will be in by the time we get down there.'

'Toodle-ooo,' called Mac, chucking Slapper's screwed-up paper after us. I caught it with one hand, dropped it in the confidential waste sack and gave him a friendly two-fingered salute. Mac was leading the airport surveillance team and they wouldn't have to leave the nice warm office for at least another half-hour. Slapper and I were overseeing the baggage search. Once that was done we would go and stand in an office overlooking the Customs hall where, watching through a mirrored window, we would make sure that the uniformed staff were intercepting people from the right flight. If any of them found any papers that looked like the ones we wanted they would secretly signal to us and allow the passenger to go on their way so that we could follow them if they fitted the profile. So far there had been nothing.

Thirty minutes or so later, a baggage crew had completed a search of the bags as they were unloaded off the plane with another nil result. I was getting quite proficient at popping the locks now and had even developed the same casual attitude to the contents of the suitcases which some of the other officers had. As the luggage disappeared up a conveyor belt towards the baggage reclaim carousels, Slapper and I walked though the airside corridors to the Customs hall.

It was empty.

The passengers from the flight would be here at any moment. Slapper, who knew a lot more about the way the airport worked than I did, went to one of the back offices, picked up a phone and dialled a number. I waited out by the baggage benches. I could hear his end of the conversation – as could half the airport.

'Yeah, where are they? . . . Lunch?! Are you fooking kidding me?! . . . Well, where are the relief? . . . He said what? . . . I'll rip his fooking head off. Tell them I want four of 'em down here now!'

I heard him throw the phone down. He appeared at the doorway.

'Can you fooking believe it?' he said. 'The uniformed staff are booked on another job and there's no one to take their place. It's bloody outrageous. It would never have been bloody allowed when I worked here.'

'So what are we going to do?' I asked. 'Will any of them get here in time?'

'Nah. They won't come.'

He thought for a moment and then said, 'You know, we are Customs officers.'

I realised what he was suggesting.

'Oh come off it! I've never searched a suitcase in my life! And anyway, look at us.'

Because we were working 'behind the scenes', we were both dressed in scruffy clothes, bomber jackets, T-shirts, jeans.

'Well you're the senior officer Harry, it's down to you, but if it turns out Volkan was on this flight and we miss him . . .'

I knew this wasn't really allowed, but I quite liked the idea of taking a chance. I weighed up the risks of missing him against the risk of alerting him because we didn't look like the usual crew in the Customs channels. Then I saw a row of Customs officers' jackets hanging in one of the back rooms. They had obviously left them there whilst they went to work elsewhere. I had a shirt and tie in my kitbag; Slapper probably had something similar. Regardless of how we were dressed, this seemed like the sort of thing a real ID officer would do.

'All right,' I decided. 'But we'll use those jackets. And wear your bloody airport pass. At least most people recognise those.'

We were ready just as the first passengers started wheeling their baggage trolleys through the channels. Slapper stood behind a bench on one side, I stood behind a bench on the other. We stopped anyone who looked like they fitted the profile and called them over to a bench, although we were careful to call one or two who didn't fit the profile as well, in order to disguise what we were up to. Strange as it may seem, I had never searched anyone's bags before. Having come straight into the ID from MI6 I just hadn't done an apprenticeship at a port or airport. At least I was quite fast, which made me look a little more professional, but then I knew the bulky luggage had already been searched. It was the hand luggage we were really interested in. Even so, after I had finished, one American businessman remarked, 'You know fella, in twenty years of travelling on airplanes that's the most thorough search of my bags I've ever seen.'

At the time I took it as a compliment but, looking back, I find it slightly worrying – either I had just missed something he was smuggling and he was taking the mickey or everyone else who searched his bags was doing a really, really bad job.

Then, as I looked up from searching a briefcase, I saw a man who fitted the profile. Early fifties, Mediterranean appearance but, most importantly, he looked distinctly ill at ease. As he entered the Customs hall and realised that some people were being searched, there seemed to be a moment of calculation before his face took on the look of a bored traveller once more. He concentrated on shuffling through with his baggage trolley, keeping his head down and trying not to make eye contact with either of us. In my gut I felt that this must be Volkan.

I signalled for him to come over to my bench. He did so very reluctantly, saying something in very poor English and pointing at his watch. I ignored him and asked if he had packed the bags himself, the standard opening question at all Customs baggage checks. I went through the bags quickly, but it was a zip-closed document folder he had tucked under his left arm that I really wanted to look at. He was very reluctant to part with it and again jabbered away in a Mediterranean language. The more he talked the more it seemed like an act to me; I was sure he was more intelligent that he was pretending to be. I began to congratulate myself on my finely-honed ID senses. Finally he passed over the document folder.

I opened it up and riffled through the contents. I intended to get one quick look at the architect's plans – which I was sure were in there – and then I would send him on his way, into the waiting arms of the surveillance team. But I didn't find architect's plans. He had porn in there. Nothing too horrific, only consenting adults, but definitely not allowed in this country. He knew that I had found it and now I faced a problem. It hadn't occurred to me that we might come across a different type of smuggler whilst searching for Volkan. We didn't have time for me to take all his details and issue him with paperwork, but I didn't want to just let him go. He looked at me for a moment, obviously surprised that I wasn't already slapping the cuffs on him. He started to make some sort of hurried excuse, but I simply held up my hand for him to be quiet. I took the magazines out of the folder, dropped them ostentatiously into a bin behind the bench, zipped up the folder and returned it to him. Then I waved him on. Of course it was strictly against normal Customs procedures, but I didn't think he'd be writing a letter of complaint. He gathered the rest of his luggage back on to his trolley and raced away through the channel as if he knew it was his lucky day.

After about thirty minutes the passengers were cleared through. We didn't find Volkan or his documents, but at least we had tried.

'Any problems?' asked Slapper, undoing the his tie and running a finger around his astonishingly grimy collar.

'No,' I said, as we walked away down the corridor back towards the Unit offices. 'Still, I did find something for Mac's collection.' I held up the pornographic magazines. They would have to be dropped in at the Queen's Warehouse on our way past, where they would be added to the always massive pile awaiting destruction. Slapper took one look at the magazines and shook his head.

'Nah, they're not Mac's style – no chickens in 'em.'

By the end of the day none of the flights had yielded any leads on Volkan and none of the targets had moved anywhere near the airport. At the very least we had hoped that we might spot some of his minders around the airport, but the surveillance teams had spotted nothing. Either they were as good as they were rumoured to be or he had never been there. We didn't believe that Volkan's team were better than us, so we had to accept that Peter's team had been wrong. We were, therefore, fairly surprised at the following morning's briefing to be told by John: 'We have it confirmed. Volkan arrived yesterday. He's here, somewhere in London, right now.'

Mac snorted indignantly. 'You're joking. What did he do? Come in by hang-glider?'

'According to Peter, Zulu 28 is going to see him today. Volkan's staying at a safe house. He's brought a full team with him because he's worried about the job and wants to make sure no one's on to him.'

'How does he do it?' asked Sid. 'One of the best known criminals in Europe, we're all bloody well after him, we've got port and airport alerts out everywhere and he just waltzes in and out of the country on a false passport. Do we have any bloody immigration people or what?'

'Well, he's here and we've got to get out to Zulu 28 pronto. He could move at any moment. I asked some of the Novembers to go out very early this morning to cover him after your late finish last night. Make sure you don't lose him today.' Then he added; 'Did a couple of you guys dress up in somebody else's uniforms and search some passengers at the airport yesterday?'

Slapper raised his hand.

'It was all Harry's idea, boss. I begged him not to do it.' At least he said it with a grin. John looked at me quizzically and I explained about the uniformed staff not being on hand. He nodded.

'OK, well the Collector in charge at the airport is screaming blue bloody murder about it, insisting that you had no right to do it and that he's going to have your badges for it.' He let this hang in the air for a moment and then added, 'But I've told him to piss off. If anyone asks, I authorised you to do it. If his people won't do their job up there, then we fucking well will. Now get out on the ground. This could be our last shot at Volkan before he goes back.'

So we raced out of the office and plotted up in our well-rehearsed positions around Zulu 28's house. You could tell that everyone in the team was keyed up. We were annoyed at missing out on Volkan the day before, but we were also paranoid about this counter-surveillance team which was supposed to be with him. They must have been at the airport and we hadn't spotted them. Worse still, although John hadn't said anything, we all knew we were playing for high stakes: if we were spotted the chances were that Volkan would call off the Liverpool import-ation, warn Haase and the Brixton crew, and six months of work would go down the pan. Of course we could have backed off from Zulu 28 and let the meeting go ahead – everything would have seemed fine to Volkan and his minders, the importations would go ahead and we could nab both the Liverpool and the Brixton gangs. But whilst that was the safe option, it would mean that we couldn't build a case against Volkan, and he was the one we had to get if we wanted to seriously damage the flow of heroin into the country. John clearly felt it was worth the risk.

And then there was the small matter of the Division's pride: we had lost the first round to Volkan when he had slipped into the country. We were determined not to lose another.

The good thing about Zulu 28's address was that the remote video cameras we had planted allowed us to hang well back from the road where he lived. Halfway through the morning, the OP crew reported the arrival of Zulu 27, his older associate, in one of the Mercedes the syndicate liked to use. He parked outside Zulu 28's flat and it looked like everything was set. But when the two of them left at around 11.00 a.m. – even though it was important to stay with him and although Zulu 27 tried to help us by driving at a sedate pace – the team hung so far back, watching for the counter-surveillance people, that we were in danger of losing him. You can't afford to drift too far from the target in heavy London traffic, and we didn't even have the luxury of a surveillance motorbike backing us up because Ralph was up in Liverpool. It was no surprise at one stage to hear Chris say, 'Fox 3: All mobiles close up for crying out loud!'

We must have all felt guilty because every mobile in the tail responded.

'Fox 5.'

'Lima 11.'

'Fox 7.'

'Lima 3.'

Five mobiles and no bike against a counter-surveillance team brought in specially from Turkey. The odds weren't in our favour and the worst thing was, we just couldn't spot them. At least if we had seen one of them we could have relaxed, it was the not knowing that was killing us. Mac was the first to crack; after about ten minutes he snapped, 'Where the hell are they? Can't anyone see anything?'

There was nothing but static on the radios.

'All right pipe down, Lima 11,' called Chris. But even he couldn't help adding, 'Everyone keep your eyes open. Call anything suspicious.'

At first we thought that Zulu 27 must be heading for Sammy's address as the Mercedes drove slowly towards the centre of London and then headed east. But in Knightsbridge they parked their Mercedes in one of the backstreets and then set off on foot. We put out a foot-team of our best people. I was sharing a mobile with a new lad from the Novembers who we had borrowed for the day to make up the numbers. He wanted to go out as well, but I told him to stay put. This was too dangerous to risk a 'newbie' making an error. The foot-team followed the two familiar figures as they made their way through the backstreets, crossed the Fulham Road and went into a hotel. Sarah and Ripper, the most smartly dressed of the foot-team, went in shortly after them.

As the foot-team had been moving, those of us who had stayed in the mobiles had been driving around the perimeter of the area, ready to deploy more people on foot and watching for the counter-surveillance. We had never seen this hotel used before so we were sure it was part of some security move.

Then we had our first sighting.

'Lima 11: I've got a new suspect at red fourteen proceeding to red fifteen. Definitely clocking vehicles and he's wearing a radio earpiece.'

Shortly afterwards this was followed by a whispered call from

Dave, one of the new but experienced recruits to the team, who was part of the foot surveillance outside the hotel.

'Lima 7: I have an IC3 male at the front of the hotel, third-floor window. Definitely watching the street. All foxtrots be aware.'

So they were there. It was almost a relief to finally see them. But we couldn't let that force us to hold too far back; it was no good being so afraid of them that we lost the target. I pulled up in the road behind the hotel with a view on the rear exit. I was a long way from the doors, but it was just about good enough. I was parked illegally, but sometimes on surveillance you can't avoid it and it wasn't too suspicious in this part of London. But two men sitting in a waiting car might be. My new partner might be better off elsewhere for a while.

'Go for a walk,' I said. 'Take one of the shops on the main drag. You can join a foxtrot team if necessary, but if it sounds like they're heading back to their car, get here pronto.'

'Sure thing.'

He got out of the car and disappeared away from the hotel towards the main road. I pulled a briefcase across the seat next to me and pulled out some of the big coloured office brochures and forms, pretending to scribble on some paperwork. Through my radio earpiece I could hear Sarah commentating on the two targets within. Apparently they were just sitting in the reception area, waiting.

For the next ten minutes or so we all simply waited; the counter-surveillance team looking for us, us trying to spot as many of them as possible. By now we had about ten possible sightings. They couldn't all be right – at least we hoped they couldn't. That would be a pretty big team.

One of the individuals who had been sighted by the foot-team earlier walked past: a big man, in his thirties with a large black moustache, dressed in a black leather jacket and grey trousers. He glanced into the car, but there was nothing for him to see except the papers I had carefully laid out. I watched him proceed past the back door of the hotel and along the road. Still there was no sign of Volkan. We were all getting more and more nervous. At any moment one of us might do something that could blow the whole operation. Where the hell was he?

There was silence from Sarah. I waited, but now it occurred to me that it was a while since I had heard an update from her. I told myself there was no need to panic yet. But I kept an eye on my watch and two minutes ticked by with no news. I received a call from my partner, who'd found himself a shop on the main road to hide in, so there was clearly nothing wrong with the car set. Two minutes more passed. It was too long.

'Fox 3, Lima 3.'

'Fox 3.'

'I have no comms foxtrot.'

Slapper chimed in from his position in one of the side-roads:

'Fox 12 likewise.'

There was a brief pause before Chris replied. He was obviously trying to set up a link with Sarah and Ripper.

'OK, Fox 3, I have comms and will relay.'

This was typical. The radios were playing up just when you needed them the most. It could just be that Sarah was sitting in a radio blind-spot, it could be anything. Now it meant that we had to relay all communications just at a time when the counter-surveillance people were likely to be scanning for radio activity. It increased the risk of a show-out and didn't do our nerves any good.

I sat there listening to the static and waiting for the next update. All the time I was watching the mirrors for Volkan's people coming up behind me, as well as keeping an eye on the rear exit from the hotel. I was trying to calculate how long I could sit here as a 'businessman' before it looked suspicious. No more than ten minutes, I reckoned, and then I'd have to swap places with another mobile. They'd also probably be clocking registration numbers; I'd have to remember to switch to ghost plates next time we stopped.

'Relay, Fox 3: Zulu 27 has just received a telephone call at hotel reception.'

'Lima 3 received.'

'Fox 12.'

I glanced in the mirrors and saw the patrolling goon appear out of a different side-street. Once again I became the businessman immersed in his order book. That did it. Next time he came round I was going to have to move.

I was aware of something happening and glanced up from my paperwork. A taxi had moved slowly down the street from a rank about a hundred metres away and pulled up outside the rear exit. The doors of the hotel revolved and disgorged two Mediterranean-looking men. I wasn't sure about one of them, but from fifty metres away the other one looked like Zulu 28. He couldn't be on the move without a relay from the foot-team, could he?

I looked over at the goon. He was stopped a few metres away but had his back to me. I risked a call using the concealed radio switch beneath the dashboard.

'Fox 3, Lima 3: are the targets mobile?'

'Negative on that Lima 3. Still no change.'

The taxi started to pull away from the kerb and towards me. Was it Zulus 27 and 28? I couldn't be sure. Although I had been close to them several times, this sighting was for about one second from fifty metres away, and that distance was too far for detail. It was two swarthy Mediterranean men and they were both smartly dressed, but then this was Knightsbridge – so were fifty per cent of the men in the area. The taxi eased past me in the narrow street. The goon had moved on again so I risked ducking down for a look as they passed. Because of the angle and the fact that the taxi was higher than my car

I couldn't see faces, but the man nearest me had a red striped tie, just like Zulu 27.

'Fox 3, Lima 3: Zulus 27 and 28: Possible sighting toucan, at red one seven.'

Toucan was brevity code for a taxi, red one seven meant the junction with the main road. If it really was them on their way to the meeting with Volkan, we would lose them due to the sheer volume of London traffic unless we went with them now.

This time, due to one of those freaks of radio reception, I actually heard Sarah's reply to Chris through the hiss of the static.

'Tell Harry to shut the fuck up – we've got 'em cold.'

Chris acknowledged.

'Fox 3.'

'Fuck!'

I slammed both my hands on the steering wheel, all thoughts of counter-surveillance momentarily forgotten. Two years ago I would have listened to Sarah and just sat tight. But that was when I was a new trainee. Now I might not have counted as an old hand, but at least knew what I was doing. All I had seen was a figure taking three strides across the pavement from the door to climb into the taxi, but I knew the way Zulu 28 moved. I felt in my gut that it was definitely him and the red striped tie of Zulu 27 just confirmed it for me. Still repeating curses under my breath, I put the car into gear and swung into a tight U-turn which brought me into the right direction. However, I was already far behind the taxi, which was held at the traffic lights at the end of the road, waiting to merge into the heavy lunchtime traffic of the Fulham Road.

'That's Lima 3 going mobile. Possible Zulu 27 and 28 in toucan, registration to follow.'

Ahead I could see the traffic lights change and the taxi pulled out into the main road.

'And that's the toucan through red one seven, towards red

two three.' Towards red two three meant that he was heading north, probably towards the traffic chaos of Hyde Park Corner.

I glanced in the rear-view mirror. My U-turn was pretty showy right behind the target vehicle like that, especially with a minder right on top of me. Sure enough, I saw a grey Mercedes pull away from the side of the road to move in behind me. I just got through the lights as they went from amber to red. The Merc behind came straight through on red, almost catching the oncoming stream of traffic. The car was two up, both males. It was too far away to see if they were Turks, but that move did it. They had ticked too many of the right boxes and were surely part of the counter-surveillance. Now I was in trouble.

I could hear Chris urgently calling Sarah, demanding confirmation that she had both Zulus in sight RIGHT NOW, but he also called Mac and told to him to go with me. Mac didn't argue; he simply acknowledged and moved. That made me feel better. Chris and Mac clearly had the same doubts I did, but as we moved away up the Fulham Road I was too far from the hotel to catch what Sarah might be saying in response to Chris's repeated enquiries.

I could see my recruit from the Novembers standing on the pavement as I cruised past and a moment later I heard his plaintive call on the radio, but I couldn't stop to pick him up or even acknowledge him, not with possible counter-surveillance right on my tail. I used the car set to tell him to stay put and then called Mac to pick him up. Mac was starting from the other side of the hotel and, in the heavy traffic, he was so far detached that he wasn't really backing me up anyway; an extra second or two wouldn't hurt. The traffic wasn't moving very fast, but it was nose-to-tail and there was absolutely no room for anyone to manoeuvre. If anyone became detached in this traffic then they were well and truly out of it. I was on my own. I only hoped I was right. Glancing in the rear-view mirror I could see the grey Mercedes was still right behind me.

All the time, as we slowly moved forward, I was trying to see things as the counter-surveillance team would. How much trouble was I in? I was dressed smartly and if they checked with the goon he had only seen me doing paperwork. So far so good. I had done the U-turn and clipped the lights but that was still the sort of thing a businessman might do, especially one who was late for his next appointment, for which he had just been reading the paperwork. It was consistent – just. I had to hope that they hadn't got my number-plate earlier because they would surely be noting it down now. Whether or not they had spotted me earlier, I mustn't play this part too long.

Suddenly Chris's voice cut in across the static.

'Fox 3: that's a loss on Zulus 27 and 28. Lima 3 stay with your mobile.'

I sighed with relief. I gave them the cab's registration number and the approximate position. I asked for a position check from the other mobiles but, as I feared, they were so far back they might as well be on another planet.

'All mobiles south of red one eight, proceed with caution.'

It was Mac. Now what?

'We've got a green Audi. Two up. Definitely on the lookout. Moving slowly in traffic.'

That tore it. None of the mobiles further back was going to be able to move easily with another counter-surveillance vehicle in the tail. Someone was going to have to do something if I were to be rescued. It was no good just sitting there. Chris obviously thought the same thing.

'Fox 3: going alternate.'

That meant he was cutting out of the traffic and going through the backstreets. He would take a very wide swing away from the target, which would allow him to pull all the illegal manoeuvres we usually used to make time in built-up areas: driving on the wrong side of the road, through red lights, the wrong way up one-way streets. It was unlikely that any counter-surveillance would see him as he was heading away from the target and, if they did see him doing something which made them suspicious, the fact that he was heading in a different direction would hopefully put them off the scent. The trouble was that taking alternates when you were one up, as Chris was, was a fifty–fifty chance – you took whichever road was free, relying on your sense of direction to keep you going in approximately the right direction, hoping to pick up a familiar landmark or road name. There was no time to navigate. Sometimes it worked. Sometimes you ended up in an even worse traffic jam than before.

'Fox 5 going alternate.'

Jess was trying the same thing. That was two of our best officers out of it. I only hoped that one of them made it.

Meanwhile we were out of Fulham Road and were heading along the Brompton Road, still towards Hyde Park Corner. The traffic was picking up speed as the jam cleared but I still couldn't afford to let the cab get too far ahead of me.

Several drivers cursed me as I refused to let them into the traffic stream. At times like that in London traffic it's a matter of strong nerves. Behind me the Merc wasn't giving any ground either. I could feel the back of my neck itching as I sensed the two of them watching me, wondering how long I was going to stick behind their man.

At Hyde Park Corner the cab turned north and I still had no one in the backup position. I had to go with him. We picked up speed on Park Lane. This was definitely the breaking point. Glancing in the rear-view mirror I was sure that this was one turn too many. The Merc changed lanes and began to move alongside me. I eased over to try and stop him.

'Any mobile, I need someone to move up, I've got about one more junction in this and then I'm toast.'

Well, I'd given them due warning. I should have been all right. Park Lane is dead straight leading to Marble Arch. It was a perfectly logical route. But just as I thought it was one turn too many the Merc, which had been sitting on my rear quarter, began to ease alongside me. A glimpse in the wing mirror and I could see that the passenger, definitely an Arab or Turk in sunglasses, had his head turned, watching my car. Ahead of me the cab signalled right, preparing to cross the junction and enter a side-street. I made one last desperate plea.

'At red three zero intending red four four. I need back up NOW.'

We crossed the junction with me just behind the cab. The minder had got a very good look at me. And then there was that most blessed of sounds – Chris's voice on the radio.

'That's Fox 3 now two three. Drop him Harry.'

I took the very first side-street.

'That's Lima 3, gone at red four four and off.'

'Fox 3 has the eyeball.'

I left Chris to it. Now he had to wait for backup and good luck to him. But glancing in the rear-view mirror I saw that the Mercedes had come with me rather than staying with the cab. Damn. I tried to think. The most important thing now was that I completed the picture that I'd painted for them earlier. I couldn't afford to go far, it would make my route look too odd. I slowed down as if looking for a parking space and prayed hard that I'd find one. The Mercedes had moved right up behind me and was now glued to my bumper.

'This is Lima 3: I still have counter behind me.'

'Fox 7: do you need backup?'

'No, no,' I said, forgetting radio discipline. 'Stay with the bastard.'

'OK, Harry. Received.'

Then for one of the very few times in my life my prayers were answered. A BMW pulled out of a parking space ahead of me. The top was down and the female driver – a blonde with long hair and big round sunglasses – glanced over her shoulder at me, smiled, exposing a row of perfect white teeth, and pulled away. I pulled into the parking space behind her and the Merc was forced to move past. They were soon out of my sight and I could relax. I didn't attempt to get out of the car. As far as I was concerned they could have a couple of minutes to get out of the area, and then I would move on and try to catch up with the rapidly fading radio calls of the rest of team. Having been so close I was pretty much finished, but a change of clothes and ghost plates and a switch of vehicles with someone else should at least mean that I could ride at the back of the tail for the next few hours.

Once I was sure that the Mercedes wasn't coming back I started up the car and tried to find the rest of the team. The calls were faint but readable, so they couldn't be too far away. It seemed that Zulus 27 and 28 were now out of the taxi and travelling on foot again. I radioed to let Chris know the registration of the Mercedes and that I was back in the game, although I was surely finished for any close-up surveillance.

'No worries, Harry. Arrange an RV with Fox 7, swap mobiles and switch to ghost plates. We'll try and keep you out of it.'

For the next few minutes the targets seemed to wander around aimlessly. The Merc was seen in the area several times, as was the green Audi. It was shortly after I had swapped vehicles with Sarah and Ripper that I suddenly heard:

'That's the green Audi approaching Zulu 27 . . . And that's both targets into the Audi and away . . . towards red five five . . . towards you Fox 5.'

'Fox 5: yes, yes.'

Sarah and Ripper had driven away at speed. I was trying to work out from the map book where everyone was and where the best place to rejoin the tail was. They seemed to be heading back towards me. I waited to hear the next call, but it didn't come.

'Do you have them Fox 5?' called Chris.

'Fox 5: nothing yet.'

Oh no. Not now. There was more silence.

'Fox 5: still nothing.'

'From Fox 3: I'm calling a total loss. All mobiles start loss procedure.'

I can't tell you how disappointed I was. After all that hard work, after saving one massive loss by breaking all the regulations, after not showing out for days we had finally lost him. But that's all it takes on a drugs surveillance, one moment of inattention, one missed radio call between two vehicles and they're gone.

But Chris was determined not to give in so easily. Even as the recriminations about who had missed what began over the radio he called for silence.

'Clear the air, clear the air! They can't have gone far. Lima 11 take the Marylebone Road east, Fox 5 check all side-roads west of red five two . . .'

I stared at the map book on the seat next to me. It looked like a straightforward move from the pick-up to the next junction. I assumed that Fox 5 had missed them there and they had gone on, but even so they should have been picked up at the next junction by one of the other mobiles. It didn't make sense. Then I saw that there was an underground car park between the two junctions. These guys were supposed to have intelligence service training. I wondered if they were trying an old trick. It was better then nothing.

'Fox 3 Lima 3: I'm going to check out the Charlie Papa at red five seven.'

'Fox 3 received.'

Still watching for the grey Mercedes, I drove quickly to the entrance of the car park, took a ticket from the barrier and drove in. I quickly swung around all three levels, but there was no sign of the green Audi and I raced back up towards the exit. As long as I was down here I was out of radio communication with the rest of the team. There was a little saloon car stopped at the only ticket barrier. I don't remember which make it was, but I do remember that it was in the way. I pulled up behind and waited impatiently. Whoever was in front of me seemed to be having a problem. They kept reaching a hand out of their window and putting their ticket in the machine, which promptly spat it out. Again and again it happened. Angrily, I hit the horn of the car. The driver's door of the saloon car opened and in the poor light what appeared to be a little old lady climbed out gingerly. She stood there and seemed to peer myopically at the ticket machine. There was no way you could lose your temper with such a figure but, exasperated beyond endurance, I leapt out of my car and strode up to the machine.

'Do you need some help, love?' I snapped.

The 'little old lady' turned to face me and I almost swallowed my tongue. It was the actress Dame Maggie Smith. I was so wrapped up in thoughts of surveillance that for a moment I was completely stunned. I tried to think of something witty and memorable to say so that for the rest of the day she would be talking to people about the charming young man she had met in the car park, but all I managed to say was, 'Blimey you're Dame Maggie Smith!'

She peered at me over the top of her glasses.

'Yes dear, I know,' she said pointedly. 'Do you think you could help me? This wretched machine won't process my ticket.'

I took it from her. It was horribly crumpled, but once I had smoothed it out the machine accepted it and the barrier raised.

'Thank you dear,' she said, smiling sweetly. 'You are a perfect gentleman and I, as you quite rightly observe, am Dame Maggie Smith.'

With which she climbed into her car and drove off. I stood there for a moment, having completely forgotten about the Audi until a toot on a car horn behind brought me back to reality. I drove back out into the sunshine and my heart leapt as I heard that Sarah had found the targets again. They were on the Edgware Road, heading north, with the Mercedes following. I raced in that direction, keeping an eye out for the Audi, but I needn't have bothered. By the time I caught up with the team Zulus 27 and 28 had already been dropped at their destination, which was an expensive block of flats just a stone's throw from Regent's Park. Sarah had redeemed herself from the loss at the hotel by taking them all the way to the building until she confirmed them entering a flat on the ground floor. Now that they were settled, Chris used the breathing space to rearrange the team a little and call for extra troops from the office. We plotted up around the building and settled down to wait.

Mac joined me in the car to help change the profile a little. I decided to impress him.

'You'll never guess who I just met in the middle of the surveillance.'

'Who?' he asked.

'Dame Maggie Smith!'

'Who the bleedin' hell is Dame Maggie Smith?'

Oh well.

Control keeps a record of all OPs which might prove useful in future operations and, by chance, there was an OP overlooking the block of flats in which we were sure Volkan must be staying. Unlike most OPs this one was luxurious. It was in a fully-furnished flat ten floors up, on the corner of a building with one set of windows overlooking the target and the other giving a commanding view of the main approach road. It was owned by a City banker who rarely used it. He was quickly contacted and gave permission for his apartment to be used. In fact he was a real star. He didn't ask any questions and said we could use it for as long as we needed. The apartment was packed with antiques and expensive electrical goods, including an enormous television, and the team were genuinely impressed, treating the fixtures and furniture with even more care than they normally did. It had a kitchen, a bathroom and somewhere comfortable to sit when you weren't manning the cameras: this was the sort of OP we wanted to be able to use again.

Although we hadn't seen Volkan in person yet, all the indications were that the building across the street was where he was staying and receiving visits from his senior lieutenants. Now we needed to make the best possible use of this opportunity – it was unlikely to be repeated. So we sat and we watched. Volkan's security teams continued to patrol the area, but safe in our OP there was no chance now that they would spot us. We carefully photographed everyone who visited the building and logged the registrations of their vehicles. We then passed these details to Peter so that he and his team could trace the details of every visitor and eliminate those who lived in the other flats. Those who remained were studied in more detail and then added to our growing target list. Volkan only stayed in the country for three days, but by the end of his visit we knew we had identified many of the leading figures in his organisation.

Volkan himself only emerged from the flat once and that was for dinner at a Turkish restaurant, with his host. They didn't go very far and there was no counter-surveillance so we assumed it had nothing to do with business. We couldn't even put any of our Turkish speakers into the restaurant. It was run by a very close-knit clan, who seemed to know all their customers personally; a white face would have been highly suspicious. So we simply shepherded him to and from the restaurant. We got some photographs, but Volkan's lack of activity meant that very few of the team had actually seen him close up.

By the end of the three days Volkan had given his blessings to the next two importations – one to Liverpool and one to

Brixton – and we had a very clear idea of the extent of his organisation in the UK. On the third day he was due to fly out to Italy to inspect his organisation there. John decided that we should let him run without a surveillance team on him. We had already gleaned so much from his visit that there was no point in taking a risk. John merely wanted two officers to be present at Heathrow to confirm that he had left the country, and to see who took him to the airport and confirm which alias he was using. We were also to arrange for his bags to be secretly searched, but we didn't expect someone like Volkan to leave anything for us to find. I was assigned to the job with Stuart, an HEO who had just been recruited to the team as the new Fox 4.

It seemed like a routine job. Thanks to research by Peter's team we knew the time he was leaving and which airline he was using. Stuart and I spaced ourselves around the check-in area, with a view of the check-in desks we knew he would be using. Bang on schedule Volkan arrived with his host, a man who – Peter was convinced – still didn't know what Volkan's real purpose was. We watched him at the check-in desk. He had left it late, as most experienced air travellers do, and Stuart and I expected him to make straight for the gate where he was boarding. But instead he left his host with one of his cases and went over to a bank of public telephones. He passed right by me and, seeing as he didn't seem to have brought any counter-surveillance with him, I turned and followed him.

I took the phone next to him and covertly watched as he punched in a number. I had hoped to see what it was, but other than noting that it was a UK number, it was just too fast for me to see. He gabbled away in what I presumed to be Turkish as I pretended to have a conversation on the neighbouring phone. We were only about three feet apart and I was able to get a really good look at him close up, something which doesn't happen very often on target operations. He was as expected: in his fifties with pale grey hair, cut in a very tidy style with a side parting. He had an unmarked face and was wearing steel-rimmed spectacles. As I stood there, still pretending to have a conversation on the other phone, I risked looking directly at him. It seemed to me that the glass of his spectacles was very thin. Either they were very expensive or they were part of a disguise. All in all, he looked exactly like what he was pretending to be, a wealthy international businessman. As he finished his call our eyes met for a moment, but Volkan didn't seem to attach any importance to it.

Then he was gone, back to his friend and off to his flight. It broke our hearts to let a major target fly out of the country, but if we took him now we'd never get the gangs in Brixton and Liverpool, and they had to remain our top priority. But he would almost certainly have to come back again. We now knew at least one of his aliases and, when he did arrive, we probably had enough evidence from this trip to arrest him.

I hoped it would be soon.

9

Knock, Knock, Knock!

No drugs job ever runs smoothly and this operation was no exception. When Volkan left the country we were all pretty excited. He had given the OK for the importation to go ahead and Peter's team had a tip about when the drugs would arrive. The knock looked like it was only days away and we were ready for it. But then there were problems, most of them caused by the criminals. First the date was changed, then there were disputes over money, then Peter lost one of his sources and it wasn't clear when the importation was going to be. It was incredibly frustrating. We had everything we needed to finish the job but the opposition just couldn't get their act together. What added to the frustration was that Peter couldn't officially tell us what was happening because of security procedures, so most of what we heard was office gossip and half-truths. Day after day we would go out to watch one target or another and gather more evidence with no real idea of what was happening except that it was happening quickly. And every day risked a show-out which might scupper the whole operation.

We were pretty badly strung-out. Simultaneously running what amounted to two jobs, against tough opposition, had been threatening to catch up with us for some time. The prospect of knocking the job at last had given the whole team a temporary burst of energy, but as that prospect receded the exhaustion and declining morale set in more firmly than ever before. At the morning briefings you could see that everyone looked haggard. Nobody was joking as much, tempers were fraying and little incidents once again blew up into major rows. We were back where we had been three months ago. There were petty squabbles over equipment. Gabi threw a petulant fit over people not clearing cars out properly at the end of the day, which was rich coming from someone as untidy as her. Dave took a swing at someone when they complained that he turned up late for his shifts at one of the OPs. That was the state we were in.

You could see it out on the street as well. It was now summer and surveillance was hot, sweaty work; the heat merely reinforced the fatigue. People weren't making as much effort to cover each other on the surveillance tail. There were a couple of minor accidents, both of them when people were parking the cars up in the garage at the end of the day. No one was getting more than four or five hours sleep a night. Even if you went home on time you were so wired with adrenalin from the day's surveillance that you didn't get to sleep. It was sheer tiredness. We needed one of two things: either we had to knock the job or the majority of the team needed to be pulled off the operation and given a complete rest.

After weeks of waiting Peter thought he had a solid lead on the next importation date. Now we needed to work out how we were going to take it down. John called a final briefing session. Most of the planning was complete, but we were still lacking vital pieces of information despite all our efforts: we didn't know how the drugs were coming in or who was going to pick them up. Worse still, Haase was being as careful as ever. He didn't want any of his regular gang associated with the drugs if he could help it. He was an experienced criminal and knew that this was always the most vulnerable part of any smuggling operation. It was expected that Haase would arrange for a mule to pick up the drugs from wherever the Turks were making the exchange. This man was then under orders to take a certain route and we expected that Haase was going to arrange for a counter-surveillance team to check for Customs or police interest.

We had only one high card in our hand: the intelligence unit were sure they knew where the handover was going to be for Haase's contact. If we could cover that then we could follow Haase's lieutenant from that meeting to wherever the load was going to be split up. There was even a chance that Haase himself would turn up there. Even if he didn't, we would have enough to tie him in.

We had a limited number of troops. As well as knocking the job up in Liverpool, there were a range of addresses that would have to be hit and searched simultaneously. We would take out Haase's gang and all Turks associated with the Liverpool job, but we had to be careful to leave the Brixton connection intact so that we could take it out later. We couldn't cover everything, so what would take priority on the day of the knock? This was a question which was really down to the Liverpool hands. They knew the ground best.

'What about the main men?' asked Slapper. 'Are we going to be putting a team out on Haase and Bennett?'

'At the moment we don't see the need,' said John. 'They are going to be particularly vigilant on the day of the knock and they won't go near the drugs. So if we follow them we risk a show-out for nothing. The key thing in this knock is the drugs and only the drugs; if we lose them we really are in trouble. It may well be that once they have the drugs at a safe house Haase or Bennett will come in person to oversee the split. Even if they don't, they are bound to be following a pretty normal routine so one of the search teams should find them at one of their addresses. Now, what about counter-surveillance on the drugs route?'

'We can do it.' said Chris. 'These guys call themselves a

counter-surveillance team but we can spot them first. I don't think they're a danger.'

Phil agreed. 'I don't think they can spot us as long as we keep our profile right – builder's vans, cars with male and female couples, baby carriers in the back, that sort of thing. These guys are looking for suspicious vehicles. Cars two up, that sort of thing.'

John wasn't so sure.

'We need something else, we've got to be able to hold back from the target. The split may not be in a warehouse, it could be on any of these estates where we just can't afford to go in.'

'Can't we bug the vehicle?' asked Mac.

'Nah,' said Paddy. 'We don't know who's collecting it, let alone which car they'll be driving. We'd have to bug their entire fleet and even then they'll probably use a clean set of wheels. It's got to be something else.'

Then Big George had a brainwave.

'What about a spotter plane?' he asked.

'Over Liverpool? You must be joking,' said Chris. 'It'd stand out like a sore thumb. We wouldn't last five minutes.'

'No wait,' continued George, 'we used one against the Colombians on a cocaine job on the Tangos. The ones the police use have really quiet engines so you never hear them, let alone see them. Equipped with the right vision devices they can give you a really clear shot of what's happening on the ground.'

Sid agreed.

'Yeah, we used one on Operation Jordash. That was a boat job. You can't get a much clearer view of the sky than from a boat out in the middle of the English Channel and they never saw a thing. In a built-up area like Liverpool I reckon there's even less chance of seeing it.'

'All right,' agreed John. 'I'll see what we can get together. We haven't used one on the job before so maybe it will give us the edge we need.'

The team was split in two for the day of the knock: London and Liverpool. Extra troops were drafted in from other teams to make up the numerous search teams that would be needed. One or two F/L officers were assigned to lead each team because we knew what we would be looking for. Early on the day of the delivery the teams were deployed out on the ground, taking care to stay far back enough from the target addresses so as not to raise the alarm.

Jackie and I were leading one of the London search teams. We had four of the Novembers to assist us and a couple of uniformed police officers. We would be arresting and searching the house of Zulu 26, the head of security for the Turks in London. After all the trouble his teams had given us it was going to be really satisfying to put him away. Of course, it was frustrating not to be in Liverpool for the knock, but we all had to face the facts: southern accents stood out up there, so northern officers had to be the best choice. Besides, officers such as Jackie and myself had spent most of our time working against the Turks in London, so it made sense that we should hit them.

The day before the knock, the General had flown into Heathrow and was staying in his favourite hotel, doubtless waiting to pick up the huge sum of money which this latest importation would produce. He would be arrested as well.

As we sat in the cars we received relays from Control about the progress of the knock in Liverpool. Our small search team was parked up on an industrial estate, not far from Zulu 26's house, in a residential area of north London. Zulu 26 had done well from his work with the gang: the house we were going to hit was a large modern detached house with its own drive. There was nothing to suggest that the person who lived there was involved in the heroin trade. I wondered how the neighbours would react to all the disturbance.

The radio crackled into life.

'From Control: relay Fox 1: handover Zulu 28 Zulu 3 complete.'

We already knew that Zulu 28 had collected the drugs from whoever had brought them into the country. Now he had clearly arrived at the pub which we knew was going to be used for the handover, as it had been many times before. Zulu 3 now had the drugs and would be making his way back into the centre of Liverpool. We were expecting him to head for one of the gang's many safe houses in Walton. But we couldn't be sure. At the moment we had heard nothing about counter-surveillance, but that didn't mean they weren't there.

'Come on you bastards,' muttered Jackie, 'don't muck it up now.'

'They'll be OK,' I said. 'Paddy will knock this even if he has to do it single-handed.'

One of the police constables wandered over from where his squad car was parked. He put one hand on the roof and looked down into the car.

'Going to be long now is it?' he asked.

'Sometime in the next thirty minutes I reckon.' I had thought that they would be bored stiff backing us up but they seemed genuinely interested, especially when they found we were expecting something like fifty kilos of heroin from the job. But that was often the way it was between rank-and-file police and Customs officers. For all the talk of 'turf wars' between the different managements, we all got along pretty well out on the ground.

We sat and waited and waited. Thirty minutes came and went. Then shortly afterwards the mobile phone went. It was Phil. I knew he was part of the main surveillance team and as soon as I heard his voice I asked, 'Have you knocked it?'

He sounded breathless but jubilant.

'I'll say we have, Harry. It's fucking chaos up here. You won't believe it but we nearly lost the lot. Zulu 3 didn't go to the safe house which we knew about and they had spotters out on the estate, so the team pulled too far back and we bloody lost it! We had that bloody aircraft up there, supposedly backing us up, but they couldn't see it either. You should have heard the panic. Then, just at the last moment, the guy on the plane looked the other way out of the aircraft and saw the target car. They were already carrying the drugs out the back. Blimey did we move! Formula One wasn't in it, but we got them and the whole consignment. Easily fifty Ks of Paki brown, I'd say.'

I could barely hear what he was saying because as people had gathered that it was news of the knock they had crowded around the car, asking for the latest details.

'Any sign of Haase and Bennett?'

'No, not yet, but they're bound to turn up at one of these addresses. There's doors going in all over Liverpool. You can tell the London teams to get stuck in.'

'Will do.'

I called Control to pass the message to the waiting search teams and then quickly summed up the details of the knock for the crowd around the car. Then they all raced back to their cars and we roared out of the industrial estate towards the target address. From the moment of the knock in Liverpool news would have travelled fast; it was only a matter of time before someone phoned our man and let him know that it had all gone wrong. We pulled up in the drive outside the house and raced to the door. There had been plenty of time to assign the different tasks and while Jackie and I went up to the door, two of the Novembers raced around the back of the house to stop anyone getting out that way. The police waited at the gate. They were there to make the whole thing look official and to intervene if anyone made it past us out of the front. Another of the Novembers was standing behind us with a 'magic key', a small battering ram used for smashing locks open. We would give Zulu 26 ten seconds to get the door open. Any longer than that and he might be destroying evidence so standard procedure was to put the door in.

I looked at Jackie to see if she was ready. She nodded. I hammered on the door.

'Customs and Excise!'

There was some confused shouting from within. Jackie and I both counted. Ten. We signalled to the officer from the Novembers who smashed the magic key into the wood around the door lock and blasted the door open. Inside, Zulu 26 was racing up the stairs. I shouted at him and he immediately stopped with his hands up, obviously scared to death that he was going to be shot.

'Come back down here!' I shouted.

Very sheepishly, with his hands still raised, he walked back down, eyes wide with fright. One November pushed past him to see if there was anyone upstairs, the other raced down the hall to search the downstairs rooms. For me the important thing now was to calm him down. As soon as they realise they're not going to be hurt most suspects come quietly.

'It's all right mate, put your hands down.'

Jackie formally arrested and cautioned him as we put the cuffs on and gave him a quick rub-down search for weapons. He would be given a more thorough search as soon as we got him to the police station we had chosen for his interrogation.

I gave him a nice big smile. 'You were in a bit of a hurry weren't you? Anyone else in the house?'

He shook his head. I knew from the file on him that he was married.

'Where's your wife?'

'Shopping', he mumbled

'Is she due back soon?'

He shook his head. Damn. That made life more difficult.

'I have a warrant to search these premises. Is there a neighbour or someone you would like to be present during the search?'

Eventually after much to-ing and fro-ing we managed to find a next-door neighbour who agreed to be in the house until his wife got back. We carefully asked Zulu 26 if there was any money or any valuables he wanted to secure before the search began. There was his wife's jewellery, which was given to the neighbour to watch over, but other than that he insisted there was nothing in the house. Getting this sort of thing out of the way prevented any allegations later. Jackie led him away to a car with one of the Novembers so that she could take him to the police station and get him booked in. In the meantime we would get on with the search. The Novembers had made a pretty good start on the downstairs rooms so I had headed upstairs, wondering what he had been going for when we had smashed through the door. I started in the main bedroom.

To search a room properly, you don't simply walk in and start throwing things around. The first thing you do is stand in the doorway and look. You imagine where you would hide something if this were your room. You make a note of these places at the start because once you get into searching a room it is easy to forget and you only get one chance at it. These days there are a range of devices, such as false electric points and chests with concealed drawers, which can be used for hiding valuables. Other favourite hideaways are the backs of televisions or radios, so you have to be prepared to take a screwdriver to almost every piece of furniture, looking for concealed drugs or paperwork such as airline tickets, notes of meeting times or receipts proving that a suspect was in a particular place at a particular time. Once you've decided what the hot-spots are, you then work your way around the room in one direction, searching absolutely everything from top to bottom. It is painstaking and often boring work, but you never know just when you are going to find that vital piece of paper which will seal the case, so you keep going.

In this case, after an hour and a half of carefully searching through the room, I found nothing other than some bits and pieces of paperwork. I took one last walk around the room to check that I hadn't missed anything. As I walked past the bed I noticed that there was a squeaky floorboard. It felt as though it was actually loose. Of course, under the floorboards is a classic hiding place, but in this case there was a fitted carpet and a lot of furniture in the way. But it was strange that this was the only loose board in the room.

I really didn't want to search any more, particularly since this was probably a waste of time, but I knew that if I didn't take a look at this board then the thought would niggle at me for the rest of the case and I would wonder if I had missed a vital clue because I'd skimped the job. So I started hauling furniture around until I had a clear area to work in and then I used a screwdriver to start prising up the edge of the fitted carpet. Things got slightly brighter once I had the first part of the carpet up. It seemed to me that the underlay was rather dirtier in this area than elsewhere — as though grubby hands had been pushing it back into place — and it only appeared to be lightly tacked down. Using the tip of a claw-hammer and a pair of pliers I started taking out the tacks which held it in place. Finally I was able to roll back the sheet of foam and get at the floorboard which had been bothering me. As I had suspected, it wasn't nailed in place and I was easily able to lift it with the edge of the screwdriver. I reached between the joists below. Nothing. Then I turned my hand around and reached in the other direction. There was definitely something there but it didn't feel like money, it felt like plastic. I pulled out a plastic bag. Inside there was a necklace. It looked expensive. As I peered into the darkened space it looked like there were several more bags in there.

I called for one of the Novembers to bring a camera and also to fetch the neighbour in. The trouble with making finds like this is that if there is cash or valuables the crooks always allege that there was more there than you found and that you had pocketed some of it. If it was drugs they simply claimed that you had planted it, so the best thing to do when you found a concealment like this was to get witnesses in as soon as possible. It didn't stop the mud being thrown in court, but at least it helped.

I pulled about half a dozen bags out of the hole, each one containing two or three pieces of jewellery. Judging by the weight these were the real thing and, looking at the number of precious stones and gold in each piece, they must be worth a great deal. Then I reached in and brought out a thick bundle of banknotes. This was more like it. Bundle followed bundle, mainly ten- and twenty-pound notes. We had to get a larger evidence bag to hold it all. It looked to me like Zulu 26 had converted his share of money into something which was easier to carry if he had to make a run for it, keeping some in each for emergencies. If we traced this I was willing to bet that almost all the jewellery would come up as stolen. The neighbour, a nasty-looking piece of work, just stood by the door and watched impassively.

'You heard him say there was no money in the house didn't you?' I asked. He just shrugged and said nothing.

Having pulled all the bundles out of concealment we had to count them, another laborious task. There was a lot of money and if we made an error about either the amount or the type of note a court might exclude the lot. In all it came to over seventy thousand pounds. We put an evidence seal on the bag with a sigh of relief. Now all we had to do was deliver it to the evidence room – which had been set up at the office – and it would be someone else's problem.

We didn't find any heroin, but then we hadn't expected to and, overall, the search had gone smoothly. We certainly had less trouble than one of the teams in Liverpool. When they entered their premises, the suspect had leapt out of a second-storey window to get away from them. Mac and Slapper had been waiting in the garden for anybody trying to escape that way, but he had seen them coming for him and had vaulted over a neighbouring fence which was so high that Mac swore he must have had springs in his shoes. It was amazing what adrenalin could do for fleeing suspects. Anyway, Mac and Slapper scrambled over the fence and went tearing off after him. He tried to lose them in several twisting back alleys and at one point they had to cross several fences, cutting across people's gardens. Startled faces peered out of windows as they hurtled past, scattering toys and plants in their wake. Finally the suspect dived into an abandoned building on some waste ground. Apparently it was a nightmare, an absolute warren of rooms on three storeys, covered with graffiti, with all the doors and windows long since gone. Slapper stayed outside in case the suspect tried to make a break for it, while Mac crept inside trying to find him. He listened for noise, but there was nothing. He searched carefully, room by room, expecting the suspect to leap out with a brick or a length of pipe at any moment. Finally he came to a room in which there was a battered old metal cupboard against one wall. Thinking it was too corny to be true, Mac crept up to it and threw the doors open. The suspect was crouched inside.

'The guy you're looking for ran back down the stairs just a moment ago,' he said.

'Shut up,' said Mac contemptuously, 'and put your wrists in these handcuffs.'

At least we hadn't had that sort of trouble. As I was kicking the carpet back into place the mobile trilled. I was surprised to hear John's voice on the other end of the line.

'How's it going?' I asked.

'Perfect,' he replied. 'We're still looking for Haase and Bennett, but in the meantime we've pulled in the rest of the gang and we're tearing lots of houses apart. One of the teams has just found some interesting documents. They relate to an old contact from Haase's gang. He's done time for armed robbery and attempted murder. Apparently he's recently gone down to London and we reckon he could be the man who's been sent after Paddy. There's what appears to be a contact address for him and it seems to be fairly current. There are also a couple of registration numbers which might be connected. Get over there and check it out, Harry. The only description we have is that he's IC3. But be careful, this guy's one of the heavy mob and the word has gone out that we've knocked this job – there was no way we could keep it quiet on this estate, so he may well be on the lookout. Don't get seen, just check out whether anyone's at the address and have a look for known vehicles in the area, then contact me. Don't try to be a hero.'

There was no point in taking anyone else for what was only a recce and anyway, there weren't any bodies spare, all the Novembers were needed to finish the search. It certainly was only about ten minutes' drive away. IC3 meant that he was Afro-Caribbean. It wasn't much to go on. The address turned out to be a ground-floor flat in a modern apartment block. I parked in the next street and checked the vehicles parked in the road as I walked towards the building. I walked into the car park at the base of the block of flats and had a quick look around. Nothing matched the numbers I had been given. I had a mini tape recorder and I read out the registration number of the twenty or so vehicles which were there so that I could get them checked through Control later. There was nothing out of the ordinary: hatchbacks, saloons, a plumber's van. There was an entry control system on the main door of the building, but it must have been broken because it opened easily when I gave it a pull.

I walked quietly up to the front door of the flat. There was no name outside, just a doorbell. I put my ear to the door. At first there was nothing. Then I heard sounds of someone walking along the hallway or room on the other side of the door. I quickly pulled away and walked further down the corridor, thinking that whoever was in there was on their way out. But no one emerged.

The problem was finding out who was in there. I went outside and decided to risk walking across the grassed area surrounding the building. I worked out which windows must belong to the suspect flat. One of them was heavily frosted, probably the bathroom, but I could tell that there was definitely someone moving around in there, even if there was no way of telling who it was.

There was a phone box on the corner. I went to it and rang Control. I gave them the car registrations whilst watching the exit of the building. It only took Control a few minutes to run the details through the Police National Computer. Bingo. One of them had been reported stolen in Liverpool two months ago. It wasn't proof, but it was another good indication. I rang John and let him have the news.

'OK, Harry, since I called you we've had some further information, which suggests he's down there. Stay where you are. If he leaves, get the vehicle number and try to stay with him as long as you can. I'm going to try and get you some backup.'

It was only a few minutes before he called again.

'Get down to the local nick. We've managed to get SO19 to assist. Brief them on the situation, then, once they have clearance from their senior officer, knock it. Remember, it remains our operation, so don't let them hijack it. I'm trying to drum up a couple more bodies who'll cover the flats while you're briefing them.'

SO19 was the firearms section of the Metropolitan Police; John was really serious about this. Twenty minutes later I got a call from a couple of Kilos. The Kilos weren't even on the same branch as Drugs F/L so John must be throwing his weight around. Chrissie and Frank were two very young officers who must have joined the Kilos since I had left. I told them to meet me down the road, out of sight of the flats but from where I could still watch the entrance. The car pulled up and I filled them in on the details, stressing that if someone came out who they believed to be our man they must not try to arrest him on their own. If he went to the Liverpool car they were to try and follow and then I'd bring the cavalry and we'd get SO19 to intercept him in the street.

I drove to the local police station and showed my badge at the desk. The armed response units were already there in the briefing room, kitted out in their body armour and blue assault helmets, with their MP5 machine-guns strapped across their chests. The officer in charge asked me to brief them. As I stood there, in front of twenty or so armed officers, it suddenly occurred to me that I didn't actually know very much. I couldn't give them a detailed layout of the premises; I couldn't tell them the exact nature of the intelligence we were working on; I didn't even have a photograph of the suspect we were supposed to be arresting. In fact, I didn't even know what he looked like other than that he was Afro-Caribbean. Still, it was too late to worry about that now. I did the best I could, letting them know the story so far, including the death threats against Knowles. I explained about the suspect's record and the information which had placed him in this area. On the whiteboard I quickly sketched a map of the layout of the building – as far as I knew it – indicating windows and entrances. I told them I had two officers still covering the main entrance and the car park.

I thought they would want to do their own recce, but the officer in charge seemed to want to get the job done right away. I had hardly finished explaining the scenario to them before we were all trooping out down the stairs and into the station yard, where two white Transit vans were waiting.

Then, as always seems to happen on these operations, there was a delay. It was something to do with getting operational clearance. Apparently the senior officer for this area wanted to know what SO19 were doing on his patch and was insisting on some paperwork. It became clear that this might take a while so I decided to head back to the block of flats to help the Kilos. The officer in charge gave me one of his radios so I could stay in touch when they were ready to move.

Twenty minutes later the two vans drove into the car park and I dashed over to them as the armed officers piled out. They seemed to have decided what the plan of attack was going to be because several of them started sprinting across the lawns, taking positions by the windows.

'Stay close to me in case we need you for an identification. Do not enter the flat until I give you the order to do so,' said the officer in charge.

'Suits me,' I replied. The Kilos gave me a look, as if asking what they should do, and I told them to stay in the car park.

'You never know. This bugger might come out of another window or something and go for a car. If he does and these guys don't shoot him, call me on our radio net. Follow him if he leaves but don't, for Christ's sake, try and stop him. I don't want you getting between an armed murderer and these guys.' Then, realising I was making it all sound a bit more frightening than it probably was, I smiled and added, 'After all, think of the paperwork.'

In the corridor outside the flat the armed officers were already in place. The senior officer and I stayed at the far end of the corridor. One of them had a magic key. It was one of the new hydraulic models which have a blade that is inserted in the gap between the door and the frame and simply punches the door clean off its hinges. The officer in charge shouted into his radio, 'Go, go, go!' the door crashed inwards and the officers poured through, shouting, 'Armed police!' At the same time as they broke in through the door, other officers smashed in all the windows of the flat and climbed through. There was what sounded like a scream and much crashing about as doors were flung open and rooms briskly searched. After no more than a minute the sergeant in charge came out again.

'OK, the premises are secure. You can come in now,' he said. 'We've apprehended a suspect.'

The man they had arrested was lying full-length on the kitchen floor with his hands plasticuffed behind his back. His trousers had been wrenched down around his ankles to ensure that he wasn't carrying any concealed weapons. But, rather than an Afro-Caribbean man in his thirties, this was a Caucasian man in his fifties.

'Is this him?' asked the officer in charge.

'No it certainly isn't,' I replied, trying to pick the man up off the ground.

The man was shaking from head to toe and mumbling something again and again which sounded like, 'I'm only the plumber, I'm only the plumber.' It would have been funny if I hadn't felt so sorry for him. Being on the receiving end of that kind of assault would terrify anyone. One of the police officers and I helped him on to one of the chairs by the kitchen table. The kitchen was on the corner of the building and the floor was covered in broken glass from the two windows which had been put in. It must have seemed as if the place had exploded. No wonder he was scared. I have to say that the police were great once it was clear that he was an innocent civilian, offering to call an ambulance for him and even making him a cup of tea. But he didn't seem able to stop shaking, insisting, 'I'm one of the good guys I am.' I left them to it.

I checked out the rest of the flat. The police team had done a thorough job. Every cupboard and wardrobe door had been wrenched open and there was nowhere our man might be hiding. Armed officers were standing around looking disappointed.

'Thanks for your help,' I said to the senior officer. 'My team can handle the search from here.'

The armed police filed out. The plumber went with them as the police insisted that they take him back home. He clearly wasn't in a fit state to drive. The two Kilos eased their way in past them and stood looking at the devastation which filled the flat.

'You certainly get to see some action on the Limas,' said Chrissie. 'Any chance of joining up?'

'Me too,' added Frank.

'Careful what you wish for,' I said, but made a mental note to add their names to the list next time we were doing a trawl for new EOs.

'I'll call a twenty-four-hour glazier and a locksmith,' said Frank, shaking his head with wonder at what looked like a war zone. There seemed to be broken glass everywhere.

'OK, you two take the bedrooms, I'll start in the kitchen,' I said, but we had barely started the search when there was a squeal of brakes and a hell of a lot of shouting from outside. I rushed outside in time to see the armed police surrounding a bright yellow Volkswagen cabriolet. It contained two young men, one Afro-Caribbean and the other Caucasian. Neither of them could have been older than twenty and both looked terrified. I sprinted over.

'Are either of these the men?' demanded the officer in charge.

'I'm not sure, let's check,' I said, and asked the two of them for identification. Although they were young it was possible that one or both of them could be connected with the gang or the safe house. They were both students and clearly rented a flat higher up in the tower block.

'C-can we put our hands down?' asked one of them.

'I don't know,' I replied, handing back their papers. 'You'd better ask the guys with the machine-guns.' In fact, I never even told them that I was a Customs officer. To this day they must be wondering who the guy in plain clothes was who had backup from a full squad of armed police.

Disappointed once more, the police piled back into their Transit vans and roared away. I worked with them many times over the years and they were always damn good at their job, but I have to say that that afternoon I was relieved once they were out of the way. They were just too keen for my liking.

Back in the flat it didn't take us long to find evidence that our man had been there; however, it appeared from the paperwork that the flat was owned by a woman. On the kitchen notice-board there was even a recently-dated postcard, addressed to our man from someone in Spain. But there were no male clothes or anything else which might have belonged to him. It looked like he had cleared out. We gathered everything together which appeared to be evidential and stuffed it into two plastic sacks. By now it was early evening and I headed back towards the office, leaving the two Kilos to watch the flat until the locksmith and glazier arrived to secure it.

The knock had been exciting but you wouldn't believe the amount of paperwork this sort of operation generates. All the items of property which had been seized from the various house searches had to be logged and indexed. Any particularly interesting items had to be marked up so that they could be used in interviews with the suspects. Then there were search warrants to be returned to courts, complete with statements of all seized items, interviews to be conducted and reports written for senior Customs management so that they could brief ministers. Then there was the Customs and Excise paperwork to be completed. This task alone was mammoth. These days everything can be entered directly on to computer but back then CEDRIC, the Customs and Excise computer, would only accept inputs which had been laboriously entered on to a form by hand with each letter of each word in its own little box.

And all the time when everyone was working on all of these tasks in both London and Liverpool there was only one question on everyone's lips: have Haase and Bennett been found yet?

It was clear that they were on the run. Despite the speed with which the Liverpool team had moved, someone must have got a call to them and they must have had a plan in place so that they could get out of the city quickly. Our best hope was that one of the suspects we had under arrest would know something or that Peter's team would pick up a lead from one of their many sources. But as the day began to draw to a close it looked as if all of these sources had dried up. The suspects, even if they knew, were too scared to talk. Haase's reputation for brutal violence was such that none of them would have turned against him for fear of reprisal. As for Peter's team, their best guess was that Haase and Bennett were together, that they were being hidden in a safe house 'somewhere in the North' and that they were waiting for the next stage of a plan which would get them out of the country to be put into operation. The most likely destination was Northern Cyprus, a country with which the UK does not have an extradition treaty. They would be beyond our reach for good.

As the day wore on, morale began to falter. Despite all our hard work, despite all the planning and second-guessing, we had come up empty-handed. We had got the drugs – Phil been right, it had turned out to be fifty-five kilos of brown heroin with a street value of over £2 million – and we had arrested half a dozen Turks from Volkan's organisation and several leading figures in Haase's gang. But without the two ringleaders themselves it was a hollow victory. With Volkan still in business it was quite feasible for Haase to rebuild his organisation and run it from overseas.

It was about half past eight in the evening. Most of the London team were still wading through the paperwork in the F/L office. A lot of the others, utterly exhausted and feeling dejected at the failure of the case, had gone home to get some rest in the hope that someone might have some information for us the next day.

Suddenly Peter, our intelligence officer, burst into the office waving a piece of paper.

'They've found Haase and Bennett!' he shouted.

All heads in the room looked up.

'They're in fucking Manchester aren't they?' said Big George. This had been his pet theory all day.

'Are they abroad yet?' asked Ralph, which was the one thing we all feared. He and Phil had returned from Liverpool with John earlier in the day.

'They're not in Liverpool or Manchester,' said Peter, his eyes gleaming. 'They're here in London. Probably no more than five miles away.'

Several people stood up.

'You're joking,' said someone. Other people expressed themselves more colourfully.

'We just got a tip,' said Peter. 'Apparently they laid up most of the day in Liverpool. Now they're being brought down south by someone. They're using the back routes because they're afraid of being stopped by the police on the main ones, but they must have passed inside the M25 boundary no more than ten minutes ago.'

'Whose driving them?' asked Phil.

'We don't know,' said Peter.

'Where are they headed?' asked Sid.

'Don't know that either,' said Peter unhelpfully.

'So how sure are you about this?' asked George.

'One hundred per cent certain. They're here all right. They could drive right past this office at any moment. And, what's more, we have a registration number. The car is X-Ray 20.'

X-Ray 20 was an nondescript Honda saloon. Just one of the many vehicles the Liverpool gang had used over the past few months.

'Have the police been informed?' asked Jackie.

'Yes, but you know what it's like. The chances of spotting them aren't good.'

'We must be able to narrow it down,' said Sid. 'Where could they be heading?'

We all tried to think of any hint from the surveillance over the past few months of a place they might be heading to.

'Well, I don't know about you, but I'm tired of paperwork,' said Ralph. He grabbed his motorcycle helmet and his rucksack.

'For crying out loud,' said Peter. 'It's a wild goose chase!'

'Great,' grinned Ralph. 'Who's coming with me?'

We all looked at each other. We were all tired of paperwork as well. We didn't think there was a hope in hell of finding Haase and Bennett out on the street, but Peter had coughed up one lead; he might come up with something else and in the meantime none of us could stand the thought of sitting around doing nothing.

'All right,' said Phil. 'There are worse ways of killing an hour. Let's go.'

10

The Getaway

We had no right to any luck that night. What had driven us out onto the streets was a combination of boredom, hope and desperation, but deep down we all knew it was pointless. It was like a giant game of blind man's buff. We studied our road maps, tried to work out what sort of route we would take if it was us trying to avoid police interest, and then headed off in that direction. Some people parked up at particular major junctions and watched the traffic, hoping for a sighting of the targets, but we knew it was useless. Our real hope was that Control would suddenly pass another piece of information, perhaps a sighting by the police, but the radios remained silent.

And then it happened.

We had been out for almost an hour and were scattered all over London when we received a radio message that none of us could believe.

'Control relay Lima 9: Contact, contact. Zulus 1 and 2 complete X-Ray two zero now proceeding south towards green three three.'

Lima 9 was Ralph's call-sign. He'd found them! Half of us didn't believe it could be true – it must be some sort of hallucination – but navigators all frantically flipped through map books anyway, trying to find where he was. The targets were south of the river on a minor road running parallel to the A23.

'Control relay: contact now heading green three four.'

That meant they were continuing to head south. All over London cars suddenly swung round in roads or just accelerated away, past traffic that must have wondered what the heck was going on. All of us headed towards Croydon. Some of us were south of the river, but most of the mobiles were north. Haase and Bennett were believed to be armed and we certainly knew that Haase would do his utmost never to go inside again. So there was no way Ralph could stop them on his own.

At the time the message came through Jackie and I were just off the Elephant and Castle roundabout in south London. We were one of the closest mobiles. I quickly swung us out on to the main road. It was about ten o'clock in the evening by now and there was only moderate traffic, although there seemed to be lots of black cabs out. I tried to make up time by going through a couple of red lights, but one of the cab drivers must have said something over his radio and, as we approached the next set of lights and were racing up the clear inside lane, a cab very deliberately swung over in front of us. I practically had to stand on the brakes to avoid running into the side of him. As the rest of the traffic closed around us we were effectively baulked. I knew these lights of old – they had a long change. We were going to lose at least a minute, and even then we'd be stuck in this knot of traffic as we tried to get away.

I gave three quick toots on the horn and wasn't surprised to receive a single-finger gesture in reply. There were steel railings along the edge of the pavement so there was no chance of using that route. We just didn't seem to be going anywhere. Not for the first time I cursed the fact that our vehicles weren't issued with flashing blue lights and sirens for just this sort of emergency.

'Sod this,' muttered Jackie.

She knew this junction as well. If Haase and Bennett were

armed then a couple of minutes delay might really mean the difference between life and death for Ralph. She climbed out of the car and dashed forward to the driver's side of the taxi. She banged hard on the driver's window with her fist, holding up her warrant card with the other hand. I had the window down and I heard her shout:

'Move this heap of shit right now or I will have your fucking licence!'

I saw the driver raise his hand as if to say 'OK' and the cab eased forward and over to the right. I accelerated forward into the gap, paused as Jackie dived back to the car and then, with me leaning on the horn to warn oncoming drivers, we roared through the junction and on to the open road beyond.

Meanwhile we could hear other developments over the radio. Phil was asking for the location of the car to be passed by Control to the police units, with a warning that the suspects were probably armed and that there were other Customs vehicles en route. But what was really worrying us was that we hadn't had any more communication with Ralph. We checked with Control, but they confirmed that they had heard nothing. Jackie and I were getting nearer and nearer to Croydon but we couldn't pick anything up on our car set. The radio sets which were carried on surveillance motorbikes were notoriously weak and that's probably what it was, but we were all praying that Ralph hadn't been hurt. Then, just as we were entering the outskirts of Croydon, we picked up his signal for the first time.

'Any mobile Lima 9 receive?'

'Lima 9, Lima 3.'

'Thank God for that.' He gave us his position and we asked if he still had the targets in sight.

'Lima 9, no, no. I had a loss about four minutes ago. Last seen they were still going south, but I couldn't stay with them. Some bastard RTA'd me.'

RTA stood for road traffic accident. Someone had knocked him off his bike.

'Are you OK, Ralph?' asked Jackie.

'Yeah, I'm fine. Nothing dented but my pride. You search the roads west of green four zero, I'll go east.'

'Lima 3 acknowledged.'

We frantically raced around the area, with more and more mobiles arriving all the time until the whole team were there. But none of us saw any sign of the target vehicle. All the time the loss continued we sensed that Haase and Bennett were driving further and further away. As we increased the radius of our search to compensate, so it became more difficult and our sense of desperation grew. Eventually Phil had no choice but to call it off. It's hard to describe the complete and utter frustration we were all feeling. Phil rang Control to see if the police had any news, but there was nothing. We had been given the most incredible slice of luck when Ralph caught sight of the car and now we had lost it. Although it was difficult to see how we could have done things differently, it felt as if it was our fault for blowing the chance. Phil summoned us all to a meeting in a car park near the East Croydon railway station. We all wanted to hear Ralph's story.

He was the last to arrive. Whatever had happened, the bike didn't look too badly damaged, although when we got out and examined it closely we could see where the fairing was scratched and damaged. Despite the fact that it was a cold night, when Ralph took his helmet off and loosened his leather biker-jacket the sweat was streaming off him.

'Give us a fag someone,' he gasped. Then, once he had got one lit to his satisfaction and taken a deep drag on it, he sagged back against the seat of his bike and said, 'I never want to go through another evening like this. What a fucking waste of time.'

'How the hell did you spot them?' asked Phil.

'Well, like the rest of you, I expect, I was trying to work out roughly where they would be and all the time I was drifting south. I mean, they've come inside the M25 so chances are they're heading somewhere in London, not down to the coast, or why come into an area that's so heavily policed, right? So I'm riding along looking for inspiration and waiting for Phil to call it off, when I suddenly catch sight of the number-plate of the car in front of me and it's fucking X-Ray 20! I nearly fell off the bike. I recognised the car straight away. I was following it up in Liverpool three days ago.'

He took another drag on the cigarette.

'So the next thing I do is look in the rear window and there is Haase. I mean, you know his haircut and the shape of his head; there's no mistaking him once you've seen him, is there? Bennett is clearly next to him in the back and there's a driver up front, although I have no idea who that was. So while I'm promising God that I will never ever do a bad thing again, I ease back and try to get a message out. And what do you know? I couldn't raise any of you, couldn't even raise Control, and I wasn't even that far south of the river. So I was going nuts. I couldn't stop to call because then I would have lost them. All I could do was keep going, stay as far back as possible and keep transmitting, praying that someone would pick it up.'

'Must have been some surveillance,' said Sid approvingly.

'You're telling me. I was so far back I was practically on the moon. Occasionally I was riding lights-off if I thought I could get away with it for a while. The only good thing was, although I was a long way back, if they turned a corner I had the acceleration to catch up and regain the eyeball. So there we were, rolling along, me going completely nuts trying to raise you lot or hoping to see a police car, and suddenly I thought I was going to see a copper murdered. We were heading towards green five two, alongside the park – there's almost no traffic about – and this policeman suddenly just steps off the pavement into the road, with his hand raised right in front of X-Ray 20.'

'Bloody hell,' murmured Phil.

'Too right,' agreed Ralph. 'My first thought is, they're going to think they've been rumbled and they'll run him down. But they eased up and pulled into the side of the road where he's pointing. Then this copper goes round to the driver's side of the car and leans down to talk to whoever is in the front. I'm about a hundred metres back, just waiting for the sound of the gunshot. You know Haase isn't going down unless we get the drop on him and I felt sure this was going to kick it off. There was nothing I could do. I could have raced up there to warn him but, not only would that have blown the tail, but also it would have been more likely to provoke a shooting than to stop one. Anyway, I don't know what they were stopped for but, after a little chat, he stands up and waves them along. He'll never know it, but this was probably the luckiest night of his life. I don't know what happened to that "All Points Bulletin" the police are supposed to have put out, because it never reached this guy. Shortly after that I raised Control, so I knew you lot and about a dozen police cars would be on the way. I was mightily relieved.'

'So how did you lose them?' asked Phil.

'Aaach, it's my own stupid fault. I was feeling really chuffed at finding them and following them all that way, but I knew the cavalry was coming so I just got over-confident. I was riding with lights off, well back, watching their tail-lights and listening for sirens. Some guy came out of a side-road and I clipped the front of him. Fortunately I wasn't doing any speed at all so he just scattered me across the tarmac. I mean, you know my usual opinion of collisions between motorcycles and cars – I don't care what happened, it's the car driver's fault, right? But in this case I have to say, I don't think there was a lot he could have done about it. Anyway it was only a love tap. He was rushing out of his car straight away and giving it the "Oh my God are you all right" routine, but of course all I'm worried about is where X-Ray 20 has disappeared to. I gave it full welly and everything, but they'd gone. I didn't even stop to give my number so I've probably been reported to half of London's Old Bill by now. That's it. End of story.'

He ground the butt of the cigarette beneath the heel of his motorcycle boot.

'So what now?' he asked. 'Do we sit here and wait for another lucky break or what?'

'I've been on the phone to John,' said Phil. 'It's a stand-down tonight. There's nothing we can do here and we're all pretty tired. It's an early start tomorrow and we just pray that something comes up overnight. At least we know the bastards are still in the country.'

We all paired up and sorted out cars for the ride home. I decided to take a spare car back to the office, find a Z-bed and sleep there; it was too late to go home. I also wanted to stay close to the office. For some reason I felt sure that this wasn't over yet.

I was woken at four-thirty the following morning by the phone going off in the office. I rolled over, staggered off the Z-bed, dragged the nearest phone off a desk and mumbled hello.

'It's John — any update?'

'No. The police are still looking and we've got some of the Oscars doing a tobacco job down in Croydon tonight. Phil's asked them to keep their eyes open for anything, but so far no news.'

'You're in early, Harry?'

'No I'm here late. I haven't been home yet.'

'OK, well, I'll be in the office about six-thirty with an update.'

'I'll be here.'

I put the phone back on the desk and then blinked repeat-edly, trying to get the sleep out of my eyes. My stomach was grumbling again. I grabbed three paracetamol from a packet on the desk and swilled them down with some flat Coca-Cola left over from the night before. There was no way I was going back to sleep until the pills took the edge off the pain, and by then it would be time to get up anyway. I decided to potter off to Control to raid their coffee machine; once that had really woken me up I knew a nearby café which would be open and where I could get an early breakfast. As I staggered around trying to find my shoes I stubbed my toe on the bed. It looked like it was going to be a really lousy day.

By the time I'd had breakfast and brought the morning papers back to the office, the first of the team were beginning to arrive. It seemed that we all had the feeling that this would be the final act of the operation and it was worth making the effort to be in early on that one day. But from the moment people arrived there was almost nothing to do. Some people made an effort with the huge backlog of paperwork left over from the knock, but no one's heart was really in it. Mostly people dozed and kept an eye on the phone. None of us could believe that it had come to this. We had put in months of work; we'd had good luck and bad luck and it just wasn't fair that the main villains were about to get away with it. This was just about our last chance – someone in the gang, somewhere, would have to make a mistake.

But time ticked by and still the phone remained silent. A couple of members of other teams who had recently worked on the case drifted in and sat around with us, waiting for news. Even Don rang me up from the Kilos to ask if there was any news. Now that the job had been knocked there was no need for operational security. Word had got round the entire Division that the fate of two major drugs targets was in the balance.

Slowly, very slowly, time ran out.

'Well look at it this way,' said Sid with a yawn, 'if they get out of the country then perhaps it's for the best. If we had nicked 'em, chances are they'd be out again in five years. This way they'll be out of the country for good. There's no way they'll come back because they know they'll be arrested.'

'Won't stop them running the gang by remote control from Cyprus or wherever though, will it?' said Phil.

Finally it got to eight o'clock. The phone rang. John was now in the office and he picked it up. We all watched him expectantly. He said 'yes' and 'no' a few times and scribbled a few notes. Then he put the phone down. He didn't look too pleased and it hadn't been a very long call.

'It's not good, I'm afraid,' he said. 'No one's got a lead as to where they are. All anyone knows is that they laid up overnight and are expecting to be taken out of the country later this morning, probably by light aircraft. Peter is speaking to West Drayton about tracking aircraft movements, but you know what it's like, once they're in the air we're effectively powerless. The only other help Peter could give is that Haase and Bennett probably ended their journey approximately thirty minutes after the loss last night, and he thinks, but I stress *thinks*, that it could be a B&B or a hotel rather than a private house. He's hoping that the police might get more details later but he's promising nothing and anyway, we're expecting Haase and Bennett to be on the move within the hour.'

Having heard the whole thing, most people gave mild groans of disappointment. This really did seem like the last straw.

'We aren't dead yet,' said John, trying to keep everyone's spirits up. 'I'm going to ring Liverpool to see if Paddy's team have got anything at all from the paperwork there. Something's got to give; there's got to be some clue or some suspect's got to talk. The moment I hear an update I'll let you know.'

With that he strode out of the office. Those people who

weren't members of F/L drifted away over the next few minutes. They knew we were as good as dead in the water. Those of us on the team went back to sitting and waiting. There was no point in rushing out on the ground, at least not yet. Thirty minutes after the loss could place them almost anywhere.

All I could keep thinking about was Frank Davies, the drugs baron who had slipped through the Kilos' fingers when he was spirited out of the country by helicopter, just after the knock. If he hadn't later been killed in Spain he would have gone on to run his drugs empire from abroad, just as Haase and Bennett were going to do now. All the misery and suffering caused by their business would go on and what was the point of all that effort we put in? Here I was, on my very next case, and it looked like the bad guys were going to get away with it again. It was ridiculous. There had to be something I could do to stop this. I kept thinking that if this were a film the hero would suddenly do something to turn the tables. He wouldn't just sit waiting.

The only advantage I could think of was the hint which Peter had given us that they might be staying in a hotel. It was a million-to-one shot and Ralph had surely claimed the entire team's ration of luck when he spotted X-Ray 20 the previous night. But even though what I was planning to do was quixotic, it was better than doing nothing.

I slipped out of the room and went to Control. They kept a large number of reference books, amongst which was a complete collection of UK telephone directories and Yellow Pages. Normally the staff in Control would tear your arm off rather than give you one of their phone books. Quite rightly, they tended to think that they would never see them again once they were out of their sight, and there was no telling when they might next need one. But I'd been spending quite a lot of time with these guys over the past few weeks and so when I explained that it was for a last-gasp attempt to try and nab Haase and Bennett, the officer behind the desk reached out and grabbed the volume I was asking for and handed it over, along with dire threats about what would happen to certain parts of my body if I didn't bring it back.

I took the book back to the office and sat at my desk. There were about six pages of hotels in the Croydon area. I knew my chances weren't good. In the time we had before Haase and Bennett would be on the move I could probably only get through one or two pages. Secondly, it was notoriously difficult to get hotels to talk about their guests: most receptionists were trained not to divulge details of guests to enquirers. Of course I could tell them that I was a Customs officer, but how could they be sure of that? Finally, I didn't know what names Haase and Bennett would be using, so I would be falling back on my ability to describe them. Overall, my chances were probably little more than zero, but I couldn't think of anything else to do.

'I'm going to start ringing some of these hotels,' I said. 'It can't hurt now. They'll be out of the country in a couple of hours. Anyone got any objections?'

'Waste of fucking time,' muttered Mac. Most of the others just shrugged or kept silent. They knew it was a waste of time too. Only Sid came over and said:

'Give us a page, Harry. I'll have a go.'

I tore out a page from Control's precious phone book and handed it over. Then I said a silent prayer, picked up a pen, started at 'A' and rang the first hotel.

Twenty minutes later I was on to the Ds and getting nowhere.

John walked in and looked pointedly at his watch.

'All right, boys, get out on the ground. Pick any part of Croydon you like, we might as well cover the ground as sit here. If there's a last-minute call from anyone it will be better if we're on the move.'

People stood up, gathered their kit and began to file out.

'If it's all the same, I'll keep calling these hotels.' I said. 'You never know . . .'

'Suit yourself, Harry. We need an act of God now, I don't care how it arrives.' John shrugged. He looked around the room. 'Billy, stay with Harry. Bring him out if we get a shout.'

'Sure thing.'

Billy brought his coffee over, put his feet up on the other side of the desk and closed his eyes. Soon, after yet another refusal to divulge information, I was ready to give up.

'Just one more call, Billy,' I said.

He nodded, but didn't open his eyes.

The next hotel I rang was just a name from the list: it didn't have a fancy advertising box like some of the others. I spoke to a man who sounded East European; his English was barely comprehensible.

'Hi, my name is Ferguson, I'm an Officer of Customs and Excise. I'm ringing from Custom House in London. We're looking for two men who may have checked into your hotel last night. It would have been at about eleven o'clock. One medium height, short black hair; the other heavy set. Do you have any guests answering that description?'

In what in another situation would have been a comedy foreigner's accent, the man replied, 'Oh yes, I am having these men here very much at the evening.'

I was stunned. He couldn't possibly have understood what I was asking. So I repeated the question.

'Oh yes, sir. Very much so,' came the reply.

'These men are staying at your hotel?'

Billy opened his eyes and leaned forwards, suddenly wide awake. He picked up the extension earpiece that was fitted to all ID telephones, so that he could listen in on the conversation.

'Oh no, sir, no. That is not right.'

Now I was really confused.

'These men are not at your hotel?'

'I was having them last evening. These are your men, I think, but I am having no room so I am sending them across the road to the other hotel.'

This couldn't be true. It had to be a wind-up.

'At about eleven o'clock?'

'Yes, eleven o'clock.'

'What's the name of this other hotel?'

He gave it to me and I put the phone down after thanking him profusely. I found the other hotel on the list.

'Come on, Harry, get going,' shouted John, sticking his head round the door.

'Just one more, guv'. I've got someone who says he sent two men, answering the right description, to this other hotel. It's probably bollocks but it's worth a call.'

'All right,' said John, 'but get your skates on. You're no use to us sitting here.'

'It is bollocks,' grinned Billy.

I punched in the number then repeated my little speech.

'I'm sorry, we're not allowed to give out information about guests,' said the receptionist. I knew that some of the team were only minutes away.

'Listen love, I can have an officer round to the hotel in five minutes to deliver this request in person, but I have to tell you that these men are extremely dangerous and probably armed. We really need to know now, before you have an incident on your hands.'

There was a pause as she thought about this.

'Hold on one second, I'll get the duty manager.'

I held the phone to my shoulder and looked round the room. John had appeared at the door again and was listening with interest. The duty manager's voice came on the line and I repeated the story.

'All right,' he said, after a long pause. 'We do have two men answering that description staying in the hotel, and they did arrive at about eleven o'clock last night. We're just preparing their bill now. I'm afraid I can't give you their names, but what do you propose we should we do? Should we call the police?'

I tried to sound calm.

'Don't do anything. I'll have officers there within the next few minutes. If they do try to leave, do anything you reasonably can to delay them. Tell them the computer's playing up or something. We have men in the area and even a minute could be vital, but don't do anything to put your staff in danger.'

I put the phone down. John had heard everything and was already on other phones, barking out orders to Control.

'Harry, get down there and get into that hotel,' said John holding the receiver under his chin as he waited to be connected to another number. 'Make sure you secure all the evidence, CCTV footage, credit card receipts and, after the knock, turn the room over in case they've left anything behind. We've got a call in for armed police support on the hurry-up, but I don't know if they'll make it. Tell Chris that, armed police or not, the targets mustn't leave that car park. I don't want this turning into some sort of *Italian Job* car chase around Croydon.'

'Sure thing guv',' I shouted, but Billy and I were already halfway down the corridor. There was no way we wanted to miss this. We raced down the stairs to the underground car park. Billy had made sure that, since we were last out, he had saved the fastest car on the team: a black BMW. Unless you were in the right area, such as central London, it stuck out like a sore thumb, but it could really shift and in the hands of a former paramedic like Billy there was nothing faster on the road for getting through heavy London traffic.

'Hope you've put your crash helmet on, Harry.' Billy grinned as he slammed the car into reverse. My head snapped forwards as he took it backwards up the ramp and spun it around at the top, horn blaring as he roared out of the gate and swerved past an incoming lorry.

Billy and Jess were always competing with each other to be the top driver on the Division, but they rarely got the chance to put themselves to the real test. The next twenty minutes were, for me, a blur of red traffic lights, snap ninety-degree turns and thumping lifts on to the pavement to get around slow traffic. If an accident didn't kill me, whiplash probably would. Faced with heavy traffic, Billy's answer was to simply go down the middle of the road, horn blaring, headlamps on full-beam. And it worked. People seemed to understand that something very unusual was happening and they got out of the way. Even so, at one stage we lost a wing mirror as we drove too close to something – I never saw what it was. Billy stayed calm all the way through, no hint of shouting, cursing or red mist. He always seemed to be in control and, although some of the manoeuvres he pulled were damn close to walls, other vehicles and sometimes pedestrians, I never felt that we were going to hit anything. It was the best piece of driving I ever saw during my time on the Division.

As we approached central Croydon we began to pick up the radio transmissions of the other vehicles that had arrived ahead of us. We knew Haase and Bennett were probably armed but not once did I hear anyone express doubt about going in. John had requested armed police backup, but they were difficult to get hold of at the best of times so the chances of them being available at ten minutes' notice seemed practically impossible.

Phil was trying the get them organised. We weren't armed so we had to hit them hard and fast:

'Lima 13, Fox 3 take up positions either side of the junction at amber five six. Fox 6 you and I will approach from behind, hold your position at green five five. On the command Lima 13 and Fox 3 will box X-Ray 20 from the front, Lima 5 and Fox 6 will box from behind. Don't be afraid of hitting

X-Ray 20 and wedging him in between us, the impact might buy us a few seconds and we have to make sure he goes nowhere. All mobiles acknowledge.'

Sid was in the hotel reception, keeping tabs on when Haase and Bennett were going to leave.

'From Lima 4, Zulu 1 has paid the bill. Expecting targets mobile in the next five minutes.'

'Control: relay from Fox 1: armed response unit ETA your location five minutes. Request briefing location.'

Billy glanced over at me.

'Jesus,' he muttered.

This was going to be really tight. The chances were that the armed police would arrive just after the knock, but it was out of our hands now. Phil had the eyeball on the main doors of the hotel. Billy and I waited in the car park of a hospital just down the road. Our job at the knock was to swing out of the exit of the car park, which was directly opposite the point in the road where the other mobiles would stop X-Ray 20. We would either provide extra bodies for the arrests or, if it looked like X-Ray 20 was manoeuvring to escape, Billy would ram them from the side and put them out of the game. Defence lawyers would have a field day claiming excessive force and other abuses, but we were unarmed and with firearms present we couldn't afford to take any chances. As usual on the Division, speed, shock and weight of numbers were going to have to make the difference.

Then everything seemed to happen almost at once.

'From Fox 6, I have the armed police at my position.'

'Fox 5: that's X-Ray 20 to the front of the hotel.'

'Lima 5, Fox 6: never mind the briefing, tell them to hit X-Ray 20 NOW!'

'Fox 5: Zulu 1 and Zulu 2 complete X-Ray 20 . . . and that's X-Ray 20 mobile.'

'Lima 5: KNOCK, KNOCK, KNOCK!'

The police had excelled themselves. Luckily for us, they were actually waiting on stand-by for another job just a few minutes away. They had driven like maniacs to get to us in time and their unmarked Transit van had arrived at Big George's position just as Chris saw Haase leaving the hotel. All George had time to do was to leap out of his car, tell the police which vehicle it was and that 'you need to fucking hit it now!' There was no time for complicated briefings, diagrams on whiteboards or any of the rules of engagement the police normally insist on. They were tremendous. The senior officer told his driver to get moving and the Transit rolled forward, with George close behind in his car. Apparently the plan was for the van to pull across the exit and block it whilst the armed police poured out of the back and into the car park. But in fact, the timing was so close that X-Ray 20 actually pulled out of the car park exit and found itself just behind the white Transit.

The rear doors burst open and the armed police piled out. They put in all the windows of X-Ray 20, shouting at the tops of their voices and shoving gun barrels into the faces of the occupants. All around them Customs vehicles roared forward to surround the area and cut off other traffic. As we all climbed out of our cars the doors of X-Ray 20 were wrenched open. Haase and Bennett were sprawled on the roadway, lying spread-eagled amongst the smashed safety glass and being searched for weapons. I looked around, trying to work out what the next problem would be. There were civilian cars scattered across the road, facing in various directions where they had screeched to a halt. The horror-stricken faces of drivers were visible through the windows. All around us pedestrians were either running for cover or simply standing and staring, wondering what the hell was going on. It was all over as quickly as that.

Once we had got the traffic of Croydon flowing again, arrangements were made for Haase and Bennett to be transported back to Liverpool to be interviewed. Now that they were in custody, I was one of the officers sent north with them to reinforce the team up there. Liverpool was the site of the importation, so that was where all investigation and prosecution would take place. Although we had the drugs, the criminals and months of surveillance evidence on our side, we knew that the really hard work was just beginning. From now on they would have lawyers on their side who would begin the process of trying to find out how much we knew and then gradually chip away at it. Any little error in paperwork or procedure – which could get vital evidence excluded – would come back to haunt us. This was the part of the process where we didn't fully understand the rules. This was where all sorts of tricks could be pulled. It was the part of the process we hated.

Everyone on the team was assigned one of the major targets for interview. Jackie and I were assigned to interrogate the General. He had been picked up at his hotel and was now sitting disconsolately in his cell in Liverpool, in a state of shock. He had never even known he was under surveillance but, as he saw more and more of the gang arriving around him, he must have realised that his arrest was part of a massive operation.

Finally, after long delays for briefing by defence solicitors and various administrative difficulties, the time for the interview arrived. I was determined to do this right. I knew that Haase and Bennett were being spoken to just down the hall and, as you would expect from professional criminals, they were saying nothing. But this was different. This was Volkan's money man. We might not have Volkan – yet – but this man held the clues to how the organisation worked. This wasn't going to be a five-minute, no-comment interview if I could help it. He wasn't a career criminal like the others and I thought he could be induced to talk if I built up slowly enough.

From the moment I walked into the room he looked

flustered. This wasn't the cool businessman I'd seen passing through the airport or eating in smart restaurants. This was his worst nightmare come true. He knew this was heroin and would be aware of what sort of sentence he could be looking at. His lawyer was sitting next to him and there was a clerk to take notes. My biggest problem was that, for all his association with other members of the gang, we didn't have much on him – just the money in the grocery packets which, strictly speaking, wasn't illegal.

I started the interview by asking him a lot of basic details: where he lived, what his career had been, things his lawyer couldn't object to him saying. I wanted him to get used to the idea of talking to me so that by the time we got to the sensitive subjects he would know it looked suspicious if he clammed up. Once we had covered these basics and he had started to relax a little, I decided to edge towards the things we were really interested in. Out of the corner of my eye I noticed his lawyer watching me closely. I gave him a sheet of paper listing details of his travel over the past six months: Italy, Holland, Germany, Spain, Poland, Britain, various places in Europe. These details were freely available, but I wanted to give him the impression that we knew everything.

'You travel around Europe a lot. Why?'

'I am retired from the army. I do some business and I am also a tourist.'

'You've been to Italy six times this year. What have you been going to see?'

'I like to see lots of things.'

'OK. I know Italy pretty well.' I saw his pupils dilate as he registered this point. He thought I was about to try and catch him out. 'Which museums have you been to?'

'I don't go to museums.'

'Art galleries then?'

'I don't go to art galleries.'

'Well where do you go?'

'I just go to see the sights.'

'What sights?'

He thought for a while.

'Just places.'

The truth was that each of his visits had only been for a day or so. As with his visits to the UK, I was willing to bet that he barely had time to see outside of his hotel room or the nearest expensive department store. He wouldn't meet my gaze. He knew that his lies were terribly weak.

'Do you know this man?'

I put a surveillance picture of Zulu 28 on the table. He glanced at it.

'I'm not sure.'

'Have a good look at it.'

'No, I don't know him.'

'You're sure?'

'Sure.'

'So how do you explain this?'

I put another surveillance photograph on the table showing them together, then another and another.

I sat there, unable to believe my luck for most of the interview. Suspects never talk in interview these days; they know their rights inside and out. It used to be that we would have more success with people arrested from the Continent, where there is a convention that you answer the questions put to you by the police, but now in the UK such suspects are generally advised by British lawyers who tell them to shut up, and that's just what they do. The General's lawyer kept advising him that he didn't have to say anything if he didn't want to, but the more the interview went on the more dispirited the General became; in a quiet voice he answered almost every question I put to him. At one stage I glanced at the lawyer, who had just made a very determined effort to get the General to shut up and had been ignored. He had the good grace to roll his eyes with a slight smile and make a gesture as if to say, 'What can I do?' I smiled back. We both knew this situation was unusual. It was like an old-style interview before all the modern rules were brought in.

I still remember the moment when the General finally crumbled. I showed the surveillance photographs of him checking in for his flight. They clearly showed the luggage he was using. I then showed him close-up pictures of the luggage, taken behind the check-in. His baggage tags were clearly visible and he admitted they were his. Then I showed him the photographs of the opened suitcase, with the boxes and jars of money laid out inside. I still remember the look of shock on his face. For the first time he seemed to realise that he had been under surveillance for months, not just on his most recent visit, and that we knew everything about him.

It took a long time and several interview tapes, but I wanted to go slowly so that I could set him up for questioning about the real goldmine we had found in his luggage. We had his diary, which was packed with entries about his journeys around Europe and the money he had collected. I took him through it page by page, every entry, every bit of cash. There was one final, coded entry which confused me and which he seemed determined to protect. On some pages there were number of stars; these occurred only on days when he was travelling abroad for Volkan. I kept pressing him on it and he became more and more determined not to answer. The more he kept evading the questions, the more I felt that I was on to something important. I kept stressing that he had admitted to so much already that his refusal to answer entries about this code just made everything look more damning.

Finally he said, 'Please, officer, if I tell you what this is and I show it is nothing, will you promise me as a gentleman that it will not leave this room?'

There was a tape machine on the desk between us, not twelve inches away. He had seen me load it with two cassette tapes at the start of every session.

'Of course,' I said.

'These stars, they are . . . they are about women.'

He had been giving the local prostitutes a star rating. I looked round and caught Jackie's eye. She shook her head incredulously and looked up at the ceiling.

It had been a long day. I stepped out of the interview room at the end of the last session, yawned and stretched. When this was over I was going to sleep for a week. I looked along the corridor and saw Haase sitting there, waiting to be taken back to a cell. He was no more than ten feet away. It occurred to me that during months of surveillance this was the closest I had been to him. I hadn't worked in Liverpool much during the case and when I had, Haase had been a distant figure in the street, a silhouette in a car or a blip on a tracker screen. It seemed strange that you could identify the target of a major operation and barely see him, but that's the nature of modern surveillance.

Up close he appeared to be exactly what his reputation said he was: a very hard man. He sat bolt upright with his hands on his knees, staring straight ahead, ignoring everyone. He had certainly been difficult to catch. For a moment I wondered what would happen if you could take all that determination and cunning and use it for something good instead of for evil. Despite his reputation for extreme and sudden violence, he had a girlfriend and a daughter to whom he was supposed to be devoted.

When I spoke to the desk sergeant some time later, he remarked, 'I'll say this about him, he's an evil bastard who, if you looked at him slightly wrong in a pub, wouldn't think twice about knifing you. But, if we had some old dear locally who was done over during a burglary, we could go to him and if he knew anything he'd tell us. Weird isn't it?'

I wondered how all those pieces fit together. But then Haase was led away and that was the last I ever saw of him.

11

The Runaround

Felixstowe docks on a dull, grey morning seemed like the depressing fag-end of the British Isles. It wasn't a cold September day, but it was certainly windy and wet. A persistent drizzle got into everything. You only had to be out of your car for a few minutes and you were soaked.

It had taken much longer than expected to get the job to this point. In fact, another six weeks had passed as Volkan reassessed the security of his organisation in the light of the collapse of the 'Turkish connection' in Liverpool that July. At first Sammy and the other Turkish contacts had lain low. We had continued to keep them under routine surveillance but there wasn't really much to see and, in a way, we were glad of that; coming off the back of the Liverpool job we needed time to rest and recuperate. People had weeks' worth of leave backed up and Volkan's pause in operations gave us time to get rid of some of this. Hours became more regular for a while and people were even able to take their summer holidays. Some of the harder-working members of the team, such as Paddy, took leave dating back to Christmas, which gives you an idea of just how dedicated to the operation some people had been.

Nicky and I had even been able to try to put things back together. The turning point had been an accident involving one of the children. They had been playing in the garden one summer's evening, leaping and climbing around in the garden. It was so warm that neither of them were even wearing T-shirts. Nicky was home from work and making something in the kitchen when she heard a shrill scream. She rushed outside to see our daughter, Sally, lying on the patio in a pool of blood. For a moment Nicky couldn't work out what had happened. Sally had an enormous gash in her side and looked as if she had been slashed open with a knife. Nicky grabbed a towel and frantically wrapped it around Sally to staunch the flow of blood before calling for an ambulance. I received a panicked call from her in the office, saying that one of the children was badly hurt. I saw John and told him what had happened. He told me to sign off and get down there as soon as possible – something which I'm sure he would have done before but which wouldn't have been as easy only a few weeks ago.

By the time I arrived at the accident and emergency department an hour later it had become clear what had happened. Sally had been climbing around on the garden furniture with her brother and at one point had jumped off of a wooden chair, trying to grab a flower which was growing out of a crack in a nearby brick wall. She had fallen against the wall and, as she did so, caught her side on a rusty protruding nail. As she fell to the ground the nail had ripped her side open by a length of several inches. She needed about twenty stitches. It was a freak accident and looked absolutely dreadful, but after stitches had been put in she was out of any danger although obviously still shocked. We were able to bring her home the following day. When I had arrived at the hospital Nicky was still very shaken. The delay for an ambulance had been so long that she had hailed a passing taxi to get to the hospital, and the ride with our blood-soaked daughter in her lap had left her very distressed. Her first words to me, once she had told me that Sally was going to be all right, were to ask for a hug. I said something like, 'Are two people who are going to get divorced allowed to hug then?' and she just threw herself into my arms and burst into tears. Then we just talked and talked for the next few hours as we sat by Sally's bed. Of course, one incident didn't make everything right straight away, but it was a start, and the easier pace of life – while Volkan made up his mind what to do – really helped us.

Finally, after about a month of lying low, Volkan's syndicate in London went back to work. They may have lost Liverpool, but they still had the Brixton connection. The first we heard that they were getting ready for a delivery was from Peter who told us that Volkan was sending one of his main lieutenants from Europe to personally oversee the operation. He was coming from Holland and so, although labelled as Zulu 66, he promptly became known to the team as 'the Dutchman' because almost all the other targets were Turks. Sure enough, we were able to follow Sammy one afternoon as he went out and met the Dutchman at a café near Olympia. Very obligingly, they sat at a table on the pavement and we were able to get some nice clear photographs of the meeting. It was unusual for Volkan's organisation that this man was not a Turk. Instead he was a heavily built, blond-haired man in his forties, probably someone Volkan had learned to trust through his Dutch drugs connections. He must have hoped that sending someone from outside the Turkish community would throw us off the scent; however, the fact was that the Dutchman was followed from the very first moment he set foot in the country.

The next piece of good news was that Peter managed to get a lead on how the heroin would be coming into the country. The gossip in the office was that they had spoken to their equivalent agency in Holland, who had put a telephone tap on the Dutchman once we had identified him, but they may have got the information by analysing what had happened on the Liverpool importation. Either way, he was able to provide us with a date and the registration number of the lorry which would be carrying the drugs. We didn't know where the drugs would be concealed on the lorry or where they were going to be dropped off, but identifying the vehicle was a considerable step forward. All we had to do was stay with the lorry and wait.

The bad news was that Volkan had called for 'maximum security' on this drugs run following the failure of the Liverpool operation. He couldn't afford to lose another part of his empire. In the drugs world, once you get a reputation for sloppiness or weakness you are finished. Either people won't deal with you because they can't trust you, or one of your lieutenants is likely to replace you because you are costing everyone money. We were sure this was going to mean more counter-surveillance. We had managed to dent Volkan's security unit by making arrests such as that of Zulu 26 during the Liverpool operation, but he could quite easily have recruited more over the past month. This factor, combined with the fact that we were going to have to follow the lorry to every single place it went until the drugs were dropped off, made it sound as if this was going to be a long and difficult operation. One of the few things that kept us going was that this case could very well be the final nail in Volkan's coffin; at the very least would cripple all his UK operations.

So that was why we were plotted up outside Felixstowe docks at six o'clock on a dull September morning. The target lorry, designated as X-Ray 72, had arrived at the docks the previous evening but inward controls had told us that it wasn't due to clear until the following morning. We couldn't afford to rely on that information, so uniformed staff at the docks kept an eye on the lorry in case the driver made a move overnight. We slept at a nearby motel but had to be ready to get out on the ground at a moment's notice if the docks called us: a rota was organised so that one mobile was always out on the ground near the dock gates. In these sorts of conditions you don't really sleep, you just doze on-and-off in your motel room, waiting for the phone to ring. The call hadn't come, but we were plotted up by five-thirty and waiting for him.

We had managed to have the driver's paperwork looked at in the docks. I was sharing a car with Sid again that morning and we listened over the radio as Mac, who was the case officer, received details of the lorry's load from the Customs office at the port.

'Bad news everyone,' he announced. 'It's a groupage load. You'd better settle down for a long journey.'

'Groupage' meant that the load consisted of lots of different commodities rather all one type of thing, such as fruit or steel. Each delivery would be placed on one or more pallets and then shrinkwrapped in plastic to stop it becoming dislodged during the journey. At each stop a fork-lift truck would be used to take off the delivery for that site and to load other goods on to the lorry which were going back to the Continent.

'That seals it then,' said Sid. 'They're going to give us the runaround. That's obviously Volkan's idea of maximum security.'

I gave Sid a puzzled look. Despite three years in the job I hadn't heard the term before.

'Basically, this lorry is going to go to dozens of sites all over the country,' he explained. 'Somewhere during that journey he is going to drop off the drugs. Now we don't know where the drugs are – they could be concealed in the bed of the lorry, they could be hidden in part of the consignment, they could even be in a bin bag in the back of the cab. So if we want to get whoever is receiving the drugs, we've got to keep a close eye on the lorry every step of the way until the drugs are handed over. We're going to have to get someone in close on every flipping stop. It's going to be murder! Even at night we're going to have to watch him: all it would take would be for a fast car to pull up, a bag be handed over, then it would drive away and that would be that. And of course Volkan's security people know the route so they can simply drop in and look for us at any time they like, anywhere on the lorry's journey – it could be day one, it could be day three. If we manage to knock this, it will be a bloody miracle. If we miss the handover, the first we'll know about it will be when the lorry returns to Felixstowe again and departs on the next ferry. No wonder Volkan spent so much time planning it.'

'Well, we know where he's going, can't we just have people there ahead of him at each stop and be ready to watch when he turns up?'

'The trouble is,' said Sid gloomily, 'it sounds good in theory, but it doesn't work. Some of these yards are huge. You can't be sure exactly where he's going to park up; you can't be sure which personnel are going to handle the unloading. The pick-up of the drugs could be almost anyone who goes anywhere near the lorry. I'm sure Mac will try to leap-frog some of us ahead when he can, but going early and picking out an OP is so much wasted effort unless you know exactly where he will be parked and what the sightlines are.'

'Stand by, stand by. X-Ray 72 mobile.'

'Lima 3: received.'

'Well,' sighed Sid, 'here we go. It's a pity we aren't paid by the mile.'

Sid and I had eyeball on the entrance to the docks. We were parked in a side-road some distance away but I was able to watch the entrance through binoculars. Right on cue, the target vehicle pulled out of the dock gates and I got my first good look at it. It was a large blue and white tractor unit with a twenty-foot canvas sided trailer behind it. There were no company marking on the side and according to his papers the driver was an independent haulier. The lorry lumbered off along the A14. Sid and I called this on the radio, but stayed where we were. The start of a surveillance is one of the easiest points for a team to be spotted. The dual carriageway was the main route from the docks and if any of us had simply followed behind the lorry, one of the Turks sitting in a car on a bridge or in a lay-by would easily have been able to spot us. Instead, Jess was waiting at the next roundabout to monitor the vehicle's progress and the rest of the team were even further ahead at the next few junctions. They would fall into place once the lorry got to them. Sid and I sat and watched to see if any suspicious vehicles left the dock area shortly after its departure. Nothing did and once we heard that the lorry was well on its way we set off after it.

That pattern continued for the next four days. You would think that it is fairly straightforward work keeping a slow-travelling lorry under surveillance for several days, but in fact it was more tiring than a few hours' work in central London. Whilst the HGV proceeded at a more-or-less steady sixty miles an hour we would be constantly circling him, confirming that he was still on the move, from bridges, junctions, small roads that overlooked major highways, anywhere which meant that we weren't just sitting behind him because we knew that was where a counter-surveillance team would be looking for us. It was tiring work because, although his speed was constant, we would go from waiting for a sight of him at one moment to suddenly driving madly on a very long route to get to our next position. This, coupled with the very long days, gradually wore us down. We were desperate for the handover but it never happened. And every night, just as Sid had predicted, we had to man an OP position, usually from a car, to make sure that the handover didn't take place. No one got much sleep.

The fatigue may even have made us hallucinate. There was certainly an incident which, even after all these years, I still can't explain. One night, at about two o'clock, Phil and I were driving on a stretch of dual carriageway in Yorkshire. We were on our way to take over OP duty watching the lorry, which was in the goods vehicle parking area of a service station. Ahead of us, in the glow of the headlights, we both saw two young girls running along the grass verge at the side of the road. One seemed to be about ten years old, with long dark hair and wearing a nightdress; she was leading another little girl by the hand, who was wearing pyjamas and looked no older than five. Both their heads turned as we shot past and we got a good look at them. The smaller of the two girls looked like she was having trouble keeping up with the older one, who was having to pull her along. They didn't look like they were afraid or being chased, they were just determined to get somewhere.

'Did you see that?' I gasped.

'Yes, I bloody did. What are they doing out at this time of night?' said Phil. He had slowed down, but he kept driving.

'Stop the bloody car,' I demanded

'Christ Harry, we're not social services.'

'We can't leave them out here. How would you sleep at night?'

Still cursing, Phil put the car into reverse and we roared back up the road. There was nothing else around at this hour. We had only travelled about a hundred metres but when we got back to the stretch of road where they had been there was nothing to be seen. I got out of the car and walked onto the grass verge. In the lights of the dual carriageway I could see for some way across the surrounding fields. But there was no sign of them, no houses, no gypsy encampment, nothing.

I absolutely do not believe in ghosts and anyway, these little girls looked far too substantial. But after all these years I still can't explain how they disappeared like that. I'm sure there was nowhere for them to hide. When we got to the service station I went to a phone box and called the police. I told them what I had seen and left Control's number in case two little girls had gone missing. I fully expected to see headlines about a disappearance in the papers the next day. But we never heard another word about it. If Phil hadn't seen it as well I would have been convinced that I had simply nodded off for a moment and dreamt it.

By the end of the fourth day we were all exhausted and fed up. It was well into the afternoon. The lorry had made deliveries and collections at around twenty locations and so far we had seen nothing, despite covering every single stop and every single hour of every night. We were increasingly certain that we had missed the handover. In a matter of hours he would be back on a ferry and across the Channel. The only other option, if we hadn't missed it, was that we had been seen by counter-surveillance; that thought depressed us almost us much. Certainly we hadn't seen anyone, but we had been so careful in our surveillance, we had worked so hard, that the thought of them spotting us without us even seeing them was unbearable.

There was only one glimmer of hope. We had maintained the OP on Sammy's flat. It wasn't certain that he would be involved in this importation, even though we knew he had arranged it, but there was a chance. We pinned our hopes on that possibility.

At about five o'clock on the afternoon of that fourth day we finally received the news we had been waiting for and all our fatigue was forgotten.

'Lima 11: relay from Fox 1. Zulu 66 is at Gold 16.'

Gold 16 was the codename for Sammy's flat and Zulu 66 was the Dutchman. Clearly the OP had seen him going in and John had phoned Mac on the mobile to let him know. This looked promising. Even so, Sid wasn't satisfied because this was the first time we had heard that the Dutchman was back.

'How the hell do these people get into the country?' he asked as we drove along. 'I mean, we know who they are, we put them on port and airport lists, we have computers checking ticketing and yet they seem able to waltz in and out of the country any time they feel like it. Next we'll hear that Volkan is dropping in for tea.'

'Beats me,' I said. 'I'm just glad he's here. Now maybe we'll see something happen.'

This single piece of information raised the whole team's level of concentration and it was a good thing it did. Only an hour later the lorry pulled into a service area. Zulu 67, the driver – an overweight, unkempt man in a filthy blue check shirt and overalls – got out and went to the services building to buy some food and visit the bathroom. I followed him all the way through the building. He didn't meet anyone and when he returned to the lorry I handed him over to Mac, who had a long-range view from the car park. As I was walking back to my vehicle I heard Mac commentating.

'Lima 11: that's Zulu 67 at X-Ray 72 . . . Wait . . . he's gone past . . . He's now at the rear . . . doors open . . . and he's climbed inside, out of my sight.'

I reached my car and climbed in. Sid and Jackie had exchanged places in order to change the profile of the vehicles. She smiled and said, 'I'll bet you five pounds he's getting the drugs.'

'You're on,' I replied, 'but I really, really hope I lose.'

'From Lima 11: that's Zulu 67 out of the back, wait one . . . He's carrying a plain brown holdall . . . doors closed . . . and that's Zulu 67 back to the cab of X-Ray 72.'

I told Jackie that I would owe her the five pounds and she looked at me sceptically, but we were both relieved. We hadn't missed the handover. Somebody pressed their transmission button and cheered.

'Cut that shit out,' barked Mac. 'We haven't got him yet. Check your goddamn plot positions.'

He'd been in a bad temper for days. As an EO this case could be his big break and he'd been more terrified than any of us that we might have missed something. Now that there was still a prospect of saving the job he was more on edge than ever.

'From Lima 11: that's X-Ray 72 manoeuvring . . . and towards you Fox 5.'

'Fox 5 received.'

We followed the lorry closer and closer to Felixstowe as the evening wore on. At every lay-by or turning we thought this was it, but instead the lorry just kept plodding on. It was a pretty smart idea just having a holdall loose in the back of the lorry: if it had been found when he entered the country the driver could have claimed to know nothing about it and would have stood a good chance of getting away with it. If the conceal-ment had been complicated then the driver would definitely have been in on it. It was also simple for the driver to deal with – one quick visit to the back of the trailer and a simple handover to a car somewhere on the journey. Unless he was watched all the time, no one would see it.

Eventually he was back on the last stretch of the A14 leading to the docks. We couldn't believe it. There was no time left and he hadn't made the switch. The radio communications were full of people trying to second guess what was going to happen and Mac telling them to shut up. Then, just as we were figuring that the holdall hadn't contained drugs after all and that we really had missed the switch:

'Fox 6: That's an off, off, off and 555 amber.'

Amber was brevity code for a lay-by. 555 meant that he had come to a complete stop. Jackie and I were backup in the tail and we soon passed the lay-by. We could quite clearly see the driver sitting in his cab, smoking a cigarette and apparently waiting. It was the practically the last lay-by before the docks. We got to the next roundabout and pulled off on to a small side-road.

Now there was nothing to do but sit and plan. The first thing we needed was a view of the lorry. We couldn't park anyone in the lay-by – that would have been far too obvious – and we couldn't afford to keep driving vehicles past all the time. George was further down the road at the top of the embankment. He could just about see the lorry with binoculars but we needed something better and besides, it was getting dark. Ripper was our close-surveillance expert and Billy, who was his driver, immediately set about finding a way round to the back of the fields behind the lay-by so that Ripper could work his way into an observation position. Like all of our close-observation officers, Ripper had been trained by the army and he had all the right equipment, such as camouflage gear and night-vision equipment. About fifteen minutes after the lorry had parked we heard Billy on the radio.

'That's Fox 10 attempting eyeball.'

We knew that Ripper would be creeping over the neighbouring farmland. Billy would be his backup, acting as relay for Ripper's whispered radio calls and ready to rush in to help if Ripper was discovered. Memories of road-rage murderer Kenny Noye, who stabbed to death a police close-surveillance officer and then walked free from court, were still fresh in everyone's minds in those days.

'Relay: Fox 10 has the eyeball.'

'Received. That's Fox 6 lifted.'

Later Ripper told us how much work it had been. There were buildings overlooking his approach so he was forced to crawl on his belly for the last few hundred metres. His face was blacked up and he was wearing a full camouflage suit, making his way along hedges wherever possible. Finally he got to the ridge above the lay-by. There were some thorn bushes about halfway down the ridge. He crawled in under one of these, making as little disturbance as possible. There was a small burger van in the lay-by. Other lorries came and went from time to time, but no one even looked in his direction and gradually he settled down. Occasionally the owner of the burger van would come around the back to empty water or other rubbish, or just to stand and have a fag. At one stage he emptied a pot of boiling water not three feet from where Ripper was lying. All the time Ripper was silently working with a trowel, digging himself a shallow hide to further lower his profile. His worry was that, as the night darkened but the street lights came on in the distance, his silhouette would become visible.

At the end of the dual carriageway where Jackie and I were parked, we could often make out his whispered comments to Billy. But radio communication is a fickle thing, especially when you're dealing with small battery-powered sets like our surveillance radios. Sometimes we could hear him clear as a bell; at other times there was just a burst of static which indicated that he had said something, but the message hadn't carried to us and we had to wait for Billy to relay. The other half of the team were even further away. They were completely reliant on Billy.

The evening wore on and, whilst we were sitting waiting for the handover to take place, two more pieces of information were relayed to us which made it certain that the handover was going to happen that night. The first was that the OP at Sammy's flat had seen him and the Dutchman leaving in Sammy's car. A loose tail had taken him eastwards across London and then dropped him, on John's orders, to avoid showing out. It certainly sounded as though they were heading our way, although we couldn't believe that Sammy would be so stupid as to come and witness the handover of the drugs personally. It was far too risky. We could only assume that he was going to wait nearby to receive the money.

The second piece of intelligence was more disturbing. Peter's team had heard from one of their sources that Zulu 58 and one other unknown person had been sent to collect the drugs and they believed that he was armed. There were now so many Zulus in the operation that Jackie and I both had to ask who

Zulu 58 was. He turned out to be an associate of the head of the record store who also controlled the Brixton gang. He was thought to be an enforcer for the gang and was rated 'highly dangerous – usually armed' in our operational bible. John was trying to get armed police backup for us once again. From the time of Sammy's departure we tried to estimate when he would arrive at our position. It seemed that it would be sometime around eleven o'clock. Now we knew how long we had to wait.

Eventually, after consulting with Phil and John, Mac came up with a plan for the knock. Once the target vehicles passed the roundabout at the far end of the dual carriageway, on the way to the lay-by, two vehicles would move forward to seal it off and prevent any civilian vehicles passing through. The rest of the vehicles at that position would get ready to move in when the knock was called. At the same time, the vehicles where Jackie and I were waiting would seal off that end of the dual carriageway. We would have both ends of the trap sealed. Then, in theory, the plan was simple: Ripper would witness the handover of the drugs and the money. The vehicle with the drugs, probably driven by Zulu 58, would be allowed to leave and at that point Mac would call the knock. At our position, we would stop the car with the drugs and arrest the driver. The vehicles at the other end of the dual carriageway would race down, arrest the lorry driver and, if necessary, continue to our position to assist in the arrest of Zulu 58. It sounded straightforward but none of us believed it would be that easy.

The plan only appeared to overlook two things: firstly, that Zulu 58 and his friend were expected to be armed, and secondly, that Zulu 58 might not want to help us out by stopping his car full of heroin. Other than that it was fine. Those of us at the 'dangerous end' of the trap began to talk about what might be the best way to stop him without getting our heads blown off.

Mac came to inspect our position. He was fussing like a mother hen, but then this was his first knock as commander and he didn't want anything to go wrong. Jess and I, who were the two HEOs in charge at this end of the trap, stood and explained to him where we thought two cars should go for the roadblock. Mac shook his head doubtfully.

'It's not enough, is it?' he said.

'Well, we figure we'll leave two of the vehicles manned. If he tries to break through then they'll ram him or, if that doesn't work, they'll start the chase,' said Jess. 'You send yours through as soon as the knock is called and we should be all right.'

Mac still looked unhappy, chewing his lower lip.

'I need to have a word with you two over here.'

We walked away from the parked vehicles. Jess and I glanced at each other, both wondering what this was about.

'Look, there's bit of bad news. The armed police aren't coming. They're expecting some heavy duty mob to do a cash machine raid with a digger and everything. It's running late but it's still on and the Old Bill are saying that their job takes priority.'

'What, they're not going to send us anything? Not even a couple of officers?' I asked.

Mac shook his head.

'We *know* that Zulu 58 is coming tooled up to collect a holdall full of heroin. What the fuck do they expect us to use? Harsh language?' demanded Jess, angrily. He clearly felt this was Mac's fault for not getting us any backup at all.

'I guess this is what they pay HEOs the big money for,' smiled Mac, but there was an air of menace in his voice. I had seen his temper snap before.

'Hey, if either of you is earning big money I want to know about it,' I joked.

Jess and Mac were still squared up to each other, but the moment passed. At least we all knew what the problem was now: either Zulu 58 would stop or he wouldn't. If he didn't, it would become an out-and-out car chase, but if he did, someone was going to have to run to the car unarmed and in full sight of Zulu 58, drag him out of the car and arrest him. We didn't even have bulletproof vests with us. They had to be signed out specially from central stores and no one had thought to bring them. In my mind I could already hear a newsreader somewhere in the future: 'Why were these Customs officers killed? Why were they forced to conduct the arrest without armed backup?'

'All right,' conceded Mac. 'I'm in charge, I'll do it, I just need one of you two to back me up.'

Now it was Jess and me who looked uncomfortable. We both knew what had to be said.

'You're plot commander, Mac. It's your job to run the knock, you can't be down here in the trenches. Leave the roadblock to us. We'll sort it,' said Jess.

Mac nodded.

'I'll see if I can't get you some local uniformed police or something. It'll give you another vehicle to use if nothing else.'

He walked back to his vehicle.

'You OK with this?' asked Jess.

All I could do was shrug.

'If we just go in fast and hard, he won't even have time to pull his fucking gun, never mind fire it.'

'Oh thanks,' I said, with gentle sarcasm. 'That's very reassuring. I'll be right behind you.'

Shortly before eleven o'clock a police patrol car pulled up at our position and what appeared to be an eighteen-stone sergeant and a twelve-year-old constable climbed out.

'Evening,' said the sergeant in a broad Suffolk accent. 'Having a bit of excitement are you?'

'Jesus Christ, it's Worzel Gummidge,' muttered Jackie, under her breath.

'Shut it,' murmured Jess, walking forward to shake hands.

'Thanks for coming out. We need all the troops we can get.'

'That's all right,' said the constable. 'Nothing much happens here on a Wednesday anyway. Sounds like this might be fun.'

Jess filled them in on the job so far, including the fact that the man collecting the drugs was thought to be armed.

'If you could come with us when we hit the vehicle, it would be a big help. These guys tend to think twice about firing if they see a uniform. Otherwise they might get a bit nervous, start thinking that it's a rip-off by another gang, and then there's no telling what will happen.'

The constable was quite keen and was already nodding, but his sergeant was a county copper of the old school and he was going to do everything by the rule book.

'Well now, our instructions are to attend and help you apprehend the vehicle and to make sure no members of the public become involved in this temporary roadblock. When it comes to making the arrest, that's really down to you. If you boys haven't got armed backup I think that's got to be your lookout, hasn't it?'

I could sense that Jess was furious. Ninety-nine out of one hundred other officers would have got stuck in. It was just our luck that we got the one guy who wouldn't.

'Fine,' murmured Jess through gritted teeth. 'We'll sort it. Perhaps when we get the word to move out you could position your vehicle on the centre of the roundabout and set your blue lights going. At least that'll make it more official.'

'Oh yes,' said the sergeant, 'we can certainly do that. Mind you, if we get a call from elsewhere we will have to go and deal with it. Is this going to take long, do you think? Only the call said the arrests were imminent.'

Nothing was said for some while as we all stood in the lane and waited for news that Zulu 58 was on the way.

After a while the sergeant spoke. 'I suppose this drugs stuff must make a nice change for you rather than watches and duty-free.'

I could tell that Jess was about to turn and say something he'd regret. I took him by the arm and asked him to come and look at the roadblock positions again.

The wait seemed to last for ever. It was freezing standing around outside. Now and again we would go and sit in the cars to try and warm up, but we were all so tense that we wanted to be out and pacing around, or at least talking to the others. Finally, towards midnight, the call came through from Mac. A red Mercedes containing Sammy and the Dutchman had just gone past their position. A short while later we got the relay from Billy. The Mercedes had pulled up in the lay-by and the lorry driver had climbed out of his cab for the meeting. We couldn't believe it: both Sammy and the Dutchman were going to be at the handover. This seemed too good to be true. We could bag the lot.

Ripper radioed that he was moving closer to see if he could hear any of the conversation. When it came to court they were bound to deny that they knew that heroin was involved and say they thought they were smuggling tobacco or something. Ripper spoke Turkish and anything he could pick up now could be invaluable in convicting them later. It was a big risk – he might be spotted as he moved – but even Mac couldn't over-ride him on this. The rule on these operations was that the close-surveillance officer was the person taking the risks, so they decided where they were best placed and whether the risk was worth it.

By a freak of radio transmission, we could hear the sounds of Ripper's breathing as he crawled through the undergrowth and down the slope towards the meeting. He must have left his transmit button on. After a minute or so we heard three short tones in succession: the signal that he was so close that he could not longer talk for fear of being overheard. All communication with him would now be based on interrogation by Billy, just as I had used when covering the first meeting with the Turks six months ago. In fact, we later found that he had managed to get so close that he was actually under the lorry. But the conversations sounded as if they were in Dutch. Ripper couldn't understand any of it.

Suddenly Mac's voice broke in over the net.

'That's Zulu 58 through blue seven driving a green Mazda sports car. All mobiles put roadblocks into operation now.'

We had three vehicles and the police car to use at our end of the carriageway. We put two at the roundabout on either side, blocking the road. If he tried to go around them by mounting the grass verges, they would ram him. The police patrol car pulled up in the centre of the roundabout with its blue light running, just as we had asked. Jess and I moved the car we were using a short way up from the roundabout, towards the lay-by. We parked it diagonally across the carriageway and got out, but left the doors open. We would be the first ones to get to Zulu 58 if he stopped, but just in case he didn't stop we had to be ready to leap back in and either ram him or join the chase.

We heard Billy interrogating Ripper and relaying the latest developments at the lay-by.

'That's a green Mazda 555 at amber . . . Zulu 58 out.'

There was a short pause and then:

'That's all four Zulus together and talking. Zulu 58 has a grey holdall.'

That had to be the money. This would have been what the Dutchman had come to collect. Sure enough, Ripper reported that the Dutchman was checking the contents of the holdall.

I could hear Jess talking under his breath on the other side of the car.

'Come on you bastards, let's get this over with.'

Ripper must have moved again because the next thing we heard through our earpieces was his voice.

'That's driver into X-Ray 72 and now from X-Ray 72 with a brown holdall.'

It was obviously the same one we had seen him transferring from the concealment in the trailer earlier in the day. Everything was going to plan.

'Brown holdall to Zulu 58. He's into the Mazda and it's an off, off, off, towards you Lima 3.'

This was it then.

'Knock, knock, knock!'

Mac shouted the familiar code-words into his radio and almost deafened me. Things then happened rapidly. Jess and I were aware of the green sports car speeding towards us. It screeched to a halt about thirty metres away. For a few moments nobody moved. We were all waiting to see what the driver would do next. Then I heard Jess say in a surprisingly calm voice, 'Let's do it.'

We both sprinted forward. On a surge of pure adrenalin we crossed the distance between us and Zulu 58's vehicle in about five seconds. Jess was faster than me and slightly ahead as the driver's door opened and Zulu 58 climbed out. Driven by pure fear, I leapt for him and actually dived clear over the door, between the slope of the door frame and the body of the vehicle. I caught him around the shoulders just as Jess grabbed his right arm in an arrest lock and we tumbled to the ground, both of us shouting 'Customs and Excise!' at the tops of our voices. I grabbed his other arm and we dragged him to his feet before throwing him up against the side of the car. He was a big guy and I could feel the massive muscles of his arms under his shirt, but he gave absolutely no resistance.

There was a thunder of feet behind us and the rest of the team arrived. Jackie grabbed the keys out of the ignition and two of the others were dragging someone out of the passenger seat. It was a woman, screaming at the top of her voice. Zulu 58 was saying over and over, 'What's going on man? I ain't done nothing', but he wasn't struggling. Jess pulled his arms behind him and cuffed them before the shock wore off and he decided to fight back. I patted him down, looking for the gun we'd been warned about, but there was nothing.

'No gun!' I shouted. Jackie was called round the car by one of the others to search the girl. Even in this situation we had to be careful that we didn't act 'inappropriately'. Jackie started trying to calm the woman down, although I could see that she had a firm grip of the woman's wrist, ready to drop her into an arm-lock if she showed any signs of trouble. Someone else was checking the interior of the car, looking for a weapon. A car came screeching to a halt a few feet away. Phil and Big George piled out of it.

'You're under arrest on suspicion of being involved in the importation of controlled drugs,' gasped Jess to Zulu 58, before cautioning him. We turned him round and leant him with his back against the car.

'Drugs?!' he said. 'I thought this was a fucking car accident. I was getting out to help.'

Actually, looking down the road at the roundabout in the darkness, it did look a bit like a road accident. There were cars all over the road, their headlights pointing in different directions, doors wide open and a police car with its blue light flashing in the middle. Quite by accident we had created a trap which had fooled him into stopping. But then maybe we deserved a bit of luck.

'Got it!' shouted Big George, dragging the brown holdall out of the boot of the vehicle. Zulu 58's head sank and he just muttered 'fuck' under his breath. Jess and I walked him back to car, ready for the long drive to Ipswich police station. As we were piling him into the back of the car Jess and I both heard a faint voice over our radio sets saying, 'I need help!' We both looked at each other in confusion and then back down the road.

While the arrest at our roadblock had gone smoothly, things had not gone so well back at the lorry. With Zulu 58's car disappearing down the deserted dual carriageway, Mac had called the knock. Ripper had sprinted from his hidden position towards where the three remaining smugglers were standing, counting the money. Secure in the knowledge that several carloads of officers were racing to back him up, Ripper had shouted, 'Customs and Excise, you're all nicked!' And all by himself he had taken each of the smugglers and roughly thrown them up against the side of the lorry with their backs to the road and their hands above their heads. And then . . .

. . . nothing happened.

There had been a dreadful pause, which Ripper later described as the longest moment of his life, when it became clear that no one was coming to help him. There was the sound of an explosion from further down the dual carriageway, but no sign of other Customs officers. The trouble was that the smugglers began to realise this too, and the shock of being attacked by this little man covered in camouflage netting soon wore off. They began to lower their arms and tried to turn round. Only one car appeared and that roared straight past them and after the fast disappearing tail-lights of Zulu 58's car. Ripper watched it go, open-mouthed, then ran backwards and forwards between the suspects, like a plate-spinner in a circus, forcing them back against the lorry and screaming at them to raise their hands and stand still. Each time he did this he had less and less success. Eventually the Dutchman tried to make a run for it. Ripper grabbed him and the Dutchman took a swing at him. Ripper ducked under that and hit him in the solar plexus before grabbing him by the shoulders as he doubled up, then running him head first into the side of the lorry. As the stunned Dutchman fell to the ground Ripper spun round to where Sammy was about to Judas-punch him in the back of the head. Sammy simply threw up his arms and said 'OK, OK!' with a big grin and stepped back to the side of the lorry again. Meanwhile the driver had done a runner round the front of the cab, only to be greeted by a flying tackle from Billy, who was hurtling down the slope of the embankment.

It was at this point that Ripper called for help and within moments the other vehicles came racing along the carriageway and screeched to a halt around him, officers pouring out to make the arrests. Ripper leaned against the side of the lorry, gasping for breath, and demanded: 'Where the fuck were you lot?'

'Strange you should say that,' grinned Chris, slapping cuffs on the Dutchman, 'but a funny thing happened on the way to the office . . .'

Apparently only moments before Mac called the knock there was the sound of police sirens in the distance and a saloon car had come roaring out of the darkness towards the roadblock. It obviously wasn't going to stop and, thinking that it was going to ram its way through, officers scattered in all directions as the car hurtled towards them. The driver of the vehicle seemed to see the cars all over the road ahead and swerved at the last moment. This flipped the vehicle first on to its side and then on to its roof before it span out of control and into the crash barrier. Partly to save its occupants and partly because they might be other members of the gang who needed to be arrested, all the officers except Phil and Big George had run across to the wreck to see what could be done. The car turned out to contain a couple of joyriders who were fleeing from a police pursuit which arrived at the roadblock seconds later. It had nothing to do with the smuggling operation and was just one massive, impeccably-timed coincidence.

Thinking that others were following close behind them, Big George and Chris had stuck to the plan and had gone to the far roadblock to make sure that the drugs were secured. They had assumed that the other vehicles would rush to Ripper's aid. It had very nearly been tragic and would certainly have been if any of the smugglers had been armed. Instead it became one of Ripper's favourite bar-room anecdotes for years to come.

Jess and I took Zulu 58 to Ipswich police station and booked him in. The other three suspects duly followed. It took three more hours to process him and get the paperwork sorted. Then we trudged out of the station, piled into the cars and drove to the motel we had used at the start of the surveillance. It must have been four o'clock in the morning. We had barely eaten all day and some of us were in the lobby, having grabbed drinks from a minibar. As we were sitting there, cooling down after the hectic past five days, we heard a lot of noise out in the car park. A crowd of people, which seemed to consist mainly of over-muscled young men with crew cuts, talking loudly in American accents, burst in through the main doors. All of them had at least one, in most cases two, and, in one very optimistic case three, drunken young women in miniskirts and stilettos hanging fawningly on their arms. The men banged on the reception desk and called for their keys before disappearing in the direction of their rooms.

We all watched this in stunned silence. Eventually Chris trudged to the reception and said to the night porter, 'Who were those guys then?'

The porter reached under the counter and gave Chris a flyer which he brought back to us. Apparently they were a group of male strippers from the US called the 'Adonis Boys' or the 'Hercules Men' or something like that. I considered the perfect male figures in the photographs on the flyer and then looked at the collection of beerguts, grey faces and hollow eyes slumped in the armchairs around me. In comparison with those guys we looked like the Addams family. There was no justice.

Mac was still staring at the door through which the men and their attendant floozies had disappeared.

'You know,' he said thoughtfully, 'I think we're in the wrong job.'

Later that day we booked out our suspects and took them to the Customs offices at Felixstowe for interviews. I was going to interview Sammy. He was sitting in the interview room with his lawyer, but they were insisting that a Turkish interpreter be found. It was strange sitting across the table from him after all those months of surveillance. As with Haase, I had rarely been close-up to him before. The interpreter took a ridiculously long time to arrive, so Sammy and I had a chat to pass the time. His lawyer seemed quite happy for us to talk off-tape – Sammy wasn't going to admit anything and I wasn't going to give anything away so it was all quite relaxed.

'You been on me a long time?' he asked.

'You're about to find out,' I replied.

'Man, I was so relieved when your man said he was Customs, I thought for sure we was being ripped off. I ain't never been so glad to see you guys. I thought I was a dead man.'

'Looks like you won't be playing poker for a while anyway.'

'Oh, man! You guys were following me while I was at the casino? Fucking hell man. Where were you? Were any of you playing at the table?'

I shook my head.

'We're not that good.'

'Damn. That's a pity. Maybe my lawyer could have got some of my money back.' He gave me a big smile including several gold fillings.

I hate to say it, but he actually seemed like a pleasant man. He didn't sulk or mouth off the way most suspects did. I wondered how he'd become involved in it all. Still, it was too late now. This was his second heroin importation offence. He was going away for a very, very long time. Finally the interpreter arrived. I started the tape and read out the official caution and formal statement which has to precede all tape-recorded interviews. At this point Sammy's lawyer leant forward to make his own statement.

'I would just like to formally request the officer to ask the interpreter to repeat all his statements and questions carefully and slowly in Turkish as my client does not speak very good English.'

He didn't bat an eyelid. It was the sheer, barefaced audacity of it that left me stunned. He had been sitting right there for the last half-hour while Sammy and I had chatted about everything, from the weather to football. A few years ago I would have been outraged at such a naked twisting of the legal system to get an advantage, but now I just shrugged it off and went through my questions. Needless to say, Sammy didn't seem to know anything. I asked him what his relationship was with the Dutchman. Sammy claimed not to have met him before that day. I pulled some surveillance photographs out of an envelope and passed them across the desk to him. They showed the two of them sitting at a table together in the café, the day the Dutchman had flown into Britain. Sammy simply grinned and shrugged.

'That's not me,' he bluffed. But by then he knew he was finished anyway. I knew it and I could see by his face that the lawyer knew it too.

Once we had questioned the four of them, Mac called a meeting to decide how to proceed. During the meeting Phil took a call from John, who was co-ordinating the operation back in London. Almost a dozen addresses across London had been hit at the same time as the knock. We were ripping the guts out of Volkan's smuggling operation in Britain.

We later heard that the team searching Sammy's flat had a

particularly strange experience. They were halfway through searching the place when the doorbell rang. Stuart, who was leading the team, went to the door and opened it. There was a young, Arabic-looking man standing there, holding a carrier bag. He simply thrust the carrier bag into Stuart's hands and started to walk away. Stuart opened the bag and saw dozens of bundles of banknotes.

'Oi,' he shouted. 'What's all this?'

The Arab turned round and came back.

'It's fifty thousand pounds as agreed,' he said.

Stuart was in a state of shock and just said, 'You what?'

'Fifty thousand pounds as agreed,' insisted the Arab.

For a moment Stuart was at a complete loss, but as the Arab started to turn away again, Stuart grabbed him round the neck and dragged him back into the flat.

'You're nicked, mate,' he said as the door closed.

But it wasn't all good news from London.

'The gossip on the streets,' said Phil, 'is that Volkan's hopping mad. Apparently he's told his people that they have got to launch an operation to spring these people from court. He must be scared that what they might say will finish him in this country. Anyway, these guys have to go to Ipswich Crown Court tomorrow to be remanded, but there are no armed police available and the prison service are saying they can't be responsible for the security at this short notice. Guess who's going to have to assist them to stand guard?'

'You're joking,' said Mac.

But he wasn't. The following day we were responsible for riding in the prison vans, mounting security in the courtrooms and standing in the dock with the prisoners. The arrests had provoked quite a lot of local interest and there were TV cameras and press all over the place. But if Volkan managed to get an armed team together in time, there was nothing we could have down to stop them. Then the press would really have got a story.

Still, by the end of the day all of the suspects – including the members of the Brixton connection who had been brought up from London – had been remanded in custody and were no longer our problem. John had booked rooms for the whole team at a better-than-average hotel not far from Ipswich and once the whole team arrived there we started a celebration. It was the end of the job. After months of work we had netted both ends of Volkan's heroin operation and if he ever came into the country again we'd nab him too. It felt really good. But, even though we had the best of reasons to celebrate, we were all just too tired. Despite the efforts of the livelier members of the team, most of us could barely keep our eyes open and a few glasses of alcohol just finished us off.

As for me, the tension of the four-day surveillance on the lorry had brought back the stomach cramps yet again. I had also caught a chill standing out on the Yorkshire Moors in driving rain and hail for several hours one night, keeping watch on the lorry. I was shivering and running quite a temperature. Several people asked if I was OK; I just wanted to get to bed. I made my apologies to John and headed for my room. I had barely got through the door before I had an especially bad cramp, blacked out and collapsed. As I went down I hit my head on the wall and the next thing I knew it was an hour later.

I didn't want an ambulance – I put the fainting spell down to a combination of tiredness and stress – I went to bed early and Sid ran me home early the next morning. But my condition continued to get worse and by the afternoon I was in hospital.

A week's bedrest was what the doctor prescribed. 'Go back after that if you feel better,' he said, and in the meantime I was put through a battery of tests. These included having to swallow some god-awful liquid before being inserted into a machine so that they could take some sort of whole body X-ray, and an endoscopy, which is where a tube containing a tiny video camera is passed down your throat to survey the inside of you stomach. Then they discovered swellings in my neck and under my arms, which meant I had to have an operation so that they could cut me open and take samples.

Finally the day came for the results. I was referred to a specialist I'd never met before. I remember he had one of the whitest and cleanest offices I had ever seen. As I sat nervously on the padded chair in front of his desk I tried to read some of the papers piled there, in the hope that I might get some sort of advance warning. But it all seemed to be hospital administration. My file was lying there, closed.

The specialist smiled, stood up, came around the desk and sat on the edge of it. Doctors never do that unless it's bad news, I thought to myself, but now that I was finally there I wasn't really scared. I had already done all my worrying by then: if this was going to be bad news such as cancer, then fine, that was the way it was going to be. The worst bit would be when he told me; I just wanted to get it over with. I can't remember all the medical terms he used but what he said next went something like this:

'Has anybody explained to you exactly what we're looking for?' He smiled.

I shook my head.

'There are problems with your lymphatic system and your digestion. Clearly your body is reacting against the stress produced in your work. There is no major damage yet, but, if the current state of affairs continues, your condition is going to likely to deteriorate until it becomes serious. The only way we can see to deal with this problem is to get rid of the stress. I'm sorry, but you have to find another line of work.'

The illness meant that I would have to leave the team just as I was beginning to feel comfortable there. It meant that I wouldn't get to see if Jackie fulfilled her undoubted potential; I wouldn't get to hear any more of Ralph's jokes. Of course I would still see them around in the building from time to time, but in the ID once you are off a team, you are little more than a stranger – everyone is so busy with their latest investigation that all but the strongest friendships soon lapse. Everyone moves on.

So that was it: I needed a change of job. At least Nicky would be happy, I thought. But I was shattered. For the second time in my life I was going to have to give up a job I loved. As I walked away from the hospital I didn't have a clue about what I was going to do next.

When I arrived home and told Nicky what the doctor had said, and that I almost certainly had to give up working for the ID, instead of doing a victory dance she reacted marvellously.

'Go and see Jack,' she said. 'He'll know what to do.'

Jack was the senior officer who had overseen my transfer from MI6 to the Investigation Division. He agreed to see me in his office the next morning. After listening to my story he went and stood by the window, looking out over the River Thames while he thought. Finally he turned and said, 'Do you know the Alpha Team?'

'They specialise in intercepting weapons shipments don't they?'

'That's part of their work. Much of it is United Nations sanctions enforcement, some liaison with the intelligence services, that sort of thing. It will also mean surveillance, but not the hard target stuff you've been doing – surveillance on UK businessmen mainly. The hours are fairly regular and there's a certain amount of foreign travel. Do you think that would push your stress levels too high?'

'Absolutely not.'

I couldn't believe my luck. When I went in through the door of his office I had thought I was going to say goodbye. Jack picked up the phone right there and then and made calls to several people. After five minutes he put down the receiver and smiled.

'It's all set up. You'll start on the first of next month. Of course, we'll need to renew your security vetting, but that shouldn't take too long. Come back and have a chat sometime soon. Let me know what you think of the work.'

We shook hands.

'Looks like you'll be staying with us for a while longer then,' he smiled.

I left the office with a spring in my step. After a year which had contained some very dark moments, I felt that things were finally looking up. No more hiding in dingy flats peering through telephoto lenses, no more getting up at four in the morning to drive out to some freezing-cold industrial estate to follow a suspect lorry. And, from Jack's description of the hours, it sounded as if Nicky would be happy as well. For the first time in a long while I felt things might be OK.

After all, dealing with the intelligence services, sanctions busters and UK arms manufacturers could never be as murky as dealing with heroin, cocaine and cannabis smugglers . . .

Could it?

Postscript

No sooner was the back of Volkan's organisation broken than Drugs F/L moved on to a new target. There were always more targets waiting to be dealt with, more than we could ever possibly handle. It always makes me laugh when I hear people talking about 'turf wars' between law enforcement agencies inhibiting the fight against crime. It always makes it sound as if we were all sitting around waiting for something to do whereas in fact the exact opposite was the case – there was so much intelligence and so many targets that we could never tackle them all.

At the same time as a new operation was beginning, the Customs and Excise Solicitors Office was deep into the long and tortuous process of turning the paperwork from months of surveillance work on Haase, Volkan and Sammy into a proper court case. We had done our job, but this was a whole new ball game and the heroin smugglers' second chance of getting away with it was about to begin.

Initially things seemed to go well. One piece of welcome news was that the death threat against Knowles had been lifted. Following our raid on the flat in London, the hit man had pulled out of the job fearing that it was only a matter of time before he was picked up. As for the Fixer, our successes against both Volkan and Haase seemed to convince him that even if he did get at Knowles it could only make things worse. The old rule, that it was better to keep your head down and make money than to openly challenge the authorities, reasserted itself and the death threat was never mentioned again. The ID managers' strategy had been proved right.

The first case to come up was the Brixton connection, early in the following year: 1994. I was curious to see how they were going to try and get away with it, because the tactics varied from case to case. As one of the main officers in the case I was called into the witness box by Sammy's lawyer. I stood there and looked out over row after row of bewigged lawyers. Every suspect in the case was represented by their own barrister, together with accompanying solicitors and solicitors' clerks. It must have been costing someone a small fortune. I stood there and wondered which one was going to lay into me. Maybe all of them. It's always a nerve-racking moment just before the questioning starts. Everyone in the court is watching you, and you never know if the lawyers are merely going to ask you a few simple questions about the facts of the case or launch into a blistering attack, accusing you of everything from falsifying the evidence to framing their client. There's very little you can do to prepare because there are months and months of evidence and you have no idea what the attack is going to be. Sammy's barrister stood up.

'Officer, you were responsible for surveillance on my client on numerous dates and, if you look at the papers in front of you, you will see copies of the observation logs for each of those dates. Are those the correct observation logs?'

There was a thick pile of papers balanced on the edge of the witness box. There was no time to check them all. I flicked through them briefly.

'It certainly looks like it.'

'If you turn to the flagged observation log and to page two of that log you will see an observation recorded at 1122 hours. Was that your observation?'

One of the logs was marked with a yellow tag. It was months ago. I ran my eye down the column until I came to 1122. It was signed so it must be mine.

'Yes, it was,' I replied.

'Could you read that observation out to the court?'

'1122 hours, two unknown persons to the door of Gold 16 carrying a large flat object covered in a white cloth. Approximate dimensions one point five metres by one metre. There then follows a description of the two people carrying the object.'

'And what did you think was under the cloth?'

'I have no idea. I never saw it.'

'But it didn't appear to be heavy, did it? The people who were carrying it, an old woman and a young man, they didn't appear to be struggling with the weight of it?'

'Not that I could see.'

'So what sort of object did it appear to be? Could it, in your opinion, have been a large mirror or a painting, something of those dimensions?'

'Possibly, but I really couldn't say.'

'But you wouldn't rule out that it could have been a large painting?'

I couldn't think where this line of questioning was going and at that moment one of the barristers in the row in front of my questioner rolled his eyes dramatically, as if to say, 'Oh get on with it!'

'It could have been I suppose, but I really don't know.'

'Thank you officer, that will be all.'

And that was it. I had been pulled off an operation, driven all the way to court, spent half the day waiting around in the corridors in the court building, and that was all they wanted to ask me. All the other barristers bounced up and down, saying 'No questions your honour', and I was free to go. As I walked out of the court I frantically tried to think what the reason for the questions was. Then it dawned on me. Whenever they met, the Turks had always talked of the drugs in terms of books or paintings. They must be trying to make a case that Sammy really was a dealer in old masters and that's where his money came from. I couldn't see that they had a hope in hell of making that stick, and sure enough they didn't. The entire Brixton connection went down for various long stretches in prison, but the heaviest sentence was reserved for Sammy: because it was his second heroin importation offence he was sentenced to twenty-four years in prison.

The following year, 1995, there were two major developments in the case. The first was that Haase and Bennett were finally convicted at Liverpool Crown Court. They were sentenced to eighteen years each and had almost a million pounds in cash confiscated as the proceeds of drug trafficking. The rest of the Liverpool gang, including five members of Volkan's organisation, were sentenced to equally long terms.

The second piece of news was even more dramatic. Our smashing of Volkan's syndicate hadn't succeeded in netting him, but international organisers are almost impossible to catch because they never go near the drugs, so we weren't particularly surprised. However, we had made it extremely dangerous for him, if he ever came to the UK again. He wouldn't be nipping in and out of the country with impunity to set up heroin deals any more, and that was some comfort. Every country with whom we had an extradition agreement would be on the lookout for him, and in every country where we had a DLO (Drugs Liaison Officer) he would remain top of the target list.

But even though we had made it more dangerous for him, Volkan still needed to get out and run the business personally and eventually this was his undoing. I was working on a surveillance on my new team when a call came through that I was to return to the office.

'Feel like some good news?' asked my SIO when I arrived.

'Sure. What is it?'

'The Dutch have nabbed Volkan.'

I sat down. I found it hard to believe that we had finally got him.

'They picked him up on a routine arrest. His papers didn't check out, they ran the checks and bingo! They informed the DLO at The Hague this morning. A couple of officers have gone out and should be bringing him back tomorrow. Obviously we need to substantiate that this is him so that the trial process can start. Only six officers have ever been close enough to Volkan to identify him and you are one of them: apparently you stood right next to Volkan as he made a telephone call at Heathrow airport. You're to get yourself up to Liverpool as soon as possible for an identification parade. There's a couple of cars being arranged to take you all up there together. Get your overnight bag.'

I rang home and told Nicky that I was going to be away. She was much more relaxed about sudden absences these days. Unlike in Drugs F/L, the work on my current team meant fairly regular hours. My health was still playing up, but not nearly as badly as when I'd been on surveillance every day of the week, and we finally seemed to have found a routine for the family that worked.

I grabbed my kitbag. Several of the older hands on the team wished me luck. Apparently word had already slipped out that the infamous Volkan had been nabbed, and they knew how important this stage of the process was going to be. If he got away he wouldn't make the same mistake ever again.

Downstairs in the Drugs F/L office the six of us gathered. It felt odd to be together again. Several of us had long since moved on to other teams and, having once worked so closely together, we were now rather like strangers. We sat around and waited for John to come and brief us.

'Better pull the old case files and have another look,' I said at one point.

Mac shook his head.

'Not allowed mate.'

'You're joking!'

'Nah, we've been read the riot act, not to refresh our memories from notes or pictures because it might prejudice the rights of the defendant.'

Now he said it, I seemed to remember witnesses at crimes not being allowed to see pictures of the crime in progress, even though they had been there, because it might pollute their evidence. It had never made any sense to me then. It made even less now.

'Yeah, all the records are under lock and key,' said Mac. 'No chance of seeing anything.'

'Well, I won't ever forget him,' I said 'that was my moment of glory.'

'Yeah, you didn't have too many did you?' grinned Mac. He grabbed a set of car keys off the desk:

'Come on, let's find John and then go and get the bastard.'

We drove up north and stayed in exactly the same hotel which had been used as our base during the months of surveillance. The following morning we went to the police station. We were pretty casual, laughing and chatting. This was easy duty for us: just turn up, identify the bad guy and go home. Basically it was an excuse for a bit of a holiday. As for visiting police stations, they were like a second home to us. But this time it was different. We told the desk sergeant who we were and you could sense the chill in the atmosphere straight away. I wondered if it was because these guys remembered which case this was and the fact that we'd had to keep it a secret from them.

'Right, sit over there and you're not allowed to speak to each other.'

Several of us glanced at each other. You could tell that one or two of us were thinking of giving him a bit of lip, but it wasn't worth the hassle. Some of us stood, some lounged on the hard plastic chairs at the end of the room. The desk sergeant made a brief call on the internal phone and shortly afterwards a uniformed PC arrived to keep an eye on us. We thought that this was definitely too much. But then, a few minutes later, another man in a dark two-piece suit arrived and also stood in the room. He was clutching a ring-bound notebook and a pen. We all instantly recognised him as a solicitors' clerk. He was there to note down anything we said. If they could interpret anything as having a bearing on the case, the defence team would use it in court to say that the identification was tainted and have the whole thing thrown out. We resolutely kept quiet. We couldn't afford any mistakes now.

And so we sat and waited to be called for the identification parade. One hour passed and then two. Some of us paced up and down, others read the papers from cover to cover. Exhibiting his usual lack of nerves, Mac simply went to sleep and soon his snores were reverberating around the room. I was sure he was half-awake and doing it for effect, but none of us said anything because it was clearly irritating the desk sergeant to whom all of us had taken an instant dislike. Time ticked on. The uniformed constable was replaced twice. The clerk wandered off a couple of times to find out what was happening, accompanied by calls just loud enough for him to hear, of 'Hurry back' and 'Don't forget to write'.

Finally, some time into the third hour, another guy in a suit appeared. The clerk acknowledged him and left the room. The man was obviously some sort of lawyer because he was holding a thick, legal case folder. He held the door open for the constable, who resolutely stayed put. The lawyer shrugged and closed the door. Mac reluctantly opened one eye.

'I'm from the Customs and Excise Solicitors Office,' he began. 'I'm sorry about this, there's been a bit of a cock-up as usual. Volkan's lawyers are claiming that there's been a mistake in the identification. Not surprising really, it's his only chance – with the amount the Division has gathered on him over the years we've got him bang to rights if we can show he is the same man. Anyway, they're contesting the identification, which is why you're here, because you are the only people to have seen him.'

The lawyer swallowed hard for a moment and considered how to explain the next stage.

'The trouble is that Volkan is refusing to take part in an identity parade.'

'What a surprise,' muttered Mac. 'Put some fucking cuffs on him and let's get this over with.'

'The trouble is, we can't force him to take part. Under British law it has to be voluntary.'

'So now what?' demanded Phil. We could all sense that bad news was coming.

'Well, there are alternatives. One is that we take a photograph of him, place that on a board containing photographs of several other men who look similar, and you make your identifications from that. But his defence team won't agree to that either. In the end we have agreed a compromise which isn't ideal, but they aren't going to allow anything else and our main concern is to get him into court before the custody clock runs out.'

'It's something called confrontation. It isn't normally used. You'll be taken from here, one by one under escort, to Volkan's cell. You will be allowed to look through the peephole, then you say if that's him. It's that simple. The most important thing is that you mustn't talk to each other at any stage of the process, that's why you've had these watchdogs around you all morning.'

'Fine. Whatever,' said Mac. 'Let's get this over with.'

The lawyer from the Customs and Excise Solicitors Office left and the clerk returned.

But now we began to get more uneasy. None of us had been

through this process before. It sounded simple – deceptively simple. After all, if you looked into a cell and saw one guy, well that must be him. Why would the defence allow that if they wouldn't allow an identity parade? I began to wonder if this was some sort of elaborate trick. Were they going to show us a cell containing someone the defence had found who looked like Volkan and then ask us if that was him? We were only expecting to be shown one cell so it would be an easy trick to fall for. We'd all seen too many cases go down the drain because of clever defence lawyers. And then there was the matter of this unusual delay. Something didn't feel quite right and I didn't like the smile the clerk had on his face.

One by one we were summoned out of the room and escorted by not one but two uniformed officers, as well as another solicitors' clerk. It felt as if we were the criminals. Phil and Mac went first, then it was my turn. We walked through several corridors and two locked doors. There were several people standing outside a cell door ahead. I recognised the lawyer from our office and at least two others who must be for the defence. There were also several more uniformed police officers.

A police sergeant holding a clipboard motioned towards the closed cell door. It was metal and covered in badly-chipped dark green paint. No one said what was supposed to happen next. There was a pause and then I put my eye to the spyhole.

The man in the cell was at the far end, as if to make it as difficult to see him as possible. He looked completely different from the last two times I had seen him: his hair was long and stringy, hanging around his shoulders, and he appeared to have been trying to grow a beard. His hair was also darker than before – probably dyed. But there was no mistaking his face. Together with his build and height, I was sure it was him. I stepped back. No one said anything, but the sergeant from the reception desk held his cheap ballpoint pen over the clipboard hovering expectantly.

'Yes, I believe that's the man,' I said, in order to emphasise how certain I was.

The desk sergeant wrote it down word for word, as did the clerk for the defence.

The constable signalled with his hand and I followed him down the corridor, which ended in another waiting room with another row of plastic chairs where Mac and Phil were waiting. Eventually the process was completed and we were escorted out of the building, through the custody suite and into the police station car park. The last steel security door slammed behind us. That was it. No sooner were we out than we all wanted to know what everyone else had said. We'd all suspected a trick and had been mighty relieved when it hadn't happened. We'd all identified Volkan except for Stuart. A chorus of groans went up.

'Look, I'm sorry guys, but I honestly couldn't tell if it was him. He didn't look a bit like the last time he was here.'

Actually, I sympathised with him. The whole process had been really odd, designed to make it as difficult as possible for us to see him. Furthermore, Stuart had never got as close to him as I had. It was a good thing I had made that last minute decision to go and stand right next to Volkan, although I had never imagined it would lead to all this. Now we just had to wait for the court hearing.

'Well, five out of six should be good enough,' said Phil.

Stuart was still apologising as we headed back to the hotel.

We were summoned to court the next day for the hearing to establish whether this really was Volkan. We stood around nervously outside the court for much of the morning. The wait was loaded with all the usual tensions but the worst thing about this time was that nobody wanted to be the one on the team who made the slip that let Volkan off the hook.

Stuart came over from where he'd been deep in conversation with John.

'Apparently he's got himself a top-flight barrister up from some London chambers.' He mentioned the name of the barrister. Several of us knew him from previous cases.

'I thought Volkan's cover story was supposed to be that he is a ditch-digger from Turkey. How the hell is he supposed to be able to afford a posh brief like that? It'll have cost a fortune.'

'Who knows,' said someone. 'The rumour is the lawyer's getting a legal-aid rate over here, but half a million in a Swiss bank account on top. Can't see why he'd do it otherwise.'

Of course it wasn't true, but you always heard rumours like this at a trial. We could never understand why otherwise intelligent and successful lawyers would represent scum like Volkan and do their utmost to get them back out on the streets. In our opinion it had to be for money, although I never once saw any evidence for it.

'Yeah, well, never mind all that,' said Phil. 'Watch yourselves. This guy is good – he'll try and make night sound like day.'

Time passed very slowly. Apparently both sides were still making legal submissions. We wondered if we'd get on at all or whether a decision was going to be made without us even saying a word.

Phil and I stood at one of the windows, gazing out across the city of Liverpool.

'One day, son, all these will be yours,' I said.

'What? The curtains?' grinned Phil, with a high-pitched squeak. He'd seen *Monty Python and the Holy Grail* as well.

We were called to the witness box in the same order in which we had confronted Volkan. I was third. It was strange to find the court almost empty; no one was in the public gallery. There was a stenographer, using one of those small machines to record everything (how on earth do they work?), two barristers, both with a clerk sitting behind them, and Volkan, sitting in the the dock, between two prison officers. He looked less unkempt than when I had seen him in the cells. His hair was tied back and he wasn't trying to hide his face any more. Other than that it was just me and the judge. The defence lawyer was on his feet as soon as I was sworn in and had been asked a few basic questions by the prosecution.

'You say you saw my client twice on a visit to this country in 1993.'

'That's right.'

'And the first time you were in an observation point whilst he was in a restaurant?'

'Yes, your honour.'

That was one trick I learned over the years. Always direct your answers to the judge. It stops you getting into a slanging match with an offensive barrister and makes you sound objective rather than personal.

'So how can you say that you identified this person? The observation point was over fifty metres away.'

'Yes your honour, but I was using binoculars. It was as good as standing next to him.'

'The second time you saw him was later the same year, at the airport. How far away were you when you saw him then? Fifty metres? Eighty metres?'

He had adopted a heavily sarcastic tone. I could see the way this was going.

'He was using a public pay phone. I was using the one next to him. I was standing at right angles to him no further than three feet away, your honour.'

'So you've only seen him twice: once from a considerable distance away and only for a few seconds each time. It's hardly much to base an identification on is it?'

'Your honour, we are talking about the leader of a major smuggling organisation. We never expected to see him in this country. For a law enforcement officer, seeing a major player like that is like seeing a film star or other celebrity. It's not a moment you forget easily.'

The defence counsel pursed his lips then tried one more attack. I couldn't work out if he thought he was winning or losing.

'When you saw the accused yesterday and were asked to identify him, you didn't say "yes" and you didn't say "no". You said "I believe that's the man". That clearly expresses your doubt. You didn't know it was him at all did you?'

'I said I believe it's him because I was certain, your honour. "I believe" doesn't mean "I doubt". When a Catholic says in church "I believe in God" it doesn't mean he doubts it.'

'Are you a Catholic?' asked the barrister.

'No, your honour.'

'No, I thought not. That will be all.'

And that's pretty much how it went for all of us. Just the repeated accusation that we couldn't possibly know it was Volkan, either because we were too far away or there were objects blocking our view, or because our memories weren't reliable. We waited around for the rest of the afternoon but it was clear that a decision probably wouldn't be available until the next day. We all had casework piling up in London and decided to drive back. Secretly none of us liked the way this was going. It had a bad feeling.

I was in the office when John rang the next day.

'It's bad news, they're letting him go.'

'You're joking.'

'Sadly not, the judge accepted that five out of six officers had made a positive identification, but the defence argued that since none of you had seen Volkan in over two years that made the identifications unreliable.'

'But that's ridiculous! If I didn't see Mel Gibson for two years I'd still know what he looked like.'

'Yes and that's what our lawyers tried to argue but the judge wasn't having any of it. Anyway, what really sealed it was a technicality. Apparently, when we sent an officer over to Holland to pick him up, our officer simply accepted that the man they had given him was Volkan. But there should have been an identification parade there first, to show that he was the right man. Because there wasn't one, the extradition is invalid under the terms of the treaty or something. Anyway, he's going to go free.'

'We can't let him get away with it, John! We've *got* to find something else to pick him up on.'

'We're trying. As a result of that information you picked up during the General's interrogation, the Italians were putting a case together against Volkan's men out there. We think that they have a warrant out against him and we're trying to get permission from the Dutch to hand him over to them, but it's complicated. Interpol are fiddling with the legal details now, but meanwhile that highly expensive legal team he's hired are screaming blue murder and trying to get him out. If he does go, then he'll just disappear back to Turkey; we'll have lost him for sure.'

I put the phone down. I followed the story for some weeks, but the last I heard he was on his way back to Turkey. Once again the English legal system had come to the rescue of the criminals, just when they assumed we'd got them cold. But the real sickener was yet to come.

In July 1996, those of us who had worked on the Volkan operation were summoned to an emergency meeting. Once again it was held in the Drugs F/L office. I hadn't been back there for a year. There were a lot of new faces but Sid and Big George were still there. Talking before the meeting, none of us could believe it was going to be very good news. Most of them seemed to think it was going to be some sort of scandal: an officer found to have forged evidence or taken a bribe.

Something was in the air. The rumours had been circulating for weeks.

There was a new SIO called Angus in charge of Drugs F/L. He entered the room from the direction of the Chief Investigation Officer's office.

'Sorry to drag you all down here from your various operations. I'm sure you are all busy. I can see quite a few notorious faces as I look around. I won't keep you. I've got a piece of news which has just come in and we wanted you people to be the first to know since you are, in a way, the most affected by it. You're not going to like it, so I might as well just get it said.'

He paused for a moment with his head down, as if trying to find exactly the right words. I thought he was going to tell us that someone had died. He looked up.

'Last week Michael Howard, the Home Secretary, signed papers exercising the royal prerogative for the release of John Haase and Paul Bennett. They are effectively being pardoned and are free men. They did a deal with the prosecuting authorities in return for certain information which I can't reveal at the moment, but the judge in the case recommended that they go free . . .'

That was as far as he got. There was a roar of protest from around the room and there was nothing anyone could do to regain order. Eventually Gareth stepped forward with enough authority to quieten everyone down.

'What the hell could they fucking offer that would get them out of the nick?' he demanded.

'I really don't know the details and I wouldn't be allowed to say even if I did. All I can tell you is that it was information which has enabled the recovery of a large amount of drugs and weapons, including large-calibre machine guns. I understand that it may also have led to the foiling of a jail-break. No arrests have been made yet, but a team has been put together to follow up the information which has been provided and . . .'

The uproar broke out again. There were cries of 'Bollocks!' from several people. We knew these guys. They were career criminals. They weren't going to roll over for anyone – their lives wouldn't be worth a penny on the streets if they did. The noise grew greater and greater. There was a lot of talk of going on strike, of refusing to go out on surveillance again until the management did something about this. I certainly felt like jacking the whole job in right there and then. There was a lot of office furniture getting a good kicking as people took out their frustrations on the nearest object. What was it all worth? Every person in that room had given up almost a year of their life, and for what? We had thought we were putting away a team of the most dangerous drug smugglers in the country – something worth making the sacrifice for. In some cases we'd risked our lives to do it. Instead it seemed to me that the managers in the Division and, more particularly, the Home Secretary, valued our efforts as practically worthless. What was the point of putting these people away if there was a revolving door that allowed them to come straight back out again?

Gareth held his hands up again, shouting, 'Hold on, hold on,' When the noise finally died away he demanded, 'What does Paddy say about all this?'

The SIO swallowed hard.

'Officer Clark was the one who recommended clemency.'

This time the news was greeted with gasps and then silence. We simply couldn't believe it. Paddy, the case officer, the man who'd put so much of his life into seeing the job through. How the hell could he approve of this?

It took the ground right away from under us. If Paddy had OKed it then there must really be something in it. Certainly none of us had ever heard of an eighteen-year sentence simply being written off before. Perhaps Haase and Bennett really had rolled over? Perhaps the information really was worth something? There was no way we could protest now. Paddy was about the only person on the team who knew all the details and if he had OKed it, what could the rest of us say?

In ones and twos we began to leave the room, no longer angry, just deeply puzzled and confused. The news spread rapidly around the headquarters as everyone went back to their respective teams. Everywhere the reaction was one of shock and disgust, but mostly bewilderment. The deal just didn't make sense.

So what had really happened? Even today no one knows for sure. The Liverpool underworld claims that Haase and Bennett pulled a fast one. The story goes that the weapons and drugs which they led the authorities to, claiming they belonged to other gangs, were actually theirs. It seems that none of the information they passed led to even one prosecution and it is claimed that a weapon they said had been smuggled into a prison was actually smuggled in by them. The story on Merseyside is that by pulling this ruse they effectively got out of an eighteen-year prison sentence for just a few thousand pounds' worth of gear.

Then there is the role of Paddy. How could he support such a deal? It is certainly a mystery to me and I worked on the case. It is said that he signed papers recommending their release and saying that he thought they would no longer be a threat to society, but I still can't believe that an experienced officer like him would be taken in by such a cheap trick. Only Paddy will ever be able to say what really happened and at the moment he isn't talking.

As for Michael Howard, the release of Haase and Bennett has dogged him in a way which must be embarrassing for him. Newspaper reports about the pardon have also published that he has a cousin on Merseyside, Simon Bakerman, who is a convicted drug dealer. The reports say that Haase apparently contacted Bakerman twice soon after his release from prison.

As for me, I have nothing but contempt for Michael Howard. He is a politician who has made his name in part by taking a tough line on law and order. How could he release two major criminals for what is apparently so small a return? I just can't believe that Michael Howard values the sacrifices of the men and women in the front line against crime. I wrote to him whilst working on this book to ask for his side of the story. I didn't even get a reply. In 2004, at the Conservative Party Conference, Michael Howard had the nerve to say that his priority in law enforcement would be the war on drugs. It would be funny if it weren't tragic.

Although the decision caused outrage at the time, subsequent Labour governments have refused to conduct a satisfactory enquiry, despite repeated requests. Only one man has carried on the fight in the House of Commons to try and have the truth revealed. That is Peter Kilfoyle, the Labour MP for Liverpool Walton, which is where the case occurred. He has seen the damage that heroin has done in Liverpool over the years and knows the harm which this particular decision caused to his constituency once Haase returned to his old haunts. He has called for debates on the issue many times, but most other MPs have refused to support him. He recently succeeded in getting a debate on the floor of the House of Commons. I tuned in and watched on the Parliamentary Channel: apart from Kilfoyle and the government officers who had to be there, the chamber was practically deserted. He has asked to speak to the case officer, but has had his request refused. He has even tried to speak to Haase.

Finally, in early 2005, having secured access to Home Office papers relating to the case under the new Freedom of Information Act, Peter Kilfoyle was able to pass information to the police. At the time of writing, this has resulted in a long overdue official investigation into why the pardons were author-ised. Perhaps the mystery will finally be solved – but I doubt it: I suspect that there are too many people who will be embar-rassed if the truth comes out.

As for John Haase, he immediately returned to heroin smug-gling, robbery and extortion following his release. He was able to apply all the lessons he had learned from hearing how Drugs F/L took him down and his counter-surveillance set-up became better than ever. It was only when one of his own men turned against him that he was finally put away. Anyone who wants to see how wrong Michael Howard was should read Graham Johnson's excellent book, *Powder Wars*, which tells what Haase did after he was released. In 1999, following yet another joint police and Customs operation, Haase was arrested on drugs and firearms charges. In February 2001 he was sentenced to thirteen years in jail. He is currently in Full Sutton maximum security prison. In 1999 Paul Bennett was wanted in connection with a £1 million importation of cannabis, but had reportedly fled to Cyprus. Apparently he is now back on Merseyside and the police are no longer seeking him. As far as I can determine, Volkan is still at large and his organisation is still operating. The street price of heroin has never been lower.

The case related in this book is not an exception. The British justice system often gives major criminals a second chance. Curtis Warren, the country's most successful cocaine smuggler, walked free after a carefully organised ID sting, boasting that he was off to 'spend his millions'. He was subsequently picked up and imprisoned as the result of a Dutch police operation. Kenny Noye stabbed an undercover police officer to death and walked free because the jury believed his story that he was dealing with an 'intruder'. He was subsequently jailed for life for stabbing a motorist to death in a road rage attack. And this isn't the worst of it. These are the ones who have been caught and convicted at the second attempt. Former ID officers can tell of many cases where drug smugglers have walked free and learned where they went wrong, never to be caught again. Unless we have more MPs like Peter Kilfoyle and fewer like Michael Howard, I can't believe we'll ever have an effective justice system.

Glossary

box	the perimeter of a surveillance area
burned	spotted by the target
burning	accelerating
Charlie Papa	car park
eyeball	vehicle or footman who has sight of the target
fading	decelerating
foxtrot	on foot
gear	drugs
ghost plates	substitute car registration plates
going nine nine	taking the eyeball position
haulage	photography
IC1/2/3	person of Caucasian/Mediterranean/Afro-Caribbean appearance
knock, knock, knock	call sign to begin a raid
lifted	no longer have the eyeball position
magic box	home address
Mike Charlie	minicab
a mobile	a surveillance vehicle
off, off, off	call sign for a car under surveillance leaving the motorway
one up	car with driver only

plot	area around a target location
plot up	to find a safe parking position at a target location covering at least one exit
sheepdog	a counter-surveillance person or vehicle
show out	to be spotted by the criminals or a member of the public
sierra	speed
toasty	vehicle or officer at risk of being spotted by target
toucan	taxi
two three	vehicle is in the backup position, able to take the eyeball when required
two up	car with driver and passenger
ukele	tube station
vulture	an observation van
X-ray	call sign for a known car
Zulu	call sign for a known person

A NOTE ON THE AUTHOR

Former MI6 officer Harry Ferguson worked undercover with Customs and Excise for eight years and is now a full-time writer. He is the author of *Kilo 17*, which told the inside story of a close-knit Customs team during a major drugs investigation, and of *SPY: A Handbook*, published to accompany the BBC TV series, for which he was also one of the 'Spy School' trainers.

A NOTE ON THE TYPE

The text of this book is set in Bembo, which was first used in 1495 by the Venetian printer Aldus Manutius for Cardinal Bembo's *De Aetna*. The original types were cut for Manutius by Francesco Griffo. Bembo was one of the types used by Claude Garamond (1480–1561) as a model for his Romain de L'Université, and so it was a forerunner of what became the standard European type for the following two centuries. Its modern form follows the original types and was designed for Monotype in 1929.

HARRY FERGUSON

KILO 17

THE SECRET WAR AGAINST THE DRUG SMUGGLERS

KILO 17 Harry Ferguson
£6.99 0-7475-6856-1

Drugs, raids, guns, fear and danger – the explosive inside story of a close-knit customs team on a major drugs bust

As an Oxford-educated former member of MI6 with no knowledge of the drugs world, Harry Ferguson is promoted over the heads of more experienced officers into Customs and Excise's Kilo team, who need Harry like they need a hole in the head. But he starts to win some respect when he makes progress with an investigation into the affairs of the local Mister Big, Frank Davies. Their long hunt for evidence is punctuated by adrenalin-pumping car chases, stake-outs, chance tip-offs and a dawn raid on a fortress-like country house as gradually the Kilos begin to unravel the complex web of Davies's criminal empire.

To order from Bookpost PO Box 29 Douglas Isle of Man IM99 1BQ www.bookpost.co.uk email: bookshop@enterprise.net fax: 01624 837033 tel: 01624 836000

bloomsburypbks

SPY: A HANDBOOK Harry Ferguson
£12.99 0 7475 7523 1

Do you have what it takes to be a spy?

In this handbook to accompany the 10-part BBC TV series, 'Spy School' teacher
Harry Ferguson reveals everything you'll need to know. He shows how to lie
without being caught, how to follow someone without being spotted and how to
spot those who might be following you. He reveals the secrets of walk-ins,
gangplank approaches, false flag operations, dead letter boxes, brush contacts,
how to construct an alternative identity, how to check your house for bugging
devices and your car for bombs, how to disappear in a crowd, how to survive
the toughest interrogation and how agents are talent-spotted and recruited.
SPY is a fascinating account of the TV series, the world of espionage, and a
handbook for the spy in all of us.

To order from Bookpost PO Box 29 Douglas Isle of Man IM99 1BQ www.bookpost.co.uk email
bookshop@enterprise.net fax: 01624 837033 tel: 01624 836000

bloomsburypbks